SHOOTING STRAIGHT

SHOOTING STRAIGHT

GUNS, GAYS, GOD, AND GEORGE CLOONEY

PIERS MORGAN

GALLERY BOOKS

NEW YORK   LONDON   TORONTO   SYDNEY   NEW DELHI

G

Gallery Books
A Division of Simon & Schuster, Inc.
1230 Avenue of the Americas
New York, NY 10020

Photo credits: page x: © Mirrorpix/*The Daily Mirror*; page 30: Courtesy Adam Rose/CNN; page 62: Courtesy CNN/KGUN; page 262: Courtesy Shannon Hicks and *The Newtown Bee*. All other photos: Courtesy CNN.

Some material in this book was previously in *The Mail on Sunday*, UK.

First Gallery Books hardcover edition October 2013

GALLERY BOOKS and colophon are registered trademarks of Simon & Schuster, Inc.

For information about special discounts for bulk purchases, please contact Simon & Schuster Special Sales at 1-866-506-1949 or business@simonandschuster.com.

The Simon & Schuster Speakers Bureau can bring authors to your live event. For more information or to book an event contact the Simon & Schuster Speakers Bureau at 1-866-248-3049 or visit our website at www.simonspeakers.com.

Interior design by Akasha Archer

Manufactured in the United States of America

10 9 8 7 6 5 4 3 2 1

Library of Congress Cataloging-in-Publication Data

Morgan, Piers
   Shooting straight : guns, gays, God, and George Clooney / Piers Morgan. — First Gallery Books hardcover edition.
      p. cm.
   Summary: "Piers Morgan gives an adrenaline-fueled account of life at CNN in the style of Aaron Sorkin's *The Newsroom*, as well as his career-defining decision to take on the issue of gun control at its historical tipping point"— Provided by publisher.
   1. Morgan, Piers 2. Television personalities—Great Britain—Biography. 3. Journalists—Great Britain—Biography. 4. United States—Politics and government—2009– 5. Gun control—United States.
6. Piers Morgan live (Television program) I. Title.
   PN5123.M685A5 2013
   070.92—dc23
   [B]   2013026432

ISBN 978-1-4767-4505-3
ISBN 978-1-4767-4508-4 (ebook)

For Spencer, Stanley, Bertie, and Elise

FOREWORD

by Michael Moore

On the Saturday morning of January 8, 2011, Congresswoman Gabby Giffords was holding a meet-and-greet with her constituents in the parking
lot of a grocery store in Tucson, Arizona. Without warning, one of the men
standing in line to talk to her rushed forward, came up to the table where
she was sitting, put a gun to her head, and pulled the trigger. Pleased with
himself and the ease with which he was able to shoot a member of Congress, he decided, for good measure, to shoot another eighteen people, killing six of them, including a nine-year-old girl. Giffords, miraculously, lived.

In the days and weeks that followed, there was a lot of national mourn-
ing and hand-wringing and pronouncements about the "strength of the
American spirit to rise above such tragedies" and carry on. But there were
no calls by political leaders to enact stricter gun laws and no such bills were
proposed or introduced. Even President Obama remained silent about taking any measures, the kind of which might have prevented the bloodletting
in Tucson.

It was in this environment, just one week later, that the British journalist and TV personality Piers Morgan debuted his new nightly chat show
on CNN. Entitled *Piers Morgan Tonight,* he took over the 9 P.M. time slot
from the legendary Larry King on the granddaddy of the cable news chan-
nels. Although he had served as the editor of numerous British tabloids and
had written several books, the American public only knew Piers Morgan
as the winner on Donald Trump's *Celebrity Apprentice* and as a judge on

NBC's *America's Got Talent*. What no one saw coming was that the loudest, clearest, most passionate voice against two other things Americans had talent for—gun violence and mass shootings—was about to unleash his rage against this senseless barbarity in a way that would make everyone sit up and take notice. For the next two-plus years, Piers Morgan has, week after week (and sometimes night after night) taken on the National Rifle Association, the United States Congress, and numerous gun lovers, gun nuts, and gun evangelists. On one infamous show, he confronted—in his polite but unforgiving English way—the popular radio host and defender of the Second Amendment, Alex Jones. Jones, offended by the suggestion that perhaps America had a problem, began screaming at Morgan and looked as if he were about to pick up his stool and clobber this "foreigner" with it (I assume he couldn't have shot him, as Time Warner security won't allow six-shooters or gunfights in their New York headquarters).

Angry gun owners, alarmed at the success Morgan was having in reaching millions of Americans (in part, by educating them on how his native Britain had significantly reduced gun violence and virtually eliminated mass shootings after a massacre that took place in 1996 in a schoolyard in Dunblane, Scotland) began a campaign to remove Morgan—not just from the airwaves, but from the country itself. A petition was launched on the White House website to have Morgan "deported." Over one hundred thousand Americans pleaded with the president to put Piers Morgan on the next boat back to England. Obama was actually forced to respond to the outcry and did so by reminding the public that this alien, Mr. Morgan, enjoyed the same free speech rights as us gun-toting Americans.

Sadly, the gun violence and mass shootings continue. But after months of relentless badgering and rallying Americans to respond to this from our better side, public opinion has shifted (nearly 90 percent are now in favor of some form of stricter gun laws) and the president sent a bill to Congress to require background checks at gun shows. It failed. But that hasn't stopped Piers Morgan from using his nightly bully pulpit to rail against this madness—and (thankfully) it doesn't look like he's going to give up and return home for tea anytime soon.

SHOOTING STRAIGHT

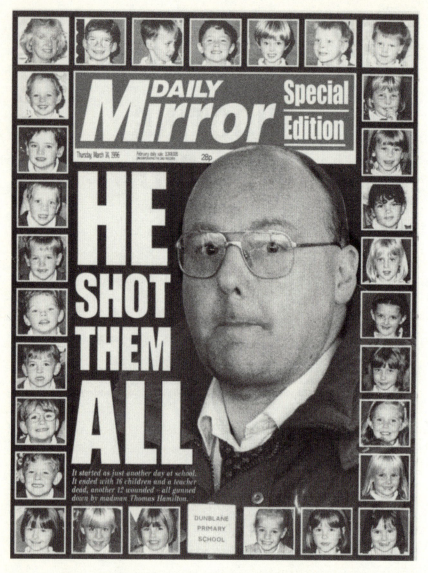

The front page of *The Daily Mirror* after the Dunblane school shooting massacre in 1996 that changed Britain's gun laws forever.

PROLOGUE

It was a quiet morning at the offices of *The Daily Mirror* in East London on Wednesday, March 13, 1996. I had been editor-in-chief of Britain's second-biggest-selling newspaper for four months.

Around 10 A.M., the news desk alerted me to a shooting incident in a small town called Dunblane in Scotland. I turned on the television to see anguished parents sprinting toward the gates of the local elementary school, and it soon became apparent that this was a terrible atrocity.

An unemployed man named Thomas Hamilton had walked into Dunblane Elementary School armed with two 9mm Browning HP pistols, two Smith & Wesson M19 .357 Magnum revolver handguns, and seven hundred forty-three rounds of ammunition.

All legally purchased.

Hamilton opened fire on a class of twenty-nine five- and six-year-old children, killing sixteen of them and their teacher, Gwen Mayor, and wounding many others.

He then shot himself dead.

My eldest son, Spencer, was just three years old at the time, and the horror of what had happened to so many innocent kids just a little bit bigger than him moved me to tears and rage. A huge national debate about guns began in Britain in the aftermath of the shooting, and *The Daily Mirror* was at the center of it.

I was determined that something meaningful would be done to try to prevent anything like this from happening again. *The Mirror* campaigned vigorously, and relentlessly, for new gun control legislation.

Eighteen months later, the British government, under enormous pressure from both the media and an almost unanimously united public, passed a ban on the private ownership of all handguns, and all small-bore pistols, giving us some of the toughest gun laws in the world.

All fully automatic guns were banned too, as were all semiautomatic center-fire rifles. To even own a shotgun or rifle for hunting and sport shooting now requires extensive background checks and paperwork.

Initially, the new laws made little impact. In fact, gun-related crime rose, peaking at 24,094 offenses in 2003-4. So the government made them even tougher—introducing a minimum five-year prison sentence for anyone caught in possession of a handgun. And it introduced an amnesty allowing citizens to give their guns in to police.

Since then, the number has fallen each year. In 2010-11, there were 11,227 gun-related offenses, 53 percent below that peak number seven years previously. The gun murder rate, meanwhile, has stayed between just thirty to fifty deaths a year, one of the lowest rates per capita of any industrialized country.

"What we have in the UK now are significantly lower levels of gun crime, levels that continue to fall," Andy Marsh, firearms director at Britain's Association of Chief Police Officers, told the *Boston Globe* in February 2013. "People say you can't unwind hundreds of years of gun history and culture [in America], but here in the UK, we've learned from our tragedies and taken steps to reduce the likelihood of them ever happening again."

There hasn't been a single school shooting in Britain since Dunblane.

When I came to America, I had no intention of becoming a public advocate for gun control. I simply wanted to be a successful television personality and, later, an effective news anchor. Yet my mission regarding guns would repeat itself here, as if inexorably, and despite the ludicrous additional obstacle of my being a foreigner questioning American constitutional rights.

This is the story of how it happened.

The King and I. My first meeting ever with Larry King,
on the day I was announced as his replacement at CNN.

1

TUESDAY, JUNE 15, 2010

This is the biggest moment of my career.

I ran two British national newspapers for eleven years, judged TV talent shows on both sides of the Atlantic, won Donald Trump's inaugural *Celebrity Apprentice,* and currently host Britain's most popular TV interview show. But right now, all of this seems like chicken feed compared to what I may be about to do—replace the great Larry King at CNN.

Larry's not just a television legend. He's arguably the most famous man in small-screen history.

For twenty-five years, he's anchored the eponymous *Larry King Live* 9 P.M. hour at Cable News Network—hosting more than seven thousand shows, and conducting tens of thousands of interviews.

But Larry's now seventy-seven, his ratings have been slipping for the last few years, and the critics have been gnawing viciously at his suspenders.

"It's time to think the unthinkable!" they cry. "Larry should retire!"

But only I, and a very select number of people, know that decision has already been made.

Because I've been offered his job.

After a series of meetings and conversations with CNN executives since April, they've concluded I'm the right man to step into the King's shoes.

There's just one problem.

I'm contracted to NBC for *America's Got Talent* for two more years, and the network's president, Jeff Zucker, is refusing to let me go.

Hardly surprising, really, given that *AGT* is one of NBC's biggest hits, and CNN is a direct rival to its cable channel, MSNBC.

In an effort to try to persuade him, I sat down two days ago and wrote him this email:

Dear Jeff,

When we sat together chatting in the *Today Show* makeup room back in January, I felt we were kindred spirits. Further investigation confirms this:

Jeff Zucker—Born April 9, 1965.

Piers Morgan—Born March 30, 1965.

JZ—Captain of North Miami Senior High School tennis team.

PM—Captain of Cumnor House Preparatory School cricket team.

JZ—Reporter for *Miami Herald* (Florida).

PM—Reporter for *Sutton Herald* (Surrey).

JZ—President of senior class, ran with slogan: "The little man with the big ideas."

PM—Campaigned for student union, with slogan: "Ambition knows no bounds."

JZ—Made executive producer of *Today Show* at twenty-six—the most watched morning TV program in America.

PM—Made editor of *News of the World* at twenty-eight—the most read newspaper in the UK.

JZ—Made president of NBC Entertainment.

PM—Made editor-in-chief of *The Daily Mirror.*

JZ—One marriage, three sons and a daughter.

PM—One marriage (soon to be two), three sons, hoping to add a daughter.

JZ—Signed Donald Trump to host *The Apprentice.*

PM—Signed by Donald Trump to win *The Celebrity Apprentice.*

JZ—Survived colon cancer.

PM—Survived falling off a Segway. (OK, you win here, though I did break five ribs and collapse a lung, and it's ten times more embarrassing.)

After beating cancer, you said: "It put my life into perspective. I want to win and win honorably. But heck, it's only television. I still want to win, but I don't want to kill somebody."

You're now doing your dream job.

I now want to do mine.

Please don't kill me, please win honorably by letting me pursue the career move I have spent my entire life striving to reach, and know that you were the man that made it happen.

I'm a journalist at heart, not a judge of piano-playing pigs—however fun and mutually prosperous that has been.

He emailed straight back. "Come and see me to discuss your future."

So I boarded a flight from London yesterday morning, landed in New York at 8 P.M., and had a fitful night's sleep.

At midday today, I stumbled down to gulp oceans of wake-up coffee at the hotel with my manager, John Ferriter.

He was bullish about the meeting with Zucker in two hours.

"I don't think he'd fly you over here just to say no. But he's going to want you to dance for your dinner. How are you feeling?"

"Nervous, but excited."

"That's the right frame of mind. This meeting will change your life."

We looked at each other, and both chuckled at the sheer absurdity of what was happening.

Then John's phone vibrated, and he took the call.

"Yes . . . OK . . . I'm very sorry to hear that . . ."

His face looked suddenly intense and very serious.

"No, I understand . . . OK . . . got it . . . thank you for letting me know."

Oh no. It sounded like Zucker had canceled the meeting.

"What was that?"

"It's nothing, don't worry about it."

"The meeting's still on?"

"It's still on."

I could tell something was wrong.

"Is everything OK?"

John stared at me for a few seconds, considering whether to tell me.

"No. It's not. Your father's had a stroke."

"WHAT?"

"That was Tracey [my UK personal assistant] and she just took a call from your mother. Your father's in the hospital, but he's OK. Your mother didn't want you to know until after the meeting. But I think you should know now, and if you want to go straight to the airport, then that's what you should do. This meeting is not as important as your father's health."

I called Mum, who was calm but firm.

"Dad's OK. It was a scary few hours, but he's stable, and the doctors are happy with his condition. I want you to go to the meeting. There's nothing you can do."

It was now 1 P.M., the meeting was at 2 P.M., and my flight home was around 7 P.M.

"Mum, forget the meeting. I'm going to try to get an earlier flight and come home now."

"*No*. You're not to do that! An hour isn't going to make any difference. Dad would want you to go to the meeting. And I want you to go to the meeting."

This was a typical reaction from a woman who has always, without a single exception, put the interests of her children before her own.

I hung up and sat back in the chair, my head now swirling with shock and adrenaline.

"If you want to go to the airport, I'll postpone the meeting right now," John said. "Jeff will understand, better than most. He's survived cancer; nobody has to tell him about priorities in life."

"My mother wants me to take the meeting," I said. "She's adamant."

"Then take the meeting, if you think you'll be OK."

"Let's go."

John and I walked the six blocks down to NBC's headquarters at 30 Rock Center in midtown Manhattan.

It was a warm, sunny day, and the streets were teeming with shoppers, tourists, and businesspeople grabbing lunch.

The nerves and excitement I'd felt earlier in the day were now replaced by a sickening, fearful jolt in my stomach.

But the one thing I'd always been able to do as a newspaper editor was divorce my personal emotions from work—whatever was going on.

I had the same kind of "show-must-go-on" mentality that actors use.

As we walked, I reflected on my parents.

My natural father, an Irish dentist from Galway called Eamon Vincent O'Meara, died when I was eleven months old of an ulcer-related condition.

It would be easily treatable today, but in the sixties it could be a killer.

He was just thirty-two, and my mother was twenty-one and five months pregnant with my brother, Jeremy.

Glynne Pughe-Morgan, a Welshman, met and married Mum a few years later, when Jeremy and I were still small boys.

He was in his midtwenties, and the magnitude of what he took on back then has grown with me ever since I've had my own children.

He's always been Dad to me. And like my mother, he has selflessly devoted his life to working ridiculously hard so his large family can prosper.

He's now sixty-nine, and this is the first time in his life he's been seriously ill. And I'm thousands of miles away in New York, on my way to a bloody business meeting.

Every part of me is screaming, "Go to the airport, try to get an earlier flight." But at the same time, I know I'm flying anyway in five hours, and I also know that Mum's right—Dad would want me to go to this meeting.

We arrived at NBC and were directed up to Jeff Zucker's palatial office.

John could tell I was in a strange place emotionally.

"You sure you want to do this?"

"I'll be fine in there, don't worry," I replied.

The meeting began with Zucker asking a perfectly reasonable question: "Give me one good reason why I should let one of my prime-time stars work for a rival network, and in particular one that we've just overtaken in the ratings."

MSNBC had indeed recently surpassed CNN to become number two in cable news.

To which I argued, with what I thought was reasonable logic, that it could only enhance my credibility as a talent show judge if I was hosting a nightly news show at CNN.

The meeting ended half an hour later with Zucker shaking my hand and saying he would let me go to CNN.

But only on the condition I continued to do *America's Got Talent* as well. And only after he'd also negotiated a hefty price tag for my services.

(I was later told by an NBC executive that I was traded for the rights to buy seven seasons of *Law and Order*, something NBC had been trying to wrestle off Turner Broadcasting—CNN's parent company—for some time.)

"Thank you," I said as I left.

"I'm not in the business of preventing people from living their dreams," he said, smiling.

John and I walked back outside. What should have been a moment of wild celebration was replaced instead with two relieved grins and a firm handshake.

"Great meeting," said John. "Now go see your dad."

I called Mum again, and she said he was sleeping and comfortable.

"I land at six-thirty A.M.," I said, "and I'll go straight from Heathrow to the hospital."

I got to JFK, boarded the plane, drank a large whiskey, took a sleeping pill, and looked out of the window—my head still swirling.

WEDNESDAY, JUNE 16, 2010

Got to the hospital around 9 A.M. and went to find Dad. He looks very frail and exhausted. His condition deteriorated slightly overnight.

He's lost the use of his right arm and is slurring his words. But the doctors are still confident he'll make a good recovery if he does all the rehab they've laid down for him.

I can tell it's been a terrifying experience, and I know he'll be worrying himself sick about his one-man but successful food distribution business.

"How did your meeting go?" he asked.

I was amazed he even remembered.

"It was good. They're going to let me do the CNN job."

"Good, good."

Dad tried to smile, but I told him not to waste energy talking about work stuff.

"Just focus on getting better."

He nodded. Dad's a very strong guy, physically and mentally. He'll come through this, I've got no doubt about that.

But I'm getting married in two weeks, and I don't think there's any chance of him attending the wedding now.

THURSDAY, JUNE 17, 2010

Newspapers on both sides of the Atlantic have been running rumors about me joining CNN.

Toby Young, author of a very funny book, *The Sound of No Hands Clapping*, about his own failed exploits as a screenwriter in Hollywood, emailed:

> In case you haven't heard this already, I pass on Larry King's own formula
> for success on television [originally imparted by him to Tucker Carlson]:
> "The trick is to care, but not too much. Give a shit—but not really."

THURSDAY, JUNE 24, 2010

Celia and I were married today.

We've been together for four and a half years.

I knew she was the one for me when I made a speech at a big magazine dinner in London soon after we first met. I tanked spectacularly and saw that she was the only one in the room laughing at my terrible jokes.

"I didn't find you funny," she explained afterward. "I found the fact you were being booed funny."

My youngest brother, Rupert, was my best man, and we shared a room together last night.

"Just wake me up on time, and don't forget the rings," I commanded.

I didn't get to sleep until 2 A.M.

At 3 A.M., Rupert's cell phone exploded into full, noisy alarm mode.

"Damn, must have set it to the wrong time," he mumbled. "Sorry."

I didn't get back to sleep.

But hey, it was a beautiful, hot day, and I was marrying a beautiful, hot woman.

And at least he remembered the rings.

We tried everything in our power to keep it all a complete secret—choosing a tiny chapel in the middle of a large remote field in the Oxfordshire countryside, only inviting fifty-six of our closest friends and family, and employing a small team of Jeremy's former army colleagues, all recently retired from covert ops in the army, to patrol the perimeter.

He himself sadly couldn't make it as he's still on active service in Afghanistan with his regiment, the Royal Welsh.

At 12:45 P.M., I was standing outside the chapel with the vicar (he was a Church of England minister, but permitted us to have a Catholic blessing) and a helicopter buzzed overhead.

When it came around for the third time, I laughed.

"Look up and wave, Reverend," I said.

"Oh? Why?"

"Because you're probably live on American TV right now . . ."

He looked horrified, and instantly began to apologize for something that obviously had nothing to do with him.

But I enjoyed the irony: the former tabloid editor utterly incapable of keeping even his own wedding from the intrusive glare of the media lens.

After a beautiful service, we drove the mile to a charming local village pub for the reception, and were met in almost every single hedgerow along the route by photographers leaping out of bushes and trees.

I even recognized one of them as a guy I used to employ in my tabloid days.

"For old times' sake, Piers?" he yelled.

After that, they pretty much left us alone, which was good of them.

I probably wouldn't have been so generous in my "old times."

There were many special moments during a very special day.

Not least was having the boys—Spencer, sixteen, Stanley, thirteen, and Bertie, ten—as my ushers. Their mother, Marion, and I were finally divorced last year, though we actually separated nearly a decade ago. Despite all that upheaval, they've remained my best friends.

Dad made it, miraculously. His right arm was in a sling, and he was barely able to walk or speak properly, but he made it. Pretty extraordinary given the state he was in nine days ago.

SUNDAY, JUNE 27, 2010

We've been on our honeymoon for three days now, and I've spent much of it on the phone with John, who's now trying to close the very complicated contractual negotiations.

Celia's been remarkably patient—she knows what a big deal this CNN thing is—but even her reservoirs of tolerance burst this afternoon.

"Tell Celia I said hi," said John, at the end of our fourth call of the day.

"John says hi," I repeated.

"I'd rather he said good-bye," she replied.

"John, only call again if you have definitive news," I pleaded, "or I'll be divorced before I start at CNN!"

TUESDAY, JUNE 29, 2010

John called at 4 P.M.

"Larry's quit."

I raced to my laptop to Google the news. And it was true.

"I talked to the guys here at CNN and I told them I would like to end *Larry King Live* this fall," Larry wrote on his blog. "And CNN has graciously accepted, giving me more time for my wife and I to get to the kids' Little League games."

He continued: "I'll still be a part of the CNN family, hosting several Larry King specials on major national and international subjects. With this chapter closing, I'm looking forward to the future and what my next chapter will bring, but for now it's time to hang up my nightly suspenders."

Asked in a subsequent interview to explain the secret of his success, he said: "I left my ego at the door. I never learned a thing while I was talking. That would be my motto."

As for whom he'd like to replace him, Larry—who had obviously heard all the rumors about me, and almost certainly knew I'd now been offered his job—replied, "If it was up to me, Ryan Seacrest."

There can be only one reason that Larry's put out this announcement—CNN must have told him that I'm coming in. And that means their negotiations with NBC must be near to conclusion.

But I've learned to never take anything for granted in the American TV business.

Until the ink is on that contract, there will be considerable reason for uncertainty. And even then, I'd want it tested by forensic scientists. I emailed John. "If you were a betting man, would you say this means I've got the gig?"

He replied: "Let me tell you a story about betting. President Calvin Coolidge, a man of few words, was at a Washington, D.C., party. Five prominent businessmen approached a rather buxom young lady and bet her that she couldn't get the president to say more than two words.

"She approached him and said, 'Mr. President, those men have bet me twenty dollars that I can't get you to say more than two words.' Coolidge stared at her breasts, then looked up, smiled, and said: 'You lose.'"

I had no idea what this meant with regard to my chances of replacing Larry King, but it did make me laugh.

TUESDAY, JULY 6, 2010

NBC asked me to interview Susan Boyle for the *Today Show,* as we're both in London.

I was a judge on *Britain's Got Talent,* alongside Simon Cowell, when we discovered Susan during a long, grimly unproductive audition day in Glasgow, Scotland, last winter.

The forty-seven-year-old woman walked out to a cacophony of sneers and jeers, and mocking eye rolls from us prejudging fools on the panel—before raising the roof with a sensational rendition of "I Dreamed a Dream" from *Les Misérables.*

Since then, she's sold ten million albums—beating Lady Gaga and Rihanna in the last year.

Toward the end of the interview, I asked her if I could audition for a competition she's running to promote her album.

Entrants just have to record themselves singing "Silent Night."

"Go on then," she urged, "let's hear yer."

I began to slowly murder the great festive hymn when after just a few seconds, Susan leaped out of her chair and began frantically shouting, "Buzz! Buzz!"—mimicking the sound of the talent show judges' buzzers.

I tried again, but this time she shrieked it even louder.

"Honestly," I said, "after all I've done for you, this is how you treat me?"

"Piers, you cannae sing," she exclaimed.

MONDAY, JULY 26, 2010

One of my favorite speeches in history is Theodore Roosevelt's address at the Sorbonne in Paris in 1910, which included this passage:

> It is not the critic who counts; not the man who points out how the strong man stumbles, or where the doer of deeds could have done them better. The credit belongs to the man who is actually in the arena, whose face is marred by dust and sweat and blood; who strives valiantly; who errs, who comes short again and again, because there is no effort without error and shortcoming; but who does actually strive to do the deeds; who knows great enthusiasms, the great devotions; who spends himself in a worthy cause; who at the best knows in the end the triumph of high achievement, and who at the worst, if he fails, at least fails while daring greatly, so that his place shall never be with those cold and timid souls who neither know victory nor defeat.

Roosevelt made that speech on April 23, 1910.

I had my first meeting with CNN on April 23, 2010.

When I told him, John said, "That's the good news. The not so good news is that Richard Nixon then quoted it in his resignation speech."

FRIDAY, JULY 30, 2010

The news is out.

Jeff Gaspin, NBC's entertainment chairman—and Zucker's right-hand man—was asked at the Television Critics Association summer press day this afternoon if NBC would be sharing me with CNN.

"Yes," was his one-word answer.

That's the first on-the-record confirmation from any of the parties involved.

MONDAY, AUGUST 9, 2010

"You're going to need a good personal publicist," John announced a week ago. I've never had one before, preferring to use the PR departments on whatever shows I work on. And, of course, relying on my own experience in the media.

But John's right: this CNN gig is going to be a whole new ball game.

We've talked to a few heavyweights in the business, but I'm concerned that they won't make me their priority.

John, who agrees, suggested a young woman called Meghan McPartland.

She works for Rogers and Cowan, whose offices are in his building.

We met for a drink last night, and I instantly liked her.

She's smart, quick, and hungry.

"It's bad news," I told her today. "You're hired."

TUESDAY, AUGUST 24, 2010

Celia's gone to Saint-Tropez to join her family on an annual trip they make there every August.

Yesterday, she was "flashed" by a revolting pervert as she walked down to our favorite little beach. He was fully naked, and performing what British tabloids like to cryptically refer to as "a sex act" on himself.

I told her she had to report it to the police, but she was reluctant.

"Knowing French gendarmes, they'll just shrug and say, 'But you were in ze bikini, yes?'"

Today, Celia trudged down to the local police station, then rang me afterward.

"It went exactly how I imagined," she said.

"What? They didn't actually say it was your fault for wearing a bikini?"

"No, but the policeman listened to me carefully, then put on a quizzical Hercule Poirot face and asked: 'Was it a high tide?' "

FRIDAY, AUGUST 27, 2010

John called.

"We're closed."

After weeks of feverish negotiations, my small army of representatives, led by the indomitable Ferret (my nickname for him), have reached provisional agreement on all outstanding issues with CNN.

We still have to sign an actual contract, but for all intents and purposes, I'm replacing Larry King.

Jim Walton, CNN's worldwide president, emailed: "I hear we have a deal! How exciting."

My mind went back to Miami Beach on a warm January day in 1994.

I was a twenty-eight-year-old show business columnist for Rupert Murdoch's best-selling UK tabloid, *The Sun,* and he'd flown me to Florida for reasons that hadn't been fully explained.

For two hours, we walked barefoot up and down the beach, talking about politics, newspapers, life, and the universe.

A few hours later, he appointed me editor of the *News of the World,* his hugely popular, globally infamous Sunday tabloid.

I remember calling Mum that night and thinking that nothing I ever do again in my career would rival this moment for sheer excitement. An excitement she eventually shared, once she'd gotten over the instinctive shock of her halo-clad little boy running the most scandalous newspaper in the world. (Mum, my biggest supporter, always sees the positive in whatever scraps I get myself into. If I told her I'd murdered ten people, she'd say: "Well, at least it wasn't eleven.")

Tonight I rang her again to break the news.

It felt even more exciting than that night in 1994, and this time, she didn't have to pretend to be excited.

CNN is an altogether more palatable career prospect for a mother to digest than *News of the World.*

MONDAY, AUGUST 30, 2010

John called. "Come down to Cut at ten P.M., and bring a pen."

When he arrived, he said: "I've just had dinner with the doctors who saved my life. Pretty incredible."

A year ago, John was lying on a bed at Cedars-Sinai Hospital in Los Angeles. He'd suffered a blood clot, complicated by a staph infection, and it had nearly cost him his life. For three months, he drifted in and out of consciousness, those same doctors repeatedly fearing he wouldn't make it.

But make it he did, only to discover that in his absence, Hollywood superagent Ari Emanuel's Endeavor company had merged with the William Morris Agency—the firm John had worked at for twenty-five years.

John was the only WMA board member to vote against the planned merger, before he fell sick and left the company in acrimonious circumstances soon after returning to work.

"Where are you going?" I asked him.

"No idea."

"OK, then this is our *Jerry Maguire* moment," I laughed, "and I'm your Rod Tidwell."

I quit WMA that day.

But almost every one of his fifty or so remaining clients chose to stay at the newly formed William Morris Endeavor company, rather than go with him like I did.

Among them, John's client for the past ten years—Larry King.

We drank wine slowly for a couple of hours until finally, at midnight, the hotel's fax machine whirred with a final CNN contract, signed by Jim Walton.

I took a pen and countersigned it.

Then I shook John's hand.

"A year ago, I took a leap of faith with you. Tonight you repaid me. Thank you. More important, you got to thank the guys who saved your life. And close a deal that fucks all those wankers who wanted you dead."

He laughed.

"It's a good night for guys who have lived, learned, and lost, and come back from the brink to achieve what was thought impossible. Thank *you*."

It's great to have a manager who's a true friend as well. I'd trust him with my life.

THURSDAY, SEPTEMBER 2, 2010

Dinner with Martin Cruddace at Soho House in L.A.

We worked together for a tumultuous decade at *The Daily Mirror*, when he ran the legal department and I ran the editorial side. And became so close that I even shared his apartment for a couple of years when my first marriage ended.

A finer, more loyal, trusted colleague and friend it would be impossible to find.

"How the fuck have you pulled this off?" he said with a grin.

"I have no real idea," I replied. It does still feel like some kind of weird dream.

"Feeling the pressure yet?"

"Nope."

"Liar."

He knows me too well.

The truth is that of course I am.

This is no ordinary job.

I'm replacing an absolute icon, and a man beloved by the American people.

The fact that I'm a younger British upstart with a history of tabloid journalism and reality television isn't going to make this takeover process any easier.

I've seen what the American media does to people it doesn't like, and it isn't pretty.

They'll give me a few months' honeymoon period until I actually get on air, but the moment I do, it's going to be a bloodbath.

If I'm not very careful, the dream will rapidly become a nightmare.

WEDNESDAY, SEPTEMBER 8, 2010

I've appeared as a guest on Larry King's show three times over the years, via satellite.

But until today, we've never actually met in person.

CNN wanted to formally announce my appointment by having me and Larry appear together. So I arrived at the network's bureau on Sunset Boulevard in Los Angeles at 8 A.M.

A phalanx of security guards led me into the building and down a long, slim corridor boasting huge photos of Larry interviewing people like Oprah.

It was immediately intimidating—the suspenders, the iconic set, the hugely famous guests.

I turned a corner, and there was Larry, sitting in a chair, having his makeup done.

"Hi, Larry," I said, walking forward to shake his hand.

"Piers, good to meet you."

It was a surreal moment.

We had a coffee together in the green room.

He was smaller than I imagined, with a slim, wiry, slightly hunched frame.

He wore a dark blue shirt, pinstripe charcoal-gray trousers, black suspenders, and a purple and silver striped tie.

"I just want you to know what a great honor this is for me," I babbled, desperate to try to hit the right tone with someone who must have been thinking: "They're replacing me with *this* guy?"

"I feel like the act who followed Sinatra at the Sands in Vegas—I know I can never do as well as you, but I'll have a go."

Larry chuckled, then we sat together for twenty minutes and talked about everything from Obama to Clinton, Iraq to Haiti, Murdoch to Mandela. He was exactly as I expected—fiercely intelligent, incredibly knowledgeable, very funny, and a quite fantastic name-dropper.

He was also surprisingly candid.

"I'll be honest, Piers, this feels like the end of a twenty-five-year marriage for me," he admitted. "I know it's time to leave, and I'm excited about having more freedom to do other things, but I'm still going to miss it. It's been my life for a quarter of a century."

"I hope I can live up to even half your extraordinary legacy," I replied.

We went out to meet the press, and Larry couldn't have been more gracious, posing for pictures, welcoming me to the CNN family, and telling everyone what a great success he thought I'd be.

I in turn repeated my Sinatra line, and tried to say all the right things.

Given how awkward these handovers can be, I think it went pretty well.

I was struck by the absolute reverence shown to Larry by all the CNN crew.

They love him, and he'd clearly earned that love with his behavior toward them.

"Larry's one of the genuinely nicest people in the business," one of the camera guys told me. "And we know, because we meet almost everyone in the business on this show."

At 9 A.M., I sat in a conference room with CNN's U.S. president, Jon Klein—the man who had led my first CNN meeting, and who had been the most instrumental since in bringing me to the network—and watched the big TV screen suddenly flash the immortal words: "CNN breaking news—Piers Morgan to replace Larry King."

It was a startling thing to watch.

Reaction around the world was swift and furious—in some cases, genuinely furious!

My oldest friends back in Newick put the news into proper perspective.

Cameron Jones, captain of the village cricket team, texted me on behalf of the lads: "A TV pundit just said you have to be ugly, have bad teeth, and live in a castle for a Brit to make it in the U.S. We're sticking some turrets on your house."

SUNDAY, SEPTEMBER 12, 2010

I was working out in the Beverly Wilshire gym this morning—I live at the hotel when I'm in L.A.—when I saw Radha Arora, the flamboyant general manager who has transformed the place in spectacular style over the past few years.

"Who's going to be your first guest?" he asked.

"Not sure yet. I'm trying for President Obama, but I suspect it's highly unlikely he'll do the show until he's seen what it's like."

"What about Oprah?"

"She'd be incredible, but I don't know her, or any of her people, and she doesn't give many interviews."

"Oprah's best friend, Gayle King, is in town right now. Why don't you ask her?"

I sent an email:

Dear Gayle,

   I believe our mutual friend Radha has warned you that I may be in touch. As you may know, I'm replacing Larry King on CNN.

   What you may not know is that I am a stupendous fan of Oprah. And I'm desperate to interview her for my launch week.

   I know she's the busiest woman on the planet, but I want to know how I can make this happen. Short of parasailing naked onto the roof of the White House, I'm prepared to do anything.

She replied quickly:

I will certainly let Team Oprah know of your interest. Please don't show up at the White House naked, you may be shot and that might hurt.

MONDAY, SEPTEMBER 13, 2010

A profile has appeared in *Vogue*, featuring a photograph of me wearing Larry King–style suspenders, and the headline, THE MAN WHO WOULD BE KING.

History, I reminded myself, is littered with the carcasses of would-be kings.

TUESDAY, SEPTEMBER 14, 2010

I went for a routine health screening in L.A. this morning, and the doctor who supervised it suddenly grew concerned when he performed the eye-watering digital rectal examination that all men loathe.

"I can feel a lump on your prostate."

I tried to stay calm.

"OK, what does that mean?"

"It may mean nothing, but I want to test your PSA levels."

"What's that?"

"Prostate-specific antigen. If the levels are raised, it could signify something more problematic is going on."

A few hours later, he called me.

"I've detected some raised PSA levels in your prostate, which again could mean nothing. But combined with the lump that I felt, they are significant enough to suggest that it may indicate a serious condition."

"Like what?"

"Like prostate cancer."

I've always wondered how I'd feel if I ever heard the "C" word, and it's as bad as I imagined.

"I don't want to alarm you," he continued, "and as I said, it may be nothing. But I want you to undergo a biopsy. And I want you to do it quickly."

"OK."

I hung up and gasped.

Tonight was the *America's Got Talent* finale, which should have been incredibly exciting and fun, but my mind was a million miles away.

David Hasselhoff, a former judge on the show, was in the same building, filming *Dancing with the Stars,* and came to say hello.

"I do miss you, Hoff," I confessed. "Working with you was like a trip to the dentist. Painful while it lasted, but essentially a force for good in my life."

"Me too, man," he laughed. "You're a wanker, but a good wanker."

To compound the misery of my day, Celia gave an interview to a British TV show called *Daybreak* this morning, in which, when asked how she felt about my new job, she replied deadpan: "I'm still reeling from the shock.

I don't know what this means for me." Pause. "I'm sure we'll survive, it's fine . . ."

All delivered with a slightly strained expression, as if she was fighting back tears.

I knew instantly it was all a joke. But unfortunately, that particular brand of sarcasm doesn't tend to travel well across the Atlantic.

And sure enough, within hours, the entertainment websites over here were buzzing with PIERS MORGAN DITCHES WIFE FOR NEW LIFE IN AMERICA–style headlines.

I was even grilled about it on the *AGT* after-show red carpet tonight.

"Is your marriage in trouble already?" asked one of the reporters.

I phoned Celia when I got home.

"Congratulations. Not only am I dying, but apparently we're also divorcing."

"Oh God, I'm sorry. I won't talk about you again in public . . ."

"I can already hear next week's *Daybreak* promo: 'Celia reveals how Piers wears her underwear, eats Chinese meals for four at night, and likes to be called Doris in bed—' "

"Those things," she interrupted, "will remain strictly entre nous."

WEDNESDAY, SEPTEMBER 15, 2010

I barely slept last night. Still reeling from what the doctor told me.

Saw John for a drink tonight, and told him.

"Look, like he said, it is probably nothing. There's no point worrying about something that may not exist."

He's right, but it's nagging at me like a large, angry worm in my ear.

THURSDAY, SEPTEMBER 16, 2010

I'm due to undergo the biopsy tomorrow. I Googled the procedure this morning and feel alarmed by some of the side effects that can result.

Then I remembered an Irish urologist who once treated me years ago in London, and is renowned as one of the best in the world in prostate-related issues.

I found his number and called him. He listened to all the details, including the lump and PSA levels, and said: "Right, do *not* have the biopsy. American doctors massively overorder these operations in situations like this, and they are almost always unnecessary. This particular procedure can also cause problems of its own. Come and see me next week when you're back in London."

I canceled the biopsy. And suddenly felt hugely better, despite having no factual evidence yet that should make me feel hugely better.

FRIDAY, SEPTEMBER 17, 2010

The single most crucial appointment for my show is going to be the position of executive producer.

That's the show-runner who makes everything tick. And for this kind of show, he or she has to be very experienced, very talented, and very driven.

I've interviewed a few candidates, but none has seemed right to me.

The name I keep coming back to is Jonathan Wald.

He's got a great pedigree, having EP'd both the *Today Show* and the *NBC Nightly News*. His father, Richard, was also once president of NBC News for four years.

I've met him a couple of times with John, who knows him well, and I like him enormously. He's very clever, super confident, and really wants the job. He also makes me laugh, which is extremely important.

Today Jon Klein said he agreed with me, and was going to offer the job to Jonathan.

SATURDAY, SEPTEMBER 18, 2010

I emailed Jonathan to congratulate him.

"Amen," he replied. "I sort of like the line Robert Redford says at the end of *The Candidate:* 'Now what?' "

MONDAY, SEPTEMBER 20, 2010

Back in London and saw my Irish urologist this morning.

"Like I thought, there's no problem here," he concluded after a series of tests. "I can't feel any lump, and many men of your age have raised PSA levels. It usually means nothing. The biopsy though can have some bad side effects. That's why I always try and avoid them unless they are absolutely essential."

"So I haven't got cancer?"

"You haven't got cancer."

FRIDAY, SEPTEMBER 24, 2010

Unbelievable.

Jon Klein's been fired from CNN.

And Jeff Zucker's gone from NBC.

The two men who made my deal happen have both departed their jobs on the same day before my show's even gotten to air.

The new CNN U.S. president is Ken Jautz, who was also in the room when I had that first interview back in April.

I spoke to him tonight and he said this changed absolutely nothing about the network's plans for me.

Still unsettling though.

SATURDAY, SEPTEMBER 25, 2010

Spoke to Jon Klein, who was upset but realistic.

"I had five good years, it's just business. You just go and prove I was right to hire you!"

I feel really sorry for him. He's a great guy, and I know he had huge belief in me.

But as he said, it's just business. And the cable news business, as I'm quickly discovering, is one of the most ruthless in the world.

SUNDAY, SEPTEMBER 26, 2010

A small memorial celebration took place in the southern English county of Kent today—commemorating the last time our troops engaged in battle with invading forces on home soil.

Seventy years ago, men from the First Battalion London Irish Rifles fought a four-man crew from a German bomber in what became known as the Battle of Graveney Marsh.

The soldiers sprang into action when a new Junkers 88 plane was shot down by Spitfires and landed on nearby marshland.

As they approached, the Germans opened fire with a machine gun, and a twenty-minute firefight ensued before the Rifles apprehended their foe.

This was the first time since Prince Charlie's defeat at Culloden in 1746 that there had been such a clash on British soil. And it was to be the last of its kind, too.

But what happened next was perhaps even more extraordinary.

The British commanding officer, Captain John Cantopher, overheard one of the captured Germans saying the plane was going to "go up" at any moment.

Realizing the Junkers 88 was an invaluable new prototype, Captain Cantopher dashed back to the aircraft, found a bomb under one of the wings, and threw it into a dyke. Thus saving the plane, which was only two weeks old, for British engineers to examine and getting the advantage on the Luftwaffe.

For his heroism, he received the George Medal, one of the highest honors for valor in Britain.

Captain Cantopher was my great-uncle, brother of my grandmother Margot. Or Grande, as we call the matriarch of my family.

She's now his only surviving sibling, and fittingly, my brother Jeremy was back from Afghanistan and able to attend the ceremony with Grande today.

John was a great character.

On the night before he was due to receive his medal, he got riotously drunk in London, arriving at the hotel at 3 A.M. and telling the concierge: "Wake me at eight A.M., I've got an appointment at Buckingham Palace with the king."

The concierge assumed he was joking, John overslept, missed the palace presentation, and the huge party organized by the London Irish had to be postponed.

WEDNESDAY, OCTOBER 6, 2010

Had my visa appointment at the U.S. Embassy in London.

My interview lasted about twenty-three seconds, just long enough for the interrogator to ask: "Have you bought your new suspenders yet?"

FRIDAY, OCTOBER 8, 2010

I've flown to New York to meet my new CNN colleagues and do some press to promote the show, which will now launch on January 17—allowing the quiet Christmas and New Year season to pass.

One of the more amusing questions that keeps being thrown at me is, "So, Mr. Morgan, are you just going to be chasing ratings?"

It reminds me of when I had to defend scoops I published as a newspaper editor and some pompous BBC announcer would always sneer: "You're just doing this to sell papers, aren't you?"

The answer to both shocking allegations is quite simple: Of course I am!

I can spout all the "it's not just about ratings" guff I like. But the truth is that if my ratings tank for a sustained period of time, I'm out.

My new glass-fronted office is on the corner of the seventh floor of the Time Warner skyscraper in Manhattan, with spectacular views over Central Park.

I discovered that I'm going to be sharing a newsroom with Anderson Cooper.

He's a terrific journalist, who made his name at CNN with his evisceration of George Bush's administration over its abject failure to help the poor victims of Hurricane Katrina.

I'd been warned that he's very shy off camera, but Anderson came over to say hello as soon as he saw me.

"If I can do anything to help, just shout," he said.

As we chatted in the middle of our joint battlefield—his side bursting with people, excitement, and energy, mine currently devoid of all those things!—I realized how much I've missed being in a newsroom.

It's been six years since I was unceremoniously ejected from *The Daily Mirror* for publishing supposedly fake photos of British soldiers abusing Iraqi civilians (I've never seen conclusive evidence to establish their inauthenticity), and it was great to feel that rush again, unique to banks of journalists at their computers chasing hot stories.

That excitement mounted as I walked around the streets of midtown Manhattan in the late afternoon, and had endless people coming up to wish me luck and offer advice.

"We love Larry!" cried one middle-aged lady. "Don't let us down!"

There's a great deal of affection and admiration for Larry in America, and the sheer scale of the challenge in replacing this man is growing on me every time I venture outside.

We needed a huge, global superstar to launch the
show and we got one with Oprah.

2

WEDNESDAY, OCTOBER 20, 2010

Jon Stewart's unique brand of acerbic, frustrated, incensed, hilarious nightly political and social commentary on *The Daily Show* has made him an extraordinarily well-trusted figure who now has considerably more cultural influence on Americans than many of his noncomedic rivals.

Tonight, he appeared on *Larry King Live,* and I watched expectantly to see if one of my TV heroes would mention the fact I was taking over the CNN show in January.

He did.

"By the way," he told Larry, "I think they made a brilliant choice by bringing in a British guy no one's heard of. When I'm thinking about floating a sinking ship, what do I want to bring on it: A guy that people are going to tune in and go, 'Who's that, and why is he speaking so funny?' "

TUESDAY, OCTOBER 26, 2010

Jonathan Wald has closed his CNN deal.

"Dress British, act Yiddish" was his first instruction today.

WEDNESDAY, OCTOBER 27, 2010

I've hired another crucial employee—my personal assistant.

Just the thought of juggling my schedules for CNN, *America's Got Talent,* and *Life Stories,* my UK talk show, made me break out in a rash.

I only had one person in mind for this insane task.

Juliana Severo is a smart, fiery, ballsy Italian American.

She was production manager of *AGT* for three years, while still in her midtwenties, and ran that maelstrom of madness with ruthless efficiency.

I need someone who's going to watch my back, make sure I never miss an appointment, and tell a *lot* of people to go fuck themselves.

Juliana's my girl.

THURSDAY, OCTOBER 28, 2010

We have a title for the show—*Piers Morgan Tonight.*

I'd prefer *Piers Morgan Live,* but my NBC contract means I won't be able to go live every night, as they have first rights to my work on *America's Got Talent* taping days. So for now this will have to suffice.

Jim Walton emailed: "The title is fine with me, but the *PMT* moniker will raise some eyebrows."

I laughed. Jim's married to a woman from England, where "PMT" is the abbreviation better known in the States as "PMS."

THURSDAY, NOVEMBER 4, 2010

John took me to the Arlington National Cemetery in Washington, D.C., this morning, where both his parents are buried. His father was a military man. And his brother Mike is a current high-ranking three-star U.S. general.

Set in 624 immaculately preserved acres of woodland, the cemetery houses the simple white graves of more than 350,000 servicemen and servicewomen and their spouses.

More than a hundred new graves are prepared each week, many currently for troops killed on the battlefields of Iraq and Afghanistan.

We came across the grave belonging to John F. Kennedy, who was buried at Arlington because he served in the navy. Only one other president is buried there—William Howard Taft.

A permanent small flame lies on JFK's simple flat stone tomb, flickering defiantly. A few feet away is a quotation of his on a small wall: "Let every nation know, whether it wishes us well or ill, that we shall pay any price, bear any burden, meet any hardship, support any friend, oppose any foe to assure the survival and the success of liberty."

I looked out at the thousands of gravestones, many of them for people as young as eighteen or nineteen, and concluded once again that there can never be any decision for a leader of a country more important to make than the one to go to war.

We reached John's parents' grave, and he knelt in the pouring rain to pay his respects.

I found the whole experience profoundly moving.

MONDAY, NOVEMBER 8, 2010

Last night, I watched *Client 9,* the new documentary movie about scandalous former New York governor Eliot Spitzer. It carries special interest for me now because Spitzer currently hosts the show that will lead into mine on CNN.

He was forced to resign sensationally two years ago after it was revealed he'd been using an escort agency despite leading a crackdown against illegal prostitution rings.

But as the film shows, before the scandal broke, he was a consistently loud, brave, and passionate defender of the downtrodden little guy against the rich, privileged, corrupt elite. Spitzer also aggressively pursued the very people who caused the global financial crisis, specifically targeting predatory lending practices by mortgage lenders.

All this made him the people's hero, and led him to be touted as a Democratic presidential candidate. But it also made him despised by many on Wall Street and in Washington, which explains why there was such undisguised relish at his political demise.

I had a good chat with him in his office this afternoon, and he's a dynamic and obviously fiercely intelligent man, determined to try to make his struggling CNN show work.

Whether he can ride out the current cacophony of criticism about his appointment remains to be seen.

TUESDAY, NOVEMBER 9, 2010

President George W. Bush has finally broken his postpresidency silence and it's been quite an eye-opener.

Bush ended up a very unpopular president, but I saw a human, and even rather charming, side to him in his various TV interviews this week, which surprised me.

A prime minister from one of the Caribbean islands once told me that he'd had dinner with Bush and Tony Blair separately within the space of six months.

"What was the difference between them?" I asked.

"Bush looked me in the eye and told me what he knew I wasn't going to like hearing, whereas Blair looked me in the eye and told me what he thought I wanted to hear."

And I suspect there's a certain truth to that. Listening to a lifetime conservative like Bush firmly defending his controversial decisions, such as going to war in Iraq and waterboarding al-Qaeda suspects, I could tell that he genuinely believed in what he was saying—even if I personally vehemently disagreed with him.

When I've seen Blair, a left-wing lawyer, try to defend similar stuff, he sounds considerably less sincere.

WEDNESDAY, NOVEMBER 10, 2010

Donald Trump invited me to a party tonight to launch Kim Kardashian's new perfume.

"How's my champ?" he shouted when he saw me coming down the red carpet. Ever since I won his *Celebrity Apprentice* show, this is what Trump always calls me.

Trump's a polarizing figure, but I love his supreme self-confidence—as confirmed by the titles of his books: *Think Like a Billionaire; Think Big and Kick Ass;* and my favorite: *No Such Thing as Over-Exposure.*

Beneath the cocksure bluster, though, Trump's a very smart businessman, and he's now seriously considering going for the biggest job of them all—the presidency.

"It's very tempting," he confessed tonight. "Everywhere I go, people ask me if I'm running. And I'm considering it. I mean, how many more houses can I buy and sell?"

A race between Sarah Palin and Donald Trump for the Republican ticket in 2012 would be a sensational one for the media, and possibly a worrying one for Barack Obama, given the huge popularity both of them have among many mainstream Americans.

One of the many fascinating things about Trump is that he's never touched a drop of alcohol, smoked a cigarette, or tried a drug. He doesn't even drink coffee.

His only vice is women.

I once asked him for the secret to his success with the ladies, and he explained:

"A lot of it is down to The Look. It doesn't mean you have to look like Cary Grant, it means you have to have a certain way about you, a stature. I see some successful guys who just don't have The Look. And they are never going to go out with great women. The Look is very important. I don't really like to talk about it because it sounds very conceited . . . but it matters."

THURSDAY, NOVEMBER 11, 2010

Appeared as a guest on my *AGT* costar Nick Cannon's radio show this morning. His wife, Mariah Carey, has just announced she's pregnant, giving me the perfect way to get straight under his skin.

"Congratulations, Daddy!" I exclaimed.

"Thank you, Mr. Morgan," he replied, instantly suspicious.

"You *are* the daddy, I presume?" I added, "I've been ruled out, right?"

Nick laughed, in the way that Mafia don John Gotti used to laugh before slicing his victims into sausages.

"You are the only man alive who I'd let say that," he said, "without whipping their butt."

"Will you both come on my CNN show?" I asked.

"Yes, definitely. Just so that if you repeat this line of questioning, I can whip your butt on live TV."

It's just as well I'm doing my own bookings, because I heard this afternoon that one of Larry King's top bookers, Nancy Baker, is now going to stay working for him on his four CNN specials a year, after indicating to us that she'd come to our show.

It's a blow, because her reputation is strong, and I will live or die by the quality of the guests.

A few hours later, we heard that another of Larry's senior bookers had also changed her mind.

I suspected the hand of Wendy Walker, Larry's longtime producer, and erupted with anger in an email to Jonathan after reading the latest rejection message.

"Right," I wrote. "Fuck them. Let's go to war. Wendy and her coterie have wasted enough of our time."

"I think you 'replied all,' so they'll get the message loud and clear," he wrote back.

Oh God, no. I didn't, did I?

I checked.

Yes, I did.

When I'd calmed down a few hours later, I realized that Wendy was only doing what she'd done with huge success for nearly two decades—look after Larry.

I admire her loyalty. And, for that matter, the loyalty of the bookers.

FRIDAY, NOVEMBER 12, 2010

Lunch with Ted Turner, the entrepreneurial genius who created CNN.

We met at his midtown Manhattan restaurant, Ted's Montana Grill, and both ate his famous bison burgers.

He added a very precise order of five french fries.

"Six makes me fat, four makes me hungry," he explained.

Ted, now seventy-two, is an extraordinary character. He's one of America's biggest private landowners, possessing more than two million acres; he won the America's Cup sailing contest and the World Series with the Atlanta Braves; gave a billion dollars to charity when such an act was unheard of; and married Jane Fonda.

He achieved all of this with his famous mantra, borrowed from Henry Ford: "Early to bed, early to rise, work like hell, and advertise."

"What's your biggest remaining ambition?" I asked.

"To rid the world of nuclear weapons."

"And of all the people you've ever met, who has been the most impressive?"

"Gorbachev," he said, without a moment's hesitation. "Many people have had an effect on parts of the world, but that man changed the whole world."

I asked him what advice he had for me.

"Do the news intelligently. Don't dumb down to chase ratings."

It was a fun, fascinating lunch.

Ted shook my hand as we left, and smiled: "I think you're gonna do just fine, young man."

I hope so.

I owe it to Ted Turner and all those who made CNN what it is.

SUNDAY, NOVEMBER 14, 2010

Feeling mischievous, I emailed Rupert Murdoch today to invite him to be one of my first guests.

Dear Mr. Murdoch,

I hope you're well. As I'm sure you're aware, I'm replacing Larry King at CNN in January. Not quite as crazy as you making me editor of the *News of the World* at twenty-eight, but bordering on it.

I would love to interview you for the show. On a scale of one to a hundred, what are my chances? If the answer is zero, I'll stop trying. Anything higher than that, I'd really like to try and persuade you.

Kind regards,

Piers

Given he owns one of my main competitors, Fox News, I won't hold my breath. But you never know with him . . .

TUESDAY, NOVEMBER 16, 2010

Prince William and Kate Middleton announced their engagement today, sparking an absolute frenzy of excitement here in the States.

This royal romance is electrifying America in a way I haven't seen since Diana and Charles walked down the aisle. The happy couple has been on the cover of almost every celebrity magazine for months, and more and more TV airtime has been devoted to analyzing every nook and cranny of a wedding that until today hadn't even been confirmed.

"Are you friends with them?" Jonathan asked. "Can you get the first interview?"

The answer is no, and no. William and I have shared a few moments over the years—including a remarkable, private two-hour lunch at Kensington Palace with his mother—but he still views anyone associated with the tabloids as vermin.

"It might be easier booking Elvis or Superman."

Jonathan laughed: "Best line from Superman. Lex Luthor to assistant: 'I ask you to kill Superman and you couldn't even do that one simple thing.' "

WEDNESDAY, NOVEMBER 17, 2010

Jonathan's been working on the set design.

"Do you want to face the audience with your desk, like Leno [I think not], and do you prefer to have your left or right side facing the camera?"

These seem like simple questions.

But they can actually be incredibly important.

"I want to sit on the same side of the desk that Larry sat, facing the guest," I said.

THURSDAY, NOVEMBER 18, 2010

Rupert Murdoch replied.

"Hi, Piers, thanks for the compliment, but your chances of getting me on CNN are zero in a hundred! However, I wish you luck with your show. Best wishes, Rupert."

FRIDAY, NOVEMBER 19, 2010

We're less than two months away from launch and still barely have anyone in the newsroom.

There's just me, Jonathan, Juliana, Maria Arceo, the senior show coordinator, and a solitary booker, Susan Durrwachter.

But we've been interviewing dozens of people, and secured some very good candidates to come on board very soon.

"We'll be fine," said Jonathan. It's reassuring that he seems to know exactly what he's doing.

SUNDAY, NOVEMBER 21, 2010

CNN has started running promos for my show.

One features me staring down the camera saying, "Come on America, call me what you like—call me nosy, unpredictable, British . . . but do *not* call me boring!"

Another suggests that I'm going to be dangerous, and keen to "seek the truth."

One of my former *Mirror* journalists, Steve Dennis, emailed me tonight from Los Angeles, where he now works as an author: "I've just suffered a flashback. That look, hands in pockets, expressionless 'bring it on' face, followed by the timely raise of the eyebrows. *That* is your withering *Mirror* editor look! It's official. You mean business. I'm warning everyone."

I laughed. It does feel like I'm going back in time to when I first walked into those newsrooms at the *News of the World* and *The Mirror*.

Fear was not an option.

They were two of the most ruthlessly professional, aggressive places in news-gathering history.

And as with CNN now, there were a lot of people just waiting for me to fall flat on my smug little face.

MONDAY, NOVEMBER 22, 2010

I've bought a pub, a few blocks from my London home in Kensington.

It's called the Hansom Cab, and my brother Rupert's going to run it for me.

Pubs have played a big part in my life.

I grew up in one. My parents ran a place called the Griffin Inn, in Sussex, from when I was five to thirteen.

During this era drunk driving was rife and barely a night went by without people fighting, illicitly fornicating, getting arrested, or simply falling over, drunk as skunks. "Lock-ins"—when pub owners let drinkers stay in the pub after the legal closing time—were the norm.

It all seemed utterly thrilling to me. Though one of my mother's most shameful moments came when the local primary school headmistress made a formal complaint that her treasured oldest son had arrived for lessons "smelling of alcohol."

It was true, I had. But only because I often spent half an hour before school "bottling up," which involved replenishing all the empty pub shelves with new bottles of beer, wine, spirits, and mixers.

When we moved a mile away to Newick, I began partaking in alcohol in a more direct way.

At fifteen, I drank my first pint of Strongbow cider with slow, deliberate glee in the corner of the Royal Oak.

It was illegal, of course. But in those days, village pubs were full of kids my age. As long as you looked even vaguely eighteen, the legal drinking age, you were fine.

I grew to love that pub with a passion.

Every Friday and Saturday, I'd pile in there with my mates and drink as much Strongbow as I could physically consume before my body gave way.

Those evenings would follow a familiar pattern.

I'd get louder and more obnoxious as the cider took its grip, until eventually someone would pour a pint over my head, temporarily blinding me in the process. I'd then wheel around, lashing out at suspected assailants until the leggy landlady, Mary, object of all our adolescent dreams, would utter the immortal words: "Piers, you're banned!" And throw me into the street.

From there, I'd stumble the mile-long walk home, occasionally lurching into a hedge.

The next morning, I'd be back at opening time to beg forgiveness from Mary—who would always capitulate, but often only when I'd agreed to do a few free shifts behind the bar.

The Royal Oak, along with cricket, became the focal point of my life.

When I chart the funniest ten evenings of my life, at least three or four would involve the Oak. At the top of the list is the time Jeremy beat his own record for drinking a pint of beer, without spilling a drop, while standing on his head, upside down.

He did it in 4.8 seconds, considerably faster than most of us could do it standing upright. And faster, he claimed, than anyone else in the British Army at the time.

Unfortunately, he then tried to repeat the exercise later that year in a restaurant in London—using warm lager instead of bitter, and a weird-shaped glass. Halfway through the attempt, the bubbles flew up his nose, and he reared up like a speared gorilla and began to projectile vomit over everyone within ten yards.

The Oak became a sanctuary as I reached my late teens. A place to escape the rigors of college and work. And, occasionally, national humiliation.

The day after I got fired from *The Daily Mirror*, I knew exactly where I needed to be to get away from the jubilantly frenzied media stomping on my professional grave.

I drove to Newick, parked my car in the Oak's parking lot, and walked down to the front door. As I entered, many of my oldest friends were waiting and delivered a perfectly timed, slow round of mocking applause.

I took a bow, the clapping increased in volume, then one of them said: "Right, you may be the most humiliated man in Britain, but it's still your round. Get the beers in, Morgan."

Even now, when I walk inside—sometimes straight from the airport after a ten-hour flight from L.A.—I breathe in the familiar fumes, see the familiar faces, and sigh with relief.

TUESDAY, NOVEMBER 23, 2010

We've hired more highly regarded bookers—Julie Zann (politics), Rachel Burstein from *Oprah* (everything), and Shant Petrossian from *Rachael Ray* (celebrity).

We also hired Winnie Dunbar, a top producer who has worked everywhere from CNN to *Oprah*. And a writer, Susan Lay.

In addition, we've successfully hired a few of Larry's key staff including Lisa Thompson, who specializes in books and world leaders; Andrea Beaumont (news booker); three bright young producers: Brad Parks, Geoff Doner, and Kathryn McQuade; Lindsay Geier, a logistical powerhouse who will run the show's guest schedule; and Deb Daly, West Coast booking coordinator.

They all have very impressive résumés, and all talk a great game. Just hope they can live up to it!

Jonathan's been handling all these hirings, but there's one over which I have taken personal charge.

Conor Hanna worked for me at *The Mirror* for years, and was a brilliant news executive who became the paper's deputy editor after I left.

He's from Belfast, Northern Ireland, and is a very experienced, reliable, and trustworthy newsman, working closely with me on huge stories like 9/11 and the Iraq War.

It's taken a while to extract him from his *Mirror* contract, but we can have him by January.

I'm thrilled. I need someone I'd trust implicitly to tell me the truth, who is a stickler for facts, and who understands me. He's that person.

"How much TV has he done?" Jonathan asked today.

"Absolutely none," I replied.

MONDAY, NOVEMBER 29, 2010

I've been working regularly with Gayle King via email about the Oprah interview, but there's still no decision. Although, I have discovered that Gayle herself is just as smart, warm, and funny as her great friend. And she definitely seems to be on my side.

But today, I received an update from her publicist, Lisa Halliday:

> Sorry, nothing to confirm yet, Piers. We are heading to Australia with our show this week—will be there until Christmas.
>
> I'll give you a call when we get back to the States the week of 12/27. Unfortunately, I won't have an answer for you until then.
>
> Hopefully we'll be able to work something out for January.

God, this is sweating it right to the wire.

My gut feeling from the tone of this email is that I won't get the interview, and they're letting me down gently.

TUESDAY, NOVEMBER 30, 2010

"If you never change your mind," said Edward de Bono, the renowned expert on creative thinking, "why have one?"

Which is why I joined Twitter today.

I've lambasted the social media site for the last couple of years as a pointless, vacuous forum for stupid Twits to tweet to other Twits.

But Steve Krakauer, my new digital producer, has persuaded me that I have to join for the sake of the show. So I took the plunge today and penned the following debut tweet: "I'm now a Twit, official."

A sentiment that sparked instant and almost universal global agreement.

Within less than an hour, I was completely hooked. It's fast, immediate, slightly wild, and great fun.

THURSDAY, DECEMBER 2, 2010

I made my debut appearance on CNN tonight, on Wolf Blitzer's show, *The Situation Room.*

Wolf's the on-screen engine driver of CNN's airtime, particularly on the big stories. So it's important I develop a good rapport with him.

I needn't have worried—he was kind and generous, with both his time and his words.

Everyone at CNN's been extremely welcoming so far, I must say.

FRIDAY, DECEMBER 3, 2010

Breakfast with Jeff Zucker.

"How's the preparation going?" he asked.

"A bit nerve-racking, but I'm loving every second."

"The critics will be out to shoot you down, mainly because you're British! Ignore them and focus on producing good shows. The ratings will come if you do that. Who do you have for launch week?"

"Nobody big confirmed yet," I said. "Still working on Obama, Oprah, and a few others."

"You won't get Obama; he'll wait and see what the show's like first. Oprah would be great, though."

"What are you going to do next?" I asked.

"I'm not sure yet. Just going to take my time, have a break, clear my head, and then see what opportunities are out there."

"Well, I can't thank you enough again for letting me go to CNN. I owe you, big time."

"I didn't want to have a judge on *America's Got Talent* full of resentment because I stopped him from doing his dream job."

"You never know, maybe you'll wash up at CNN!" I joked.

We both laughed at the absurdity of such a notion.

SATURDAY, DECEMBER 4, 2010

I've made my first Twitter booking.

Someone tweeted that they'd love me to interview Jessica Alba for the show.

I retweeted, with the comment, "I agree, she'd be fantastic."

And minutes later, Jessica tweeted back, "Thank u, I'd be honored!"

As simple as that. No agents, managers, publicists, lawyers.

Just one quick Twitter exchange and the deal was done.

As a news source, Twitter's extraordinary.

As a font of gossip, unparalleled.

As a booking force, clearly incredibly useful.

And as a way to kill time on all those tedious car and plane trips that befall my weekly life, it's a joyously entertaining diversion.

Jonathan, highly amused by my conversion to his favorite social media, penned a blog for CNN.com:

Somewhere along the way to amassing more than fifty-seven thousand Twitter followers in a little less than a week, including the delightfully British-sounding @Lord_Sugar, Piers Morgan became an American television anchor. It might have been hard to tell from his tweets—an often inexplicable amalgamation of soccer, cricket, warm beer, and other distinctly British areas of fascination—but the Americanization is under way.

TUESDAY, DECEMBER 7, 2010

Back in London to meet the staff at CNN International.

Unlike in America, most of these journalists are British, and know all about my tabloid past.

I could tell from some of their faces that my appointment has gone down like a cup of cold pea puree.

But that's OK.

I've experienced that exact same reaction before, when I first walked into the *News of the World.* It's down to me to prove them wrong.

I also sat down with journalists from countries including Brazil, Israel, Germany, Denmark, and France.

I asked one of the CNN execs afterward to confirm how many places the network aired in.

"About two hundred countries and territories," he replied.

"And how often will my show air?"

"Three times a day, including prime time."

"Wow. That's a lot of eyeballs!" I said.

"Yep. We don't know exactly how many, because rating systems don't work that well in many places we air. But we're available in over three hundred million homes."

Tonight, CNN threw a lavish launch party for me at the Mandarin Hotel.

Jim Walton repeated in his welcome speech the three hundred million potential global audience figure—causing audible gasps of undisguised horror from my numerous British TV rivals in the room.

But he won their hearts with his next line: "We listened to your phone calls, we read your emails, and we decided to do what you asked, and take Piers out of Britain!"

Cue loud roars of approval.

FRIDAY, DECEMBER 10, 2010

A message from Gayle King: "I am waving my Piers pom-poms!"

Not sure what this means.

SATURDAY, DECEMBER 11, 2010

Another message from Gayle King: "Looking good."

Now I think I know what she means.

THURSDAY, DECEMBER 16, 2010

The last *Larry King Live* show aired tonight, and it was a remarkably poignant occasion, as presidents and superstars queued up to pay homage to the great man.

The funniest moment came when Larry told Bill Clinton, "We're both in the Zipper Club."

The former president looked momentarily startled, perhaps assuming for one terrifying moment that this was a reference to their mutual love of the ladies.

Later, Larry—clearly prompted by nervous CNN executives backstage—gave the following hilarious clarification: "By the way, the suits wanted me to remind you what the Zipper Club is. It's if you've had open-heart surgery, they have to zipper you up. I thought everyone knew that . . ."

Clinton roared with laughter, then said, "I'm glad you clarified that!"

As the final moment arrived, a tearful Larry stared at the camera and said, "I don't know what to say, except to you, my audience, thank you. And instead of good-bye, how about so long?"

The lights dimmed, and the final shot was of a lone microphone twinkling in the darkness.

It brought a lump to my throat, and I'm sure to millions of others who were also watching.

FRIDAY, DECEMBER 17, 2010

My favorite U.S. sport is basketball. Probably because it's the only one of America's big four (baseball, football, and ice hockey being the others) that I've actually played.

Tonight I attended my first game in the States, and took Meghan as my guest.

She recently left Rogers and Cowan to be both my personal publicist and CNN publicity director for the show.

So I'm now her sole client.

"Every inch of press and hype right now is good for the prospects of my show launching well," I told her on the way to Madison Square Garden, where the New York Knicks were taking on the Miami Heat. "The only enemy is apathy."

"Or terrible press," she replied.

The VIP suite was bursting with famous people—Woody Allen, Paul Simon, Spike Lee, two Jonas brothers, and Liam Neeson.

I spotted Bill O'Reilly, standing with two young girls.

He's extremely tall, at least six feet four, and exudes that air of cocky, unassailable nonchalance that comes with the fact his show's been the number-one cable news program for the last decade in America.

"Let's go and talk to him," I said to Meghan.

"Are you sure you want to?"

"What's the worst that can happen?"

"That he doesn't know who you are, which would be embarrassing in this room right now."

"Don't be ridiculous!" I said. "How could he not be aware of all the promos we've been running—it's the biggest cable news launch in years!"

Meghan raised an eyebrow.

"He's Bill O'Reilly. I don't think he cares about, or watches CNN promos."

We walked over.

"Hi, Bill, Piers Morgan."

He stared down at me with an expression of undisguised disinterest.

"Yeah."

"We have something in common."

"Oh yeah, what?"

"We've both worked for Murdoch."

I could tell he wasn't remotely interested in anything I had to say, about anything.

"I'm looking forward to competing with you," I persisted.

He just smirked.

O'Reilly clearly didn't know who the hell I was, let alone view me as some kind of competitor.

This was all getting excruciatingly awkward.

"Well, nice to meet you," I concluded, before shuffling back with Meghan to where we'd been standing before.

"That went well," she said with a laugh.

"What a dick!"

"He's not a dick just because he doesn't know who you are," she replied.

A few minutes later, Meghan whispered: "O'Reilly's coming over to you."

And indeed he was, with the two young girls.

"Mr. Morgan," he said, rather sheepishly, "my daughter is a fan of *America's Got Talent*. Would you mind taking a picture with her?"

I exercised everything in my bodily power not to explode with laughter.

"Of course, Bill, no problem."

I turned to his daughter, who was blushing with excitement, and shook her hand.

"Who's going to take the picture?"

"I will," said Bill.

I posed with the two girls as O'Reilly steadied his camera. An elderly security guard in a badge-emblazoned blazer rushed over, stuck his hand in front of the lens, and shouted at him: "I'm sorry, sir, but we must safeguard the security of our celebrities!"

Meghan stifled a snort of laughter.

O'Reilly burned a deep shade of puce, and I thought he was actually going to erupt like a volcano.

"It's OK," I interjected. "I am more than happy for Mr. O'Reilly to take my photograph."

The guard didn't look happy, but allowed the picture to be taken.

"Thank you," said O'Reilly, through the world's most gritted teeth.

"No problem. You should definitely come on my CNN show now."

"Oh yeah, why?"

"Because A, it will be good for your celebrity status, and B, your daughter will love it."

He smirked.

"Right. Well, we'll see."

He walked away and Meghan and I shared a lengthy fit of giggles.

I got home and watched Letterman, who dedicated his top ten to Larry's farewell.

He opened by saying: "Larry will be replaced by Piers Morgan—I don't know who that is. Just a guy in the CNN lot."

Then: "Number six: I hope the show will enjoy continued success under . . . what's his name."

SATURDAY, DECEMBER 18, 2010

Simon Cowell called from Barbados, where he's spending the Christmas holiday.

"I've been watching endless promos for your new CNN show," he said. "This is ruining my holiday."

Knowing Simon as well as I do—he was responsible for bringing me to America in the first place, as a judge on *America's Got Talent*—I know this will be entirely true.

MONDAY, DECEMBER 20, 2010

Dan Pfeiffer, the White House communications chief, phoned to say it's a "no" to an Obama interview for launch week, though they haven't ruled out doing it later.

I don't have any really big names locked in yet, and we're just three weeks away. Crunch time.

The office is an intense place now, with the bookers frantically working their phones. I can feel the tension rising by the second. We all know how vital the launch week is.

"We've got to get someone huge," I told Jonathan tonight.

"We will," he insisted. "We've hired the best team in American cable news."

And that is true, at least on paper.

We've recently added another top celebrity booker, Haleigh Raff, to our coterie, and a fabulously entertaining editorial producer, Pamela Gross, whose husband, Jimmy Finkelstein, owns the *Hollywood Reporter*.

TUESDAY, DECEMBER 21, 2010

Anderson Cooper has interviewed me for a show that will air on the eve of my launch.

"So why on God's earth do you want to do a show on CNN?" was his opening question.

"Well, it actually goes back to 1991," I replied. "I was working on a big national newspaper in Britain. I was in my early twenties. And I was watching the Iraq War on a giant TV screen. CNN reporters Bernie Shaw and Peter Arnett were literally doing the most astonishing television I ever watched, with Scud missiles flying over their heads. And the whole newsroom came to a halt.

"And I realized watching it that the future of journalism was probably going to be through the presence of a TV screen. For the first time.

"The whole CNN thing just seemed to be incredibly thrilling . . . the twenty-four-hour rolling news. If it happened, you had to watch CNN."

"How will you measure success from your show?"

"Ratings. I've been brought in at a time when CNN has been going through a very tough time ratings-wise, and I think I've been brought in to shake up that nine P.M. hour, make it louder, noisier, more provocative, get some headlines, and get it talked about."

"Do you see yourself as liberal, conservative, or what?"

"I don't want to say because I can't vote here anyway, so it's kind of meaningless, and I really don't want to get pigeonholed once I start this show as a political interviewer who has a bias. People have asked me how CNN can occupy the middle ground and not be partisan but still make a big noise.

"And I always quote you, actually, from your reporting at Katrina, where I really didn't get a sense that you were bothered if it was a Democrat or

Republican administration. What you cared about so passionately and eloquently in your reporting was that somebody in an administration running your country was betraying these people and it had to stop. I'm not trying to blow smoke up the backside, but that was brilliant journalism. CNN's at its best where it can be just as visceral and emotive and passionate as its rivals without descending into partisan political speak."

"How much of an interview do you try to prepare?"

"I like to research very thoroughly. I would hate to have a moment with a guest where they know you don't know about a key aspect of their life because you haven't bothered to find out. I think as a journalist, I see it as an absolute prerequisite of the job to be very well briefed. Having said that, I love spontaneity and I think on television, with an interview, you can get some of the best moments from silence or from a 'Whoa, what did you say?' Anything that makes it suddenly feel unscripted, that makes it go veering off from what the viewer at home assumes is a nice, cozy setup. To me, there are the seven P's. It's my brother's unofficial regimental motto: 'Prior planning and preparation prevents piss-poor performance.' And then there's the three F's for guests. They've got to be fascinating, fun, and fabulous. If you've done the seven P's and you meet the three F's, you've got Emmy-winning stuff!"

Anderson laughed.

"You've said you're banning Madonna. Now what do you have against Madonna?"

"She's boring. There's Lady Gaga now. Everything is cyclical. It will happen to you, Anderson. There will be a new Anderson in ten years' time and I'll have to ban you as well."

"I'm boring now, I admit it. I never pretended not to be, but she's not boring. I like Madonna."

"No, she's boring. She's too old to do that kind of thing. When I saw her stripping off down to her undies again at fifty-two, I was like, enough. Lady Gaga's great, the new Madonna, with brains."

"I met Madonna a couple of times, I think she's really interesting."

"I disagree. She's banned, and that's it, and by the way it's permanent. It's a life ban. There's no way back."

Anderson then went on an interrogatory rampage through my life and career.

We had a really good chemistry, and I think he was intrigued, offended, and amused by both my background and my answers, in equal measure.

One thing's for sure—I'm not your normal CNN anchorman.

I in turn was surprised by how playful and funny he was—not always apparent from his serious news image.

Toward the end, I decided it was time to switch roles and throw a few questions at *him*.

"How much pressure do you feel to keep honest yourself?"

"How do you mean?"

I meant because of his "Keeping Them Honest" tagline on his show.

"You must be almost saint-like now. You can't be dishonest at all. All of us lie at least ten times a day. You can't."

"I've just stopped talking to people!"

"What's been the greatest moment of your life, the one you'd relive again before you die?"

"Wow."

"The single moment."

"Wow. Let me think about that. Honestly, professionally, I'd say the greatest moment was, and this is going to sound weird, but it was being in Haiti that first week after the earthquake because I think there's nothing worse than seeing people who have lived good and decent lives dying, being crushed, their bodies put away into dump trucks and literally dumped onto the side of the road. And no one knows their name. No one even knows their passing. And no one knows what will ever happen to them. And to be in a position where you could try to help people and actually call out those who are doing that kind of stuff and try to make a difference, to me professionally, that was the moment when I felt, this is exactly what I want to be doing with my life.

"And personally, the greatest moment . . . you know, I lost my dad when I was ten, and I think for any kid who loses a parent at an early age, it is transformative. It changes, I think, the person I was meant to be. I think the person I am now is very different than the person I was meant to be before my dad died.

"So if I could relive any moment, it would probably be . . ."

Anderson paused, and I could see he was suddenly getting very emotional.

"As a kid, I used to watch TV and lay my head on his stomach. And I remember listening to him breathe while I was watching TV.

"So I—I think it would be something like that."

Tears had sprung up in his eyes.

It was an extraordinary, unexpected moment. I've seen Anderson report from some of the saddest places on earth, but never seen him cry.

"Sorry about that," he said afterward, "I don't know what happened there."

"There's no need to apologize," I said. "I lost my father when I was young too."

WEDNESDAY, DECEMBER 22, 2010

Woke to an email from Lisa Halliday in Australia.

"We are happy to confirm Oprah has agreed to be your opening guest."

BOOM!

Got to the office, and Julie Zann ran over smiling: "George Clooney just said yes to launch week!"

BOOM!

Minutes later, Susan Durrwachter clapped her hands in the air and screamed *"Thank you!"* at whomever she was talking to on the phone. Then ended the call, punched the air, and shouted: "We got him!"

"Who?" I asked.

"Howard Stern."

BOOM!

I looked at Jonathan, who smiled. "See, I told you . . ."

By the end of the day, we'd also locked in Condoleezza Rice, Rudy Giuliani, Donald Trump, Rod Stewart, Kim Kardashian, Kid Rock, Joel Osteen, Mitt Romney, and Barbara Walters for the first three weeks.

An amazing turnaround from where we were a few days ago.

The bookers have done their job.

Now it's down to me, and the researchers, to deliver great interviews.

And the producers to make them look fantastic.

TUESDAY, DECEMBER 28, 2010

Flew back into New York tonight after spending Christmas back home in Britain to find the city's been deluged with snow. I've never seen anything like it—there were six-foot drifts *inside* the parking garage at JFK Airport.

Driving into Manhattan, it was as if some great ice-age apocalypse had engulfed the place. All caused by a ferocious twenty-inch blizzard. Even by the extreme standards of New York's weather, this was extreme.

"Wish we were on air," sighed Jonathan, when I phoned him.

"Why?"

"Because Americans are obsessed with weather."

WEDNESDAY, DECEMBER 29, 2010

New York's mayor, Michael Bloomberg, is being hammered by the media for his "slow" response to the snow.

Yet the streets are virtually back to normal after thirty-six hours!

In Britain, we tacitly accept that two inches of snow will paralyze our country for a fortnight.

SATURDAY, JANUARY 1, 2011

Had a big New Year's Eve party at the Monkey Bar last night, with some friends from London.

I stumbled, heavily hungover, into the arctic streets of Manhattan this morning, desperate for anything to remove the vicious headache pulsating at my every cranial movement.

Times Square was full of people, even at 9 A.M., all bustling along as New Yorkers tend to do—they truly are the world's great bustlers, all in a dreadful hurry, though most never seem quite sure exactly where they're hurrying to.

And then I looked up and saw my own gigantic body looming down at me.

LIGHTS ... CAMERA ... PIERS! screamed the billboard. WHO'S ON PIERS MORGAN TONIGHT?

Then, in smaller letters: THE NEW 9 O'CLOCK. COMING IN JANUARY ON CNN.

The image was a full-length photograph of me, taken on a rooftop last month, standing next to a bright white camera light.

My expression was meant to convey "smart, combative journalist."

But I fear it may have strayed more into "smug, supercilious, invading Brit" territory.

TUESDAY, JANUARY 4, 2011

I've flown to L.A. to start taping my first few interviews.

CNN is building identical studios for me in L.A. and New York.

The reason is that although the show's going to be primarily based in New York, I'll have to spend at least three or four months on the West Coast for *America's Got Talent*.

The New York studio's ready, but the L.A. studio isn't quite finished yet.

So I sat down for my very first interview today, with bad-boy rock singer Kid Rock, at a downtown Los Angeles hotel.

I didn't know much about him, and he knew even less about me.

Asked to record a quick video message that we could use to promote the show, he nodded, looked straight into the camera, and snarled: "Who the fuck is Piers Morgan?"

He was a handful to interview—abrasive, cocky, confrontational.

But he was admirably honest too, and fascinating about the state of modern America.

"What does being an American mean to you?"

"It means the freedom to choose whatever you want to be and to have a shot at that American dream—whether it's getting a good job, raising a family, buying a piece of land. It's just that ultimate sense of being free, more than anywhere else in the world."

"Is the American dream what it used to be?"

"I don't know—sometimes I shake a little finger at those baby boomers, I wonder if they did some damage. I think the dream's still there, it's just more difficult these days. When you're driving fast, you're going to stray off course a little bit. Jerk the wheel and get back on it. I think we're just jerk-ing the wheel right now and trying to get back on it."

WEDNESDAY, JANUARY 5, 2011
"Hello, Mr. Morgan!"

Oprah Winfrey burst through the door of our interview suite at the Montage Hotel like a fabulously exotic human cyclone—bold purple pant-suit, bright yellow blouse, hair glammed to the ceiling, flashing a smile so big and bright I feared I'd be electrocuted.

She shook my hand firmly and looked me straight in the eye. "We meet at last!"

"Thank you so much for doing this," I said, barely able to contain my excitement.

"No, no, thank *you* for asking me," she replied. "Everyone keeps telling me what a great interviewer you are, I'm curious to see if that's true!"

Gayle was right behind her, and we hugged.

"What can I say?" I said. "Other than I owe you, big time."

Oprah chuckled. "It was very smart of you to go through Gayle to make this happen."

"I knew I had to persuade Gayle that I was trustworthy."

"It worked. She was so passionate about me doing this interview, and eventually I go, 'Do you *know* him?' And she goes, 'No, I don't know him.' And I'm like, 'What's the deal here? Why are you pushing me so hard to do this?' "

I laughed. "We had a seduction by email."

"Oh my gosh!" squealed Oprah.

"No, we did *not* have seduction by email!" squealed Gayle, equally loudly.

I led Oprah to her chair, and she instantly went into game mode, check-ing her camera angles, retouching her hair, joking with my crew in an effortlessly professional yet calming way.

She commands a room like very few I have ever seen before—only Nel-son Mandela, Bill Clinton, Princess Diana, and Paul McCartney, perhaps.

"Don't make me cry," she warned. "I hear you like making people cry in interviews!"

"Pretty rich coming from you," I said, laughing.

"True, true!"

I had a few last words with Jonathan.

"Take your time," he said, "and remember we can cut out any stuff that doesn't work."

"Like when I talk to her about cricket?"

"That will never happen."

"Watch me."

Oprah's story is extraordinary.

She came from a life of abuse and abject poverty in racist Mississippi to become the most popular and influential talk-show star in the world, a position she has occupied for twenty-five years. She's worth a reputed two billion dollars, and has an empire that sprawls over every aspect of media—from books, magazines, and videos to her new TV network called OWN.

She'd agreed to give me forty-five minutes, and I didn't want to waste a second.

"How many people do you trust absolutely?" I asked.

"Probably five or six that I ultimately would trust no matter what, and if I were to be betrayed by those people, then I would say I don't know anything. There's a wonderful line in a Toni Morrison book that says, 'It stripped me of everything I knew.' "

"You've just come back from Australia," I said.

"Yes, it was one of the most loving experiences of my life."

"I love Australia too," I concurred, "because we just destroyed them at cricket."

"I'm not talking about that kind!" she said with a laugh.

"You don't like cricket?"

"Cricket is fine . . ."

I could see Jonathan out of the corner of my eye performing what seemed to be a slow, agonized form of self-strangulation.

For the last few weeks, I've been trying to think of genuinely distinctive

questions that could become my signature ones if I used them regularly
with guests.

The first I decided on was: "How many times have you been properly
in love?"

The second: "If I had the power to let you relive one moment of your
life, excluding marriage and children, what would you choose?"

It was time to unload the first one.

"How many times have you been properly in love?"

She stared at me as she digested what I'd asked.

"Boy, you're good . . . you are *good*!"

"Thank you."

"That's a good question. You know what's good about it? 'Properly.' By
'properly' do you mean was it really love?"

"Where it hurts your heart," I said.

"Oh, OK. Three."

"Stedman's one?"

"Stedman didn't hurt my heart. This is what I learned, love doesn't hurt.
So, only two."

"Who are they?"

"I'm not naming them! Are you kidding?"

She then revealed she still keeps the love letters from one of them in a
safety deposit box.

"Why do you keep them?"

"I don't know. I should burn them . . . Gayle knows if anything happens
to me, get the letters!"

Oprah's fascinating answer to my question was all the proof I needed
that "How many times have you been properly in love?" is going to be a rich
source of good material.

Later in the interview, Oprah disclosed how she'd nearly killed herself
by deliberately drinking detergent after becoming pregnant at fourteen.
"There isn't the great stigma that there was when I was in school. I was
fourteen. You're having a baby out of wedlock? Your life was over," she said.
"So when the baby died, I knew it was my second chance.

"So I went back to school and nobody knew, because had anybody
known at that time, I wouldn't have been able to be head of the student

council. I wouldn't have been able to be speaking champion in forensics. I wouldn't have been able to be Miss Fire Prevention.

"I wouldn't have been chosen as one of the two teenagers in the state of Tennessee to go to the White House Conference on Youth. None of those things would have happened, and the entire trajectory of my life would have been different."

As the interview drew to a close, I told her it would air on January 17, Martin Luther King Day.

Oprah paused, and her eyes filled up.

"Now you're going to try and make me weep . . . I could weep over that. But I'm not going to. I hold him in such reverence. I would not be here, the life that I live, the dream that I live in, that he predicted for our people, would not be possible had he not been who he was."

"If he was looking down now . . ."

"The night before I was launching my network, Stedman and I were watching a documentary of Dr. King and I turned to Stedman and said, 'He would have been so proud.' "

"Well, he would see an America where the most powerful man and woman. . . ."

"One of. One of."

"An arguable point. But to many people, the most powerful man and woman in America are both black . . . and for Martin Luther King, I would think that would be pretty much the culmination of that journey he talked about, the dream."

"I would say so too. I stand on the shoulders of those who have come before me."

A solitary tear crept out of Oprah's right eye. And she smiled, knowingly. The interview drew to a close.

"How did I do?" I asked her.

"You were . . ." She hesitated. "You were . . . surprising."

"Surprisingly bad?"

She giggled loudly. "No, just surprising! And that's a good thing, because who doesn't want to be surprised?"

"What was so surprising?"

"You don't take no for an answer! You just keep asking the same question in a different way until you get a response. Interviewers don't do that in America, so your style will surprise a lot of people."

THURSDAY, JANUARY 6, 2011

Television critics lead strange lives. They're forced to do what the rest of us never have to do—watch television they absolutely loathe. While we reach for the remote and find something more palatable, they have to stick with whatever ghastly show they feel compelled to review.

So it's hardly surprising that so many of them are sour-faced, both in person and in print.

Like most performers, my view of critics depends entirely on what they say. If they rave about me, I love them. If they bury me into a deep pit of bile, I want to have them mutilated limb by limb.

Today, I found myself at the Television Critics Association press tour in Pasadena, where hundreds of critics gather to throw verbal darts at the very same people they throw literary darts at all year.

I sat on a raised stage with Jonathan and looked out at a sea of unimpressed, unamused, bored, tired faces.

We plodded through predictable questions.

"CNN has to make more noise," I responded to someone who asked what I hoped to bring to the network. "It's up against loud, partisan beasts in the jungle like MSNBC and Fox News. To perform in that jungle, you've got to be more aggressive, louder—make more noise."

Another accused me of being "polarizing"—in a way that implied I would be upset by this assertion.

"I love being polarizing," I said with a laugh. "It's more fun. The idea of being some saintly figure in modern television must be unbearable. I think television should be provocative."

Asked about the "dangerous" promos that have been running, I said: "Guests have a choice of a safe, easy five-minute ride on another interview show to plug their movie, or they can come on for an hour and joust with an annoying Brit and, if they succeed, be the toast of America."

I could tell that some of the critics "got" my humor, and some of them most definitely didn't.

Washington Post writer Lisa de Moraes blogged later: "Based on tweets afterward, half the room fell in love with him, the other half loathed him, and think it's the beginning of the end for CNN."

Oprah, meanwhile, appeared at a cocktail party to launch her new OWN network, and was asked about our interview.

"Wow, it was one of the toughest I've done in twenty years," she said, then laughed. "Listen, I had to go and have a hot bath and take a couple of painkillers afterward. Piers is a tough cookie!"

I couldn't wish for a better endorsement.

ON YOUR SIDE BREAKING NEWS   1:27 58

REP. GIFFORDS SHOT   9

:ies are reporting up to six dead. 9 Au

I assumed the horrifying assassination attempt on a congresswoman
would lead to tougher gun laws in America, but nothing happened.

3

FRIDAY, JANUARY 7, 2011

" 'Allo, old son," Rod Stewart cried as I arrived to interview him this morning, prancing out of his Beverly Hills mansion in red tartan trousers. "Have a load of this!"

Then he produced a toy hand grenade and tossed it at me.

"Whoaaa!" I yelped, not sure what the hell he was doing.

"Relax, you big girl's blouse ... I heard your show's *dangerous*, so thought I'd come prepared!"

Later he took me up to see his secret model train set room. Very few people ever get to see firsthand the hobby he's pursued most of his adult life.

I have never seen anything like it in my entire life.

Rod has personally built an extraordinary model city, based on Manhattan a few decades ago. Inch by inch, tiny detail by tiny detail.

It's breathtaking in both the quality and the creativity.

"How many hours do you spend on this?" I asked.

"Three or four a day. Even when I'm on tour. I take all the tools with me."

Later in the afternoon, Jonathan and I drove over to Mel Gibson's house in Malibu to try to persuade him to do an interview.

He's been in the headlines for all the wrong reasons in recent months after claims—reinforced by explosive tapes leaked to the Internet—that he'd physically and verbally abused his Russian musician lover, Oksana Grigorieva, and spewed racist insults.

In terms of TV interview "gets," he's about as hot as it could be right now.

We drove up a long, hilly dirt track until we found the home and rang the bell.

Mel answered, unshaven and slightly wild-eyed.

He took us inside.

"Can I get you a beer?"

"Sure, thanks."

We sat in his living room, which was full of rare religious paraphernalia.

And for the next two hours, Mel outlined the extraordinary pain and bitterness he feels toward Ms. Grigorieva, with whom he has a child.

He was at times outrageously offensive, hilariously funny, and deeply, deeply sad.

This is a man who has been one of Hollywood's all-time top-grossing movie stars, and who had a famously long, successful marriage to Australian dental nurse Robyn, which produced seven children.

But since their separation in 2006, days after he was arrested for drunk driving, his life seems to have descended into utter professional and personal turmoil.

I've been through a divorce, so I know how raw and unsettling they can be.

Even "civilized" ones are nasty, horrible things.

Mel's divorce from Robyn was heavy enough (it's said to have cost him a near Hollywood record four hundred million dollars), but the split from Oksana, even though they never married, has been far worse.

He now has conflict with his ex-wife, his kids, and his young lover.

Not to mention with virtually the entire movie community, many of whom haven't forgiven him for his anti-Semitic outbursts when he was caught drunk driving.

We went outside to the patio and had another beer.

Coyotes were howling in the hills, and I noticed that Mel had blood on the side of his ear, where it looked like he'd been scratching himself.

He ranted some more, and at several moments had tears in his eyes.

This was a guy right on the edge, and I felt for him.

"I don't think I'm ready to do an interview," he finally said. "I don't trust myself not to explode and say stuff I'd regret."

The interviewer in me would like nothing more than Mel Gibson exploding on my show—it would be gripping television, and great for ratings.

But the father in me agreed with him. This was no time for Mel to be talking on air about this stuff.

"Thanks for listening to me," he said, taking us back to our car.

"I hope you sort things out," I replied, and I meant it.

Jonathan and I waited until we were out of earshot before both exclaiming at the same time: "What the *fuck* was that?"

SATURDAY, JANUARY 8, 2011

Flew with John to New York, and as we were still up in the air, news broke that a congresswoman called Gabby Giffords had been shot at a rally she was attending in Tucson, Arizona.

Within minutes, multiple news outlets were reporting that she'd died from her injuries, along with at least six other people, including a nine-year-old girl.

The plane had CNN, so I watched the dramatic developments unfurl in real time.

And it made me stop and think hard about the reality of the job I was about to take on.

There's no way I'll just be doing taped celebrity interviews of the kind I've conducted in L.A. this past week.

At some stage, a big story's going to break and I'm going to have to anchor it live on air for CNN around the world.

And I've never done anything like that on television—a slightly unsettling realization.

Suddenly, on Twitter, news filtered through that Gabby Giffords was still alive. Everyone began reversing their reporting and saying now that she was still in surgery and definitely *not* dead.

My mind went back to all those big breaking news days when I ran *The Daily Mirror.*

So many times, initial information was wrong, but we usually had time to correct it before we actually went to print.

On live TV, you don't have that luxury. And I can already sense that Twitter has changed the news game irrevocably.

Note to self: "This is dangerous. Be careful."

John and I discussed the potential ramifications of this mass shooting.

"Gun violence in America is out of control," I said. "We just don't have this problem in Britain. Nobody expects to be able to own a gun, very few people want to own a gun, and it's illegal for most civilians to have one anyway."

"It's completely different here," John replied. "The Second Amendment to our Constitution allows everyone the right to bear arms. And the majority of Americans have guns. It's part of the culture, whether to hunt, shoot for sport, or defend yourself."

"Do you?"

"No. I know what guns do to people. My brother's a general."

"Surely they will change the gun laws after this?"

"I doubt it."

"But you can't have a congresswoman shot in the head and do nothing?"

"Hey, we had two Kennedys and a civil rights leader all shot dead within a few years, and nothing changed."

"Why don't people want things to change?"

"Because to many Americans, rights are more important than life."

But what *is* this right?

It all comes down to the precise wording of the Second Amendment to America's Constitution, which reads: "A well-regulated militia, being necessary to the security of a free state, the right of the people to keep and bear arms, shall not be infringed."

The progun lobby insists this amendment gives every American the right to own and use guns.

The antigun lobby argues that the exact placement of the commas shows that the Founding Fathers intended the "right to bear arms" only to apply to members of a militia—which, in the eighteenth century, meant an army composed of ordinary citizens, not professional soldiers.

Those commas have thus become the most deadly, expensive, and controversial punctuation marks in the history of language.

Whatever your view, I find plainly ridiculous the idea that what Thomas Jefferson and his cohorts had in mind when they wrote the Constitution was defending the rights of Americans to legally and easily buy high-powered assault weapons to murder other Americans.

SUNDAY, JANUARY 9, 2011

First rehearsal at CNN.

It was quite a moment as I walked in to find this vast studio with "Piers Morgan Tonight" branded everywhere. A Perspex desk sat on a raised stage in the middle, and the walls were a psychedelic mishmash of mainly bright blue and green squares, intermingled with other colors. It was totally different from Larry's famous darker studio with dotted maps on the walls.

In the center of the wall was a large video screen, featuring a giant image of Condoleezza Rice, whom I am interviewing tomorrow.

"That's the magic wall," Jonathan explained. "It can do anything—play video, display still photos, banners, whatever we want. All while you're doing the interviews."

I loved it. The whole thing looked dynamic, modern, newsy, and entertaining—the perfect mix for this kind of show.

Then Jonathan played the theme music, which was a really upbeat, exciting, vibrant sound.

I sat at the desk, imagining what it will feel like a week from Monday when the Oprah interview airs.

MONDAY, JANUARY 10, 2011

My first interview in my actual studio.

I'd been warned that Condoleezza is a very private lady and probably wouldn't welcome any intrusive questions. But it's all in the way you ask them.

After half an hour of pretty heavy Iraq, Afghanistan, Bush, and 9/11 interrogation, I turned to lighter matters.

"You remain one of the most eligible women in Washington," I said.

"Well, actually I live in California now!"

"If I was to try and woo you . . . how would I?"

Condoleezza stared at me for a second or two in what looked like horror, then burst out laughing.

"Convince me that you'll spend Sunday afternoon watching football," she replied, "and I'll even cook."

"What would you cook me?"

"Fried chicken, chili, corn bread—I'm quite good at corn bread—or perhaps because of my half-Creole grandmother, I'd cook gumbo."

"What's gumbo?"

I could hear Jonathan groan. A clear sign that I'd just exposed my Britishness in the most ghastly manner possible.

"You don't know what gumbo is?" she replied, laughing.

"No."

"Go to New Orleans, they'll tell you."

"You sound like the perfect woman, you make fried chicken, you watch football all day."

"Yes! I just haven't found the dream man yet, but you know, we all keep trying."

This afternoon, Harrison Ford was asked about me by reporters in London, where he's promoting his new movie.

"Piers is promoting his show as looking for the truth from his subjects, so I shall have nothing to do with him," he said. "I'm not interested in the truth, I'm interested in selling a product. If you want the truth, go somewhere else."

Ironically, this is one of the most truthful things I've heard a celebrity say.

TUESDAY, JANUARY 11, 2011

Jonathan emailed me early this morning.

"We're doing a potentially problematic taped interview today with *The King's Speech* stars."

"Why potentially problematic?"

"Because Geoffrey Rush will be in Australia on a two-second delay,

Helena Bonham Carter will be in London on a one-second delay, and Colin Firth will be here in New York with laryngitis."

"Ah . . . I see."

It went about as badly as he predicted, all four of us talking over ourselves repeatedly, Colin barely talking at all.

And the discomfort was compounded by the behavior of Firth's publicist, who was one of the rudest, most objectionable human beings I've met in my entire life. In direct contrast to the man himself, who was charming.

The power of publicists in America is quite extraordinary.

In Britain, most of them are ranked lower than meter maids in terms of authority.

Over here, they hold supreme sway over anyone working in the media, and some of them abuse that strength relentlessly.

Cross them, and they'll fuck you over until eternity. And they do it by simply refusing to let you interview any of their clients again.

If you're in the interview business, this is not a risk you want to take.

But I was so appalled by the way this particular woman spoke to one of my producers that I decided to get in first by phoning her boss and telling her I was banning all her firm's clients from the show until we got an apology.

Then I slammed down the phone, and saw my booking team looking at me in abject horror.

WEDNESDAY, JANUARY 12, 2011

Fascinating op-ed piece about guns in the *New York Times* by Nick Kristof.

He detailed some shocking facts, sourced from several leading academics, including David Hemenway, a top Harvard professor of health policy:

- 320 or so Americans have been killed by guns *since* Tucson.
- Every day, 80 Americans die from guns, and several times as many are injured.
- There are about 85 guns per 100 people in the United States.
- Handgun sales rose by 60 percent in Arizona, immediately *after* the shooting, as people raced to beat any strengthening of gun laws.

- American children are 11 times more likely to die in a gun accident than children in other developed countries, because of the prevalence of guns.
- The chances that a gun will be used to deter a home invasion are unbelievably remote, and dialing 911 is more effective in reducing injury than brandishing a weapon.
- Suicide rates are higher in states with more guns, simply because there are more gun suicides. Other kinds of suicide rates are no higher.
- Because most homicides in the home are by family members or acquaintances—not by an intruder—the presence of a gun in the home increases the risk of a gun murder in that home.

Hemenway's ideas for how to stem the tide of gun violence enveloping the country include better background checks, a limit on gun purchases, a crackdown on gun dealers who sell to traffickers, a twenty-eight-day waiting period (as in Canada) to buy a handgun, and a ban on oversize magazines such as the thirty-three-bullet magazine used in Tucson.

He also cited what happened in Australia in 1996, following an appalling mass shooting in Port Arthur, Tasmania, that killed thirty-three people. The government banned assault weapons and bought back 650,000 of them. The country's firearm homicide and suicide rate dropped by almost half in the next seven years.

Hemenway might also have cited the school shooting massacre in Dunblane, Scotland—also in 1996.

What's interesting about these two examples is that neither was a political debate.

Australia had a Conservative prime minister, John Howard, who brought in the gun bans. Britain had first a Conservative prime minister, John Major, and then a Labour one, Tony Blair, who both worked on the gun ban legislation.

Here in America, it's very different. If you dare breathe the words "gun control," you're instantly branded a "libtard," short for "liberal retard."

If you're progun, you're a right-wing loon.

It's a hideously polarizing, very angry discourse, which conspires to ensure nothing ever gets done.

THURSDAY, JANUARY 13, 2011

Interviewed George Clooney today, and in a pre-taped tease, I said: "Probably the biggest problem for George in this interview will be how to deal psychologically with being only the second biggest heartthrob in the room."

He laughed, more out of pity than amusement, when my producers played it to him, and responded with his own tease:

"You know I've never seen Piers sober, but I'm a big fan."

Ostensibly, George had agreed to an interview on the grounds that most of it would be about his latest passion, the Sudan.

But we both knew I'd be getting personal at some stage. Nobody can ever interview Clooney without asking him about the one thing every one of his adoring female fans really wants to know—his love life.

I used the pretext of his parents' fifty-one-year marriage as an excuse (his father, Nick, was in the studio with me; George was in Los Angeles).

"Do you think you'll ever remarry, George?"

"Here we go," he groaned. "You just waited for the last segment to pull it out . . ."

"I'm allowed one, aren't I? You don't have to answer . . ."

"I'm not going to. Piers, are you married?"

"I just got remarried. That's why I asked you the question."

"Oh, you did?"

"Yeah, about six months ago."

"Congratulations. And they said it wouldn't last!"

I left it there. I'd had my fun, and he'd responded in an amusing way without actually giving an answer. Which is entirely his prerogative.

In a final commercial break, Nick Clooney mentioned it was his birthday today.

"It's your dad's birthday," I told George. "Anything you want to say to him?"

He smiled and nodded. "Yes, there is. Happy birthday!"

"Did you get him a present?"

"He did," interrupted Nick. "A beautiful first-edition copy of *For Whom the Bell Tolls,* by Ernest Hemingway."

"It was signed too," George interrupted.

"Wow," I said. "That's impressive."

"Yes. Only it wasn't signed by Ernest," chuckled George. "It was signed by me!"

The pair of them laughed loudly.

If you want to know where Clooney Junior gets his charm from, look no further than Clooney Senior—a delightful man.

After the interview finished, George suddenly said: "By the way, I loved that Susan Boyle video of her audition on your other show."

"Really?" I said, slightly taken aback.

"It was so inspiring. I was filming *Up in the Air* at the time and I kept playing it to all the crew. She's an amazing lady. Such a great story."

A single, now forty-nine-year-old woman from a tiny Scottish village being lauded by Hollywood's number-one heartthrob. Now that's an even better story.

SUNDAY, JANUARY 16, 2011

I asked people on Twitter to send me their best excuses for why they wouldn't be watching the launch of my show tomorrow.

Lily Allen, the fiery British pop star, won with this response: "I'll be eating a shit sandwich."

Tonight Celia and I sat and watched the Golden Globes, or more specifically, the host Ricky Gervais tearing into Hollywood's finest again with quite splendidly disrespectful enthusiasm.

There's something oddly self-flagellating about the way Americans like bringing Brits over to their country simply so they can be abused by them. Whether it's the likes of Simon Cowell and me harshly judging on talent shows, Gordon Ramsay screaming in the kitchen, or Ricky pricking balloons at awards ceremonies.

Everybody feigns outrage afterward, but they must secretly love it, or we wouldn't keep being hired.

As for the inevitable uproar over Ricky, my view is that if you invite a shark to dinner, don't be surprised when he eats all the guests.

The best of his many great lines tonight? "Mark Zuckerberg is reportedly worth seven billion dollars. Heather Mills calls him the one that got away . . ."

Before I went to sleep, I sent Jonathan and John an email.

> As we head into the final twenty-four hours, just want to say to you, Jonathan, that I think you've done an absolutely incredible job in building such a great team so fast. Really, bordering on miraculous.
>
> I love your passion, energy, sense of humor, and "control valve" when I start going haywire. Above all, I love your leadership.
>
> May we kick some serious butt this week, then go on kicking it for a long time to come.
>
> To you, John, I simply say thanks for landing me the greatest job I could ever dream of.
>
> It's everything I hoped it would be and more, already. And we haven't even gotten to air yet.

MONDAY, JANUARY 17, 2011

Woke at 3:50 A.M., buzzing with adrenaline. Decided to take a walk through Manhattan, which was icily cold and eerily calm. I've no idea how the show's going to go down tonight—all I do know is that we couldn't have done much more to hype it up, and I genuinely think the Oprah interview is a strong one.

I discovered late in the day that this is "Blue Monday"—supposedly the most depressing day of the entire year.

This may well still turn out to be true . . .

Tonight I gathered the whole *Piers Morgan Tonight* team in the Presidential Suite of the Mandarin Oriental and made the best Churchillian "We will fight them on the bookings!" speech that I could conjure with jangling nerves.

They're a fantastic bunch. Incredibly hardworking, determined, spirited, and passionate.

They also know that all their own immediate career prospects depend almost entirely on me now delivering the goods.

At 9 P.M., we turned on CNN and started watching the Oprah show.

No turning back now.

Emails, texts, and tweets started pouring in from all over the world.

Viewers were split. Many tweeted delightfully positive things. Others wished to inform me that I had "squinty eyes" and was a "toe-curling toady."

At midnight, John emailed me: "You will be the same guy tomorrow that you are today and that you were a year ago. The same father, the same brother, the same son, and the same partner to Celia. Always remember that."

Which is all true. I'd just prefer to be the same guy next month hosting the 9 P.M. hour on CNN as the guy tonight . . .

Once the show finished, the team burst into raucous champagne-fueled applause.

I shook Jonathan's hand.

"How the hell are we going to top Oprah?" I asked.

TUESDAY, JANUARY 18, 2011

The reviews were a mixed bag, but ratings were fantastic—three times the average figure for the 9 P.M. slot on CNN in the last year. But I'm well aware it's a marathon, not a sprint, and many people will have tuned in to take a look then disappear just as fast.

It's where the figures are in six months that matters.

THURSDAY, JANUARY 20, 2011

Tonight, I made my first appearance on David Letterman's *Late Show* and he gave me some advice:

"What you need is to have somebody punch you on the show or even better, you punch a guest," he instructed, to loud cheers.

"Would it work if it was Larry King?"

Letterman laughed loudly.

"I'd like to see you punch a seventy-eight-year-old man!"

SATURDAY, JANUARY 22, 2011

The ratings for my show predictably came down from the heights of the hugely promoted opening night with Oprah, but still ended the week some 45 percent higher than the average for the 9 P.M. CNN slot over the past six months.

As for the media, there's been an unbelievable amount of coverage.

Christa Robinson, head of PR for CNN, sent around an email today congratulating Meghan on securing me more press in the last two weeks than any show had achieved in the last year.

And it's true, she's done an absolutely incredible job.

My instinct to go young and hungry with a publicist, rather than old and experienced as many recommended, has paid off.

The bigger test, though, will come if we have to handle a crisis.

And, judging by the previous twenty-five years of my career, there's bound to be one before too long . . .

TUESDAY, JANUARY 25, 2011

I was invited to take part in CNN's coverage of President Obama's State of the Union address tonight.

"What's it like being part of the best political team on television?" asked Wolf Blitzer.

And the truth is that it feels great. I've only realized how much I missed being immersed in hard news since I started working for CNN. There's really nothing like it to get the juices flowing.

On Twitter, those who haven't seen my new show and only know me as a judge on *America's Got Talent* were incredulous.

"Is this some sort of joke?" tweeted one viewer. "What's that idiot Morgan doing on a serious news show—waiting to give Obama a big red X?"

FRIDAY, JANUARY 28, 2011

At midday, I was on a plane with Jonathan to Los Angeles for an interview with Janet Jackson, due to air next week. But by the time we landed, all hell had broken loose in Egypt.

Fueled by recent Internet-driven uprisings in Tunisia and Yemen, hundreds of thousands of protesters were swarming the streets of Cairo, Alexandria, and Suez.

The focal point for their fury quickly became Tahrir Square in Cairo, where a huge crowd gathered, demanding the overthrow of President Hosni Mubarak, who has dissolved his government.

We were supposed to be airing the taped *King's Speech* show, but this was clearly no longer an option.

"OK, we're going live," said Jonathan. "Let's go to the bureau."

As our car sped to CNN, my heart began to pound.

I turned to Jonathan and said as calmly as I could: "Is this a good time to tell you I've never anchored a second of breaking news on TV in my life?"

He stared at me.

"Seriously?"

"Seriously. I've done lots of live TV, and of course I led a huge newsroom on many big news nights at *The Daily Mirror*. But I've never actually combined the two experiences into anchoring any live TV news. Which may seem odd given I've joined CNN, but it remains a fact."

Jonathan laughed.

"Wow. OK. Well, fortunately for you, I've produced lots of it. So we'll be just fine."

We arrived at the bureau around 4 P.M. to find scenes of controlled chaos.

Jonathan and I set ourselves up in makeshift offices, and a constant stream of information began pouring into our email in-boxes.

He was like a machine—barking orders, discussing bookings, shouting at production people. I suddenly felt less panicky.

I could tell this was a guy who'd done a LOT of breaking news on TV.

At 5:45 P.M. I walked into the studio down on the ground floor and took my seat.

It was Larry King's seat in his old studio. He'd handle a night like this with consummate ease. I felt so nervous I could feel my bones rattle.

The crew was eerily silent. Almost as if they were contemplating disaster too.

I put my earpiece in, linking me to Jonathan in the control room.

"You OK?" he asked.

"I think so," I replied.

If I screwed this up, I'd be a laughingstock at CNN, and it would simply confirm what many of them feared—I was an ex-tabloid, talent-judging lightweight who should never be let near serious news.

Conversely, if I did well, I would allay those fears in an instant.

The clock turned to 5:57 P.M. and I began reading the prompter. It was changing all the time, and much of the information seemed to be wrong.

"Jonathan, this doesn't make sense," I said.

"Wait, WAIT!" he shouted back. "I'm sorting it out. Just read what's there at six P.M., OK?"

"OK."

I had to trust him, there was nothing else I could do.

My hands were clammy, my neck stiff, my head fit to burst with hideous doomsday-scenario thoughts.

It was just like my first "live" day as editor at the *News of the World* back in 1994. I was twenty-eight, one of the youngest members of my own staff, yet still the boss. Everyone looked at me that day, expecting me to fail. It was terrifying, yet exhilarating.

But I kept calm that day. And I didn't fail.

As 6 P.M. arrived, Jonathan's voice was supremely cool and collected.

"OK, buckle up."

I began reading the prompter, which had now miraculously morphed into perfect journalistic breaking news TV prose.

"Tonight, one of America's strongest allies in the Middle East is in turmoil. The winds of revolution are fanned by the power of the Internet sweeping across the Arab world—from Tunisia to Yemen.

"Now the fury is spreading to Egypt, and the nation some say is the key to peace in the Middle East is on the verge of total chaos.

"President Hosni Mubarak has dissolved the government. Protesters are tonight swarming the streets in Cairo, Alexandria, and Suez.

"What's really going on right now? Is anybody in charge in Egypt? What does it all mean for peace, for oil, for the United States and the rest of the world? This is a special edition of *Piers Morgan Tonight!*"

For the next hour, Jonathan skillfully guided me through a procession of CNN reporters around the world—from Ben Wedeman in Cairo, to Nic Robertson in Alexandria, and Wolf Blitzer in Washington.

It was fast, furious, and—to my amazement—virtually flawless.

No lines went down, no guests failed to turn up, I didn't get any names wrong.

At 7 P.M., I handed over to Anderson Cooper, and exhaled.

"Great job," said Jonathan, more out of relief, I suspect, than anything else.

"Thank you," I replied. And never have I meant it more.

TUESDAY, FEBRUARY 1, 2011

Hosting live CNN breaking news shows on Egypt has taken me mentally right back to *The Daily Mirror* newsroom.

Anchoring live TV news is actually a very similar discipline to editing it for a newspaper. Teams of reporters bring you the information, teams of production staff make it come to life visually, and you, as anchor/editor, have to navigate the viewer/reader through it in as simple and engaging a manner as possible.

Today that nostalgic feeling was cemented even further when I persuaded Tony Blair to give me an exclusive interview.

I knew him very well in our previous incarnations. In fact, I once worked out that I had fifty-six one-on-one meetings with him when he was prime minister.

But we fell out rather spectacularly over the Iraq War (*The Daily Mirror* opposed it before, during, and after) and have had nothing much to do with each other ever since. To my surprise, he agreed to come on the show tonight and talk about the events in Cairo, in his capacity as Middle East peace envoy.

"Mr. Blair," I started, "how are you?"

"Very well, Piers, how are you doing?"

"It's been a while."

He laughed. "It has indeed!"

The interview itself was informative and valuable.

Blair, for all his catastrophic faults over Saddam Hussein and missing WMDs, knows the region better than most politicians (as one friend cynically put it, "he ought to; he's bombed much of it"), and his comments that

Egyptian President Mubarak's days as a leader are over, despite him being "immensely courageous and a force for good," made headlines all over the world.

Interesting how we view these Middle Eastern dictators though, isn't it?

Mubarak, who's been in power for thirty years, has been accused of fleecing and repressing his people while lining his pockets.

Yet he's "a force for good," while Saddam was so evil we had to go to war with him.

I thanked Blair afterward for giving me what had been a genuine scoop.

"I enjoyed it," he replied. "Well, almost."

WEDNESDAY, FEBRUARY 2, 2011

Egypt is descending into total anarchy, and becoming very dangerous for journalists.

Anderson Cooper was punched in the head today as he tried to film in Tahrir Square, and there was astonishing footage late in the afternoon of a pro-Mubarak mob on camels attacking protesters with sticks.

It was like something out of medieval times.

THURSDAY, FEBRUARY 3, 2011

Barbara Walters threw a dinner party in my honor at her Manhattan home tonight, but I was unavoidably detained with another live Egypt show until 10 P.M.

I dashed straight there as soon as I finished, only to find that she'd invited the very cream of New York society, including New York Mayor Michael Bloomberg, Nora Ephron, Sir Harry Evans, and Woody Allen and his wife, Soon-Yi.

I exchanged some small talk with Woody, and then he started murmuring about going home, so I seized my chance.

"Mr. Allen, would it be completely inappropriate for me to use this opportunity to invite you on to my TV show?"

There was a deathly silence for a few seconds, then Barbara shouted, "Yes! It absolutely would be inappropriate!"

At which point, everyone laughed at the irony of this interjection. She is of course famously the most relentless, ferocious, fearless, and shameless booker in the history of television.

Woody politely declined.

As he has done to even his good friend Barbara for her entire career.

FRIDAY, FEBRUARY 4, 2011

I'll do a lot of difficult interviews in my career at CNN, but few surely to match the one today with the new prime minister of Tunisia, Mohamed Ghannouchi.

"He's going to be speaking through an interpreter, in French, with a three-second delay," said Jonathan, trying not to laugh. "But we're taping it, so we'll tidy things up in the edit. It's just a five-minute hit for tonight's show."

I asked my first question: "You've been in charge of your country for twenty-two days, Prime Minister. Have you managed to achieve stability?"

And Mr. Ghannouchi then spoke, without pausing, for ten minutes, all of which had to be translated, and communicated back to me from French to English, with their voices constantly overlapping from the delay.

This was the TV anchor's equivalent of being waterboarded.

When we finally finished, more than forty minutes later, Jonathan was laughing so hard I thought he'd have a hernia.

THURSDAY, FEBRUARY 10, 2011

Hosni Mubarak was expected to resign today, but didn't. So I hosted a rather deflated show in New York, recording this non-moment-in-history. Then raced to catch the last flight back to London at 11:40 P.M., in the expectation of having a relaxing weekend with the family for the first time since we launched.

I nearly missed the plane, as the check-in desk had closed when I got to JFK Airport.

But the woman from American Airlines smiled: "I saw you with Oprah, and she likes you, so I'd better let you through or she will be mad at me."

FRIDAY, FEBRUARY 11, 2011

I landed to discover Mubarak's quitting after all, which means I'm doing a live show at 2 A.M. from CNN's London bureau.

When I arrived in the studio at 10 P.M. my time, the team in New York had lined up an impressive array of people for me to interview for the show, including CNN reporters right inside Cairo's Tahrir Square, the Egyptian finance minister, and President Bush's former defense official Paul Wolfowitz.

The ecstatic scenes, as Egyptians celebrated the world's fastest revolution—all over in just eighteen days—were incredibly moving.

And the keen influence of social networking and modern technology is striking. This "Arab Spring," as the uprisings in Tunisia, Yemen, and Egypt have now been collectively dubbed, is the first revolution built on Twitter and Facebook—young people using their mobile phones to communicate as they plot the overthrow of their despotic leaders.

As I was mulling over how to round off this momentous show, someone sent me a tweet saying today was, by coincidence, the twenty-first anniversary of Nelson Mandela's release from prison. I'd found my ending.

After a frenetic, emotion-charged hour of pulsating history-making television, I turned to the camera and said: "In the words of Nelson Mandela, released twenty-one years ago today—'Let freedom reign. The sun shall never set on so glorious a human achievement.' "

TUESDAY, FEBRUARY 15, 2011

My interview with Janet Jackson finally aired tonight—all the big celebrity interviews I taped last month have been held back due to the Middle East turmoil—and it was a fascinating insight into the weird, fantastical world of the world's most famous showbiz family.

"What did you call him?" I asked her, referring to Janet's famously dictatorial father, Joe Jackson.

"Joseph. One time I tried to call him Dad."

"What happened?"

"He just said, 'No, I'm Joseph. You call me Joseph. I'm Joseph to you.' So, I always called him Joseph."

Later, as she discussed her lifelong battle with weight, Janet revealed she knows some female stars who eat Kleenex tissue paper to clog up their stomachs so they don't feel hungry.

"I know worse stuff they do too," she told me in a commercial break. "Stuff I don't even want to go into."

THURSDAY, FEBRUARY 17, 2011

Brian Williams, *NBC Nightly News* host, and a good friend of Jonathan's, sent me a note.

"As Mr. Wald knows too well, my tin-horn advice from the cheap seats is simple: be live every night you can. I think there's a live TV endorphin that makes us different, makes us better, and changes the stakes—simply knowing that editing is an option changes the energy of an interview."

He's absolutely right.

The problem for me is that my *America's Got Talent* taping schedule means I can't be live every night. I just have to hope and pray that changes.

Tonight, Larry King gave an interview to the BBC back home, and struck a rather less cordial tone than he had when we met.

Asked about my show, he said: "I think one of the problems was they oversold it. He was going to be dangerous. He was going to be water-cooler talk. 'Wait until you see me, I'm different.'

"He's good but not that dangerous. I think they might have been better off just starting quietly.

"That's not Piers's fault, or maybe it is. I don't know, I'm not inside anymore. He's certainly not bad, he's certainly an acceptable host. He asks good questions. Maybe he interrupts a little too much at times."

Meghan started getting calls asking for a reaction to what media people were taking as a negative verdict from my predecessor.

It annoyed me, but on her advice I decided to take the high ground, and tweeted: "Larry remains one of my heroes, so he can say whatever he likes about me."

Jonathan had an idea.

"Let's book him for our show. You interview him, let him say what he wants, you respond, be gracious, and we can all move on. There's no upside for you in having a bad relationship with Larry."

FRIDAY, FEBRUARY 18, 2011

Ratings have slipped in the past ten days.

"*American Idol*'s killing us midweek," said Jonathan. "It's a steamroller."

"Imagine how bad we'll feel when *America's Got Talent* starts up again and I steamroller myself," I replied.

Had dinner with Jamie Oliver, who is still plowing his lonely but incredibly courageous field of trying to make Americans eat healthier food. He's currently battling the school authorities in Los Angeles over the bilge they serve youngsters.

"It's so important," he said. "I've got the support of thousands of parents. But I get treated like some sort of communist spy over here. It's crazy!"

One thing I've learned quickly about Americans is that they don't care much for anyone, particularly snotty-nosed Brits like me or Jamie, telling them how to lead their lives. Just as we Brits resent anyone else telling us how to.

It doesn't mean we don't occasionally need it though, and right now I'd say America needs Jamie.

SUNDAY, FEBRUARY 20, 2011

Hollywood's hottest ticket this year, after the Oscars, is the annual NBA All-Star game between the best players from America's East and West conferences.

I knew just how big it was when I arrived with John at the Staples Center in Los Angeles to find Dustin Hoffman sitting in my courtside chair.

It's hard to know what the etiquette is in such a tricky situation.

I could hardly just kick out one of the biggest movie stars in the world.

John and I stood around awkwardly, trying to work out what to do, when a steward came over and asked if he could help.

"Dustin Hoffman's sitting in my seat," I whispered.

He nodded, as if this was a perfectly ordinary dilemma, and walked straight over to speak to Hoffman, who was with his son.

Dustin craned his ear to hear him over the noise of the crowd, then checked his ticket, looked at me, smiled, and moved down a seat.

We chatted, and he asked me where I was staying in L.A.

"I'm in your mate Warren Beatty's old suite at the Beverly Wilshire," I replied. "The one he lived in for ten years."

Dustin smiled again, knowingly. "Yes, I'm familiar with that suite. Have you ever met Warren?"

"No, but I'd love to."

"Let's go see him," said Dustin. "He's right over there."

He led me across the court to where Beatty was sitting.

"Warren, meet Piers. He's living in your old bedroom at the Beverly Wilshire."

Beatty laughed. "You *are*?"

We had an amusing conversation for a few minutes, then I headed back to my seat, where Dustin told me: "I once asked Warren whether he would sleep with any woman in the world, and after thinking for a bit, he said yes. When I asked why, he replied, 'Because you just never know!' "

WEDNESDAY, FEBRUARY 23, 2011

Larry King arrived at the L.A. bureau for our interview tonight, and got a standing ovation when he walked into the studio.

"I won't even bother introducing my next guest," I said.

Larry laughed. "Don't bother!"

"Does it feel weird being on that side of the desk?"

"A little. It's not my set. It's a beautiful set, by the way."

Larry looked around the studio.

"It was weird coming in here tonight. It's my corner, you know, Larry King Square! But it's good to be back. It's nice, it's a comfortable feeling. I spent a lot of years here."

After a few questions about the Middle East, I got around to his criticisms of me in the BBC interview last week.

"How many shows of mine have you watched?"

"About eight. And I haven't seen dangerous yet."

"But I'm following a legend!" I protested. "I can hardly come in and undersell myself. You can't follow Sinatra in Vegas and say, 'By the way, I'm not very good and this is going to be useless.' "

"Why can't you just say, 'I'm Piers Morgan, I'm coming, watch me'?"

"I've always oversold myself."

He laughed.

Then I produced my trump card.

"I want to show you who now wears the suspenders in this town, Larry."

I ripped off my suit jacket to reveal a pair of suspenders resplendent with the Union Jack.

"Oh my gosh!" he cried. Then he laughed again. "I'm honored, see, that's a tribute."

"You're my hero!" I said.

"I know that and I appreciate it. I just think you oversold it . . ."

It was time to say what I really felt.

"Well, the honest truth, Larry, is I actually feel an incredible privilege and honor that I am replacing you at CNN. In fact, I don't feel like I'm replacing you. You can't replace someone like you. And every day I do this my admiration for what you achieved grows. Because I've done twenty-two shows and I feel like I've been in a war zone. And you did seven thousand shows in twenty-five years and just the sheer stamina that took is awesome."

"Thank you."

"And I carry with me a great responsibility to try and live up to the legacy that you left."

"Thank you, I appreciate it. But when you said 'dangerous,' what did you mean?"

"I was only kidding," I said.

"Ah-ha. British humor?"

"Yes. You didn't get it?"

"I'm from Brooklyn. In Brooklyn, if you say, 'I'm dangerous,' you better be dangerous."

Jonathan exploded with laughter in my ear.

Who better to talk to about the death of Osama bin Laden than
Rudy Giuliani, the heroic mayor of New York on 9/11?

4

MONDAY, FEBRUARY 28, 2011

I first met Charlie Sheen in the early nineties, when Planet Hollywood launched a restaurant in Aspen, Colorado, and I was a cub showbiz reporter at the *Sun* dispatched from London to cover it.

He kindly agreed to do an interview with me when his "people" said he didn't have time. And he gave a great interview.

He was also one hell of a party boy, even then—Charlie had been out hell-raising until 8 A.M. before our midmorning chat, but seemed perfectly OK as we larked about for pictures with skis in the snow.

Today, I woke up in L.A. to see Charlie all over the TV news.

CBS has suspended his number-one-rated comedy show *Two and a Half Men,* following his recent behavioral misdemeanors involving various porn stars, drugs, and a hotel trashing.

But rather than take it lying down, he's come out fighting like a man possessed—which some people think he is.

He's done a couple of pretaped interviews with other networks, but in the preview clips I've seen he looks riled and angry and doesn't make much sense.

Julie Zann found his number for me today, so I dialed it and one of his daughters answered.

"Hi, is Charlie there please?"

"Yes, who is it?"

"It's Piers Morgan from CNN."

"Dad, it's someone called Pierce from CNN."

Then I heard Charlie's voice. "Piers?"

"It is. How are you?"

"I'm cool, dude, winning cool."

"I don't know if you remember, but I once interviewed you in Aspen."

He laughed. "Actually, I remembered when you got Larry's gig. That was a fun interview."

"It was, and you were very kind to agree to do it. I want to return the favor."

"OK, I'm listening—shoot."

"All these other interviews are making you look a bit crazy because of the way they've edited them. I think you should walk into my studio tonight, live, and let's do a more sensible, calmer conversation about all this."

"Live, eh? That could be fun."

"Uncensored, unedited. You can say whatever you want to say. And it will air around the world, not just America."

Charlie paused. "OK, you're on. Let's roll with this."

"Great. Is this one hundred percent? Because if it is, I'll cancel the other guests."

"One hundred percent. I swear on my kids' lives, I'll be there."

At 5:30 P.M., an hour after his call time—when guests are scheduled to arrive—and thirty minutes before my show was going live, there was still no sign of Charlie.

I stood pacing the steps as my team made a series of frantic calls to his phone and those of several of his assistants, but nobody was answering.

As the minutes ticked by, we began planning an emergency second show to run with if Charlie broke his promise. At times like this you discover the terror-induced symptoms of hosting a live news show: sweaty palms, knotted stomach, whole cans of Red Bull.

Then at 5:55 P.M., just when I'd given up all hope, a giant Maybach swept into the CNN lot and screeched to a halt in front of me.

Out stepped a weird-looking entourage, then the man himself—cigarette in mouth, cheeky grin, and crying, *"Winner!"*

He bear-hugged me on the steps, and said, "OK, bro. Let's go rock 'n' roll."

We raced him into the studio, the lights went up, and I just had time to send one tweet saying: "BREAKING NEWS: I promised 'dangerous.' Charlie Sheen just arrived at CNN for 1st LIVE television i-v on @PiersTonight—starts 6 P.M. PT."

It was an electrifying interview, one of those times when you know it's going to make big news, and anything can happen.

Charlie was as amusing ("I didn't take cocaine; I paid for it") as he was eloquently defiant ("It's been a tsunami of media and I've been riding it on a mercury surfboard").

In one dramatic moment, when I asked him directly if he was on drugs, he produced his latest laboratory test results, showing full negatives.

What the viewers didn't see was what happened in the next commercial break.

Charlie asked for a pen, scribbled on the results paper, and handed it to me. The message read, "To Piers—let's get hammered. Love, Charlie."

I had to laugh. With half of the world starving and most of the rest of it either at war, undergoing revolution, or suffering crippling financial hardship, it's important to keep a proper perspective on the Sheen affair.

We're dealing here with a Hollywood star, the highest-paid man on American TV ($1.8 million per episode), who likes to party too much.

"I wish people would spend more time on their own lives and families and not some distant planet that is me," he said.

In one fascinating moment, he watched me doing a tease halfway through the show for my colleague Anderson Cooper's Libya special coming up afterward.

In the break that followed, Charlie shook his head.

"This is so fucked up, man—how can I be news with all this crap going on?"

Ten minutes later, during another break, I asked Charlie if he was on Twitter.

"No, should I be?"

"Definitely—you'd be huge on it, trust me."

TUESDAY, MARCH 1, 2011

Incredible. After my single tweet at 5:55 P.M. last night, more than half a million extra viewers tuned in by 6 P.M. to watch the Sheen interview, and as the Twitter buzz exploded, so did the audience, which rocketed upward through the hour to our highest ratings yet in the all-important twenty-five-to-fifty-four demographic (the one advertisers most crave).

WEDNESDAY, MARCH 2, 2011

Charlie Sheen joined Twitter yesterday, and, after just twenty-four hours, reached one million followers this afternoon—the fastest accumulation of that milestone in Twitter's history.

FRIDAY, MARCH 4, 2011

Since I started at CNN, I've been eagerly anticipating the inevitable moment when my TV mentor, Simon Cowell, would come to *my* studio to be a guest on *my* show.

Tonight, he walked into our spanking-new L.A. studio, with the giant PIERS MORGAN TONIGHT banner right above the desk. Simon stopped in his tracks, his face frozen in shock, and he groaned like a wounded warthog.

"Oh. My. God. This is even worse than I feared."

"You should see the New York studio," I smirked. "It's even bigger . . ."

"Really? I do feel like Dr. Frankenstein now. This is a genuine horror story for me. Might need to lie down." Fortunately, Simon's fiancée, Mezghan Hussainy, was on hand to race onto the set and apply emergency powder to her man's enraged sweating brow. "This is my ultimate nightmare, Mish," he sighed.

WEDNESDAY, MARCH 9, 2011

My grandmother once told me: "The three warning signs a woman should look out for in a man are, one, if he wears black shoes and white socks; two, if he has a large bunch of keys jangling from his hip pocket; or, three, if he can't pronounce the letter R."

Tonight, Eva Longoria added a fourth.

"Nothing worse than a soft handshake."

"Could you ever go out with a man with a soft handshake?"

She shook her head violently. "Never, no."

I agreed. "I've told my three sons, a firm handshake will get you through any door in life, but people will never forget a weak one."

"Yes, and look me in the eye."

I stared hard into Eva's eyes, until she realized what I was doing, and laughed.

She recently split from her basketball star husband, Tony Parker, amid rumors of his infidelity, and began to cry when I brought it up.

"It was heartbreaking," she said, tears welling up. "It's the first time I'm talking about it, I'm sorry."

She took a few seconds to compose herself.

"It was so disappointing because I had such an identity in being Mrs. Parker and being a wife. And when that's taken away from you, you go, 'Who am I?' It was hard. Sorry."

More tears fell. I felt so sad for her.

FRIDAY, MARCH 11, 2011

I got back at 1 A.M. this morning from a long day judging *America's Got Talent* auditions in downtown Los Angeles, turned on the TV, and saw that CNN was reporting breaking news on a massive earthquake and tsunami striking Japan.

It looked horrendous, and as the minutes ticked by, it soon became clear this was going to be a major international disaster.

Obviously, we'd have to do a live show tonight on it, but there was a logistical nightmare to resolve.

I have to do two more *AGT* audition shows today, from 2 to 5:30 P.M. and 7:15 to 10 P.M. And NBC has exclusive rights to my time on the days I am taping its show. This was agreed as part of my deal when I signed.

There wouldn't quite be enough time to go to my CNN studio to anchor my show live from 6 to 7 P.M.

I emailed my *AGT* producers. "Can we move the audition times a bit?"

"No," came the reply.

They explained it wasn't possible due to all the planning involved in having two shows with three thousand people in each audience, and fifty acts to perform.

I knew it would be a nightmare, and understood.

I called Jonathan at 6 A.M. his time in New York.

"Any suggestions?"

"We'll have to try to do it from the theater where you're taping *AGT*," he said.

Brad Parks—who's been tasked with chugging around America with me on the *AGT* audition tour precisely for this kind of eventuality—was promptly dispatched to investigate this possibility. Within a few hours, he had the answer.

"Yes, we can do it on the roof. It won't be easy, but we can do it."

I got a few hours' sleep, and by the time I woke again, the full scale of the hell that had befallen Japan was evident.

The earthquake was bad enough, but the tsunami was even more devastating. The death toll is feared to be over ten thousand people, making this one of the worst natural disasters in modern times.

It felt incredibly jarring to be judging a talent show on such a day.

For the first time since I started at CNN, the kind of conflict I had feared had finally transpired. And I knew instinctively where my heart now lay.

I spent the afternoon judging some particularly dumb acts—a singing parrot that didn't sing and a group of human dancing Christmas trees (in March)—and taking every chance I got to check my BlackBerry as more and more dreadful updates poured in from Japan.

Everyone could tell I was massively distracted, but I focused on the judging when I had to, and kept things professional.

I owed it to my co-judges, Sharon Osbourne and Howie Mandel, host Nick Cannon, and the rest of the team to do my job properly. Even if my *other* job now seemed a million times more important.

At 5:30 P.M., Brad came and grabbed me and we raced up to the roof of the Orpheum Theatre, where he and the team had erected an extraordinary makeshift outdoor studio.

There was even a tenuous reason for me to be doing it from downtown L.A.—because there were fears that the aftershocks of the Japan tragedy might be felt on the California coastline.

I sat in my chair, Jonathan spoke into my ear from New York, and off we went—powering through an hour of the most devastating news imaginable.

I interviewed CNN's heroic correspondents on the scene, and garnered expert opinions from an array of scientists and senior politicians.

It was a powerful, informative show, and we had no issues with the set itself. The only error came when I pronounced MIT (we booked one of their science professors) as "Mitt University." The simple reason being that I'd never heard of it before.

"I'll have to teach you how to speak American," Jonathan groaned.

When I'd finished, I raced back downstairs to the theater, where the first new *AGT* audition act appeared soon afterward.

"What's your act?" I asked.

"I'd rather just show you," replied a cocky young man.

"OK."

He then used his mouth and hands to fart in the supposed manner of each judge.

The juxtaposition of this unedifying spectacle and what I'd been through for the previous hour couldn't have been more stark.

Sharon Osbourne, sensing my discomfort, turned to me and whispered: "Now *that's* what I call breaking news . . . or should I say, breaking wind news!"

I got back to the Beverly Wilshire at midnight, absolutely drained.

And absolutely convinced that this dual *AGT*/CNN working existence is not long for this world.

WEDNESDAY, MARCH 16, 2011

I've flown to Jerusalem for a world-exclusive interview with Israeli Prime Minister Benjamin Netanyahu—the first he's given since the Arab Spring uprisings began in Tunisia back in December.

I've never been to Israel before and was taken aback by the extraordinary natural beauty of the place.

I was also surprised when we stopped at a café on the road from the airport for lunch and saw it full of Arabs and Jews eating side-by-side quite happily.

"We don't all hate each other," explained my driver.

We drove to a hilltop in the afternoon to film a piece for tonight's show, and I saw firsthand just how close Jerusalem is to Ramallah.

Only a giant security block separates the two sides. It reminded me of the Northern Ireland conflict: warring neighbors parted by a bit of barbed wire and generations of bitter fighting.

Because of the time difference with New York, I had to go live for CNN from my hotel balcony at 3 A.M., overlooking Old Jerusalem, with the twinkling lights of the ancient walled city behind me.

It was magical.

THURSDAY, MARCH 17, 2011

The interview with Netanyahu was a fascinating encounter, conducted at his private residence in Jerusalem, surrounded by incredibly tight security.

The prime minister was intelligent, articulate, and charming. But he's also a ferociously tough politician, and I knew—with the world watching— that I couldn't give him an easy ride.

At one point he asked me directly what I would do to secure a settlement, clearly expecting me not to answer.

"Honestly, what do I think?" I replied.

"Yes."

"When Sadat came to Jerusalem bearing concessions, it worked. Why don't you go to Ramallah, and be the big guy? Why don't you take concessions that are perhaps more than you're prepared to give now and say, 'I'm calling the bluff here,' not just of the Palestinians, but of the international community? Because the international community is desperate for this to work. They would come with you. And yes, of course there would be problems. Yes, there would be more outrages. Everybody knows that. But in the end, somebody has to be the big guy here. And that could be you, couldn't it?"

He looked at me hard, then smiled.

"I'm pretty big," he said.

"You are."

"We'll have to see."

With so much upheaval elsewhere in the region, there's probably never been a better time for the Israelis and Palestinians to strike a two-state deal.

But these things only happen when big leaders take big steps. I might be completely wrong about this, but I get the sense that Netanyahu realizes this might be the moment to put his large hand on history.

At the end of the interview, we walked into his office.

He took me to the large map of the Middle East behind his desk and began laying his hand on various countries.

"This is Libya, which is about a hundred times the size of Israel. Egypt, about forty times the size of Israel. This is Saudi Arabia, God knows how many times. Iraq, Syria, Iran. You want to see Israel now?"

He put one finger on a tiny piece of the map.

"Here's Israel. My finger covers it, with the West Bank, everything. So it's a tiny country, surrounded, well, shall we say living in a very tough neighborhood."

It was a pretty powerful illustration of the isolation and vulnerability that Israel feels. And more so since the Arab Spring, because there's now turmoil almost everywhere around them. And that's dangerous.

On the side wall was a photo of Netanyahu and his brother Yonatan, who was an elite Israeli army commando, killed during the daring raid on Entebbe in Uganda, as he rescued hostages from an airliner hijacked by terrorists and welcomed by despot Idi Amin.

"What do you think when you see that picture?" I asked.

"Well, first that I must go on a diet!" he chuckled.

Then his eyes teared up.

"Secondly, how young we were. That was on the Dead Sea, a few weeks before he fell. I think a lot of him, and I often ask myself, what would he be doing?"

"Would a peace deal be the greatest legacy you could give your brother?"

"A peace that holds, yes."

FRIDAY, MARCH 18, 2011

Woke up to a storm of Twitter outrage over my Netanyahu interview—half the complainants saying I was too soft on him, the other half saying I was too hard.

TUESDAY, MARCH 22, 2011

Celia's pregnant!

This will be my fourth child, and I couldn't be happier.

Of all the things I've experienced in life, fatherhood is by far the most rewarding, joyous, intriguing, and occasionally infuriating.

WEDNESDAY, MARCH 23, 2011

It all began so promisingly as I arrived at New York's JFK Airport at 5:50 A.M. to catch the 8 A.M. three-hour flight to Minneapolis.

This would get me there at 10 A.M. local time, four hours before I was due to start judging *America's Got Talent* auditions.

We took off late at 9 A.M., which didn't overly concern me as it still gave me two hours' "wiggle room."

But then, after ninety minutes in the air, the Delta Airlines pilot suddenly announced that due to bad weather conditions we were not able to land at the Minneapolis airport.

"I regret to inform you," he added, "that we have been directed to return to New York."

Whaaaat?

He was serious. The plane turned around and began heading back to New York.

I emailed the *AGT* team. "Er, we have a problem. I'm going the wrong way."

At 12:30 P.M., I landed right back where I'd started.

"I don't have words to describe how sorry we the crew are about what just happened," said an attendant. "We apologize sincerely."

A statement that would have moved me more if I hadn't discovered from Juliana that many other Delta flights *were* still landing at Minneapolis, including one carrying one of my producers.

I would now miss the first *AGT* show, and there was a serious risk of missing the second one too. With two audiences of three thousand people each, a production crew of over a hundred, and fifty acts flown in from all over America to perform, this was not good.

I've never been late for a show in nine seasons of *BGT* and *AGT.* I may be annoying, but I'm always on time.

I called Jonathan to explain what was going on.

"Elizabeth Taylor died," he said. "So we need to do a special tribute show from Minneapolis when you eventually get there."

Minneapolis is on Central time, so my live CNN hour would fall from 8 to 9 P.M., right bang in the middle of the second *AGT* show.

"We'll have to tape it two hours early," I said, knowing this was far from ideal on a story of such global interest.

But I had to get to Minneapolis first.

I sat in the lounge, agitated beyond belief, tweeting my rage at Delta.

Then I boarded a second flight, due to take off for Minneapolis at 2 P.M.

After another delay, we taxied out a few hundred yards. Then stopped.

"I'm sorry, but we have a technical fault and we need to power down the plane for a few minutes," said a flight attendant.

Engineers appeared. Then we were herded off the plane again.

It was now 3 P.M. in New York, and nobody from Delta seemed to have a clue when another flight might be able to go to Minneapolis.

I called Jonathan again.

"This is a nightmare, no idea what's going on now."

His interest, of course, was purely CNN related.

"Look, I've had to consider the possibility you may not be able to do our show tonight. So I made a discreet call, and Larry could step in for you."

My head, already dangerously near boiling point, nearly exploded.

"No, no, NO!"

The last thing I wanted was Larry back in his old chair just two months after I replaced him—it would send all the wrong signals.

"I'm doing it, whatever happens."

Jonathan could tell I was in a volatile state.

"OK, OK, don't worry, it was just an idea to try to solve the problem."

Delta still couldn't tell me what on earth was going on, but indicated the next flight to Minneapolis wouldn't be leaving until at least 5 P.M. That would get me there after 7 P.M., and by the time I was at the theater and ready, I'd have missed at least half the second *AGT* audition show.

In the meantime, I'd miss any taping window for my CNN show too.

I had to make a decision.

And it seemed pretty simple to me—forget about trying to get to Minneapolis today, go back to New York, and anchor my CNN Elizabeth Taylor tribute show from my usual studio.

As my car took me back into Manhattan, I tweeted a final message to my Delta tormentors: "The gates of Hades will freezeth over before I ever darken your pitifully incompetent doors again."

Juliana called from Minneapolis.

"Delta's marketing chief is reading your tweets and wants to make amends."

"How, exactly?"

"They'll send a private plane to get you there tonight."

Given that Delta had so far cost NBC a considerable sum of money, I accepted the offer.

I recorded the Taylor special and sped to a private airstrip.

At 8 P.M., I was told there'd be a one-hour delay due to "bad weather" and the plane might not fly at all.

For fuck's sake!

But at 9:15 P.M., as sleet, hail, and snow lashed the wings, we took off (by "we," I mean me and the two pilots). By then, I didn't care if the plane skidded into Minneapolis sideways.

We landed shortly before 1 A.M. local time. Nineteen hours after I'd set off.

I can't go on trying to juggle these two shows—it's going to kill me.

THURSDAY, MARCH 24, 2011

The first act at the *AGT* audition today was a group of giant tap-dancing human elves, calling themselves The Funny Little People.

"More like The Unfunny and Incredibly Annoying Little People," I said.

In a break later, there was a knock on my dressing-room door and Howie Mandel ran in with the elves, who began jumping around and shouting, then knocked me to the floor, in my suit, and smothered me.

As I lay there, one thought steamed into my brain: "How do I get out of this madness?"

TUESDAY, MARCH 29, 2011

Ratings have come out for March, and CNN's overtaken MSNBC for the first time in fourteen months.

I've comfortably beaten my opposite number, Rachel Maddow, MSNBC's biggest star, and registered ratings of 118 percent higher on Larry King's figure for March 2010.

I couldn't have wished for a better start. But I'm very aware that it's mainly down to the huge hype surrounding my launch, and the very busy news cycle in the last few weeks.

CNN historically does very well in the ratings when there's big news around, and not so well when there's little happening.

The challenge is to make my show as compelling as possible in the quieter periods.

MONDAY, APRIL 11, 2011

Back to work after a week off, straight into a frantic day of tapings, including Whoopi Goldberg, Demi Moore and Ashton Kutcher, and Robert Redford.

And into a huge firefight with the White House, over something utterly trivial—well, to my eyes anyway.

The trouble started when I pretaped an interview with Barack Obama's half sister Maya Soetoro-Ng—who is promoting a book—and asked her about Donald Trump's controversial "birther" campaign to expose the president for supposedly not being born in America.

Trump has been surging in the polls as a potential presidential candidate, although nobody seems convinced he's seriously going to run.

"I think it's unfortunate," she replied. "He was born in Hawaii. There is a tremendous amount of proof that has already been presented. So I think that it is time for people to put that to bed, put it to rest completely."

"What do you think of Donald Trump banging on about this every day at the moment?" I asked.

"Well, I think it's a shame. And I think that my brother should definitely be president for a second term. And that's really all I have to say about it."

All fairly innocuous, and exactly what I expected her to say.

We put out a preview clip containing a few of the quotes to promote the interview, which airs tomorrow night.

Within an hour, Jonathan and I started getting angry emails from Dan Pfeiffer accusing us of "using the birther thing to drive ratings," being "pretty cheap," and concluding: "I am annoyed, others will be furious. This is not a great way to entice us to give you a presidential interview."

Wow.

I hadn't seen bullying nonsense like this from a government communications team since Tony Blair's spin doctor Alastair Campbell used to harangue me in a similar vein.

TUESDAY, APRIL 12, 2011

The interview with Maya Soetoro-Ng aired, and everyone calmed down once they realized it really wasn't the presidency-threatening nightmare they'd feared. Just a sister saying nice, protective, supportive things about her brother.

In the same show, I interviewed Governor Tim Pawlenty, and asked him if he'd ever consider being Donald Trump's running mate if the latter won the Republican nomination.

"I'm running for president," he replied. "I'm not putting my hat in the ring rhetorically or ultimately for vice president. So I'm focused on running for president."

Jonathan erupted in my ear: "Whoa, he hasn't said that before— press him."

"Governor, unless I'm mistaken, you just said you were running for president. Can we take that as an official announcement?"

"Well, I have an exploratory committee up and running. We'll have a final and full announcement on that in the coming weeks here. It won't be too much longer. But everything is headed in that direction, Piers."

All pretty unequivocal. We'd just made some big political news.

WEDNESDAY, APRIL 13, 2011

Governor Pawlenty's revelation lit up Washington today.

Then his team issued a statement saying CNN had taken his "running for president" remarks out of context and he *hadn't* announced that he was running for president.

Of course he hadn't. How silly of me.

THURSDAY, APRIL 14, 2011

I've flown to Atlanta for more *America's Got Talent* auditions and I felt tired and irritable all day. And ended up having a screaming match in my dressing room with Georgie Hurford-Jones, one of *AGT*'s executive producers, and my closest friend on the show.

It was all a fuss over nothing, and she gave as good as she got, until we both calmed down and started laughing.

But it's a worrying sign that this relentless pace of trying to do two big shows is taking its toll already. I feel like I never have time to breathe anymore.

After *AGT* taping finished at 11 P.M., I flew to Los Angeles for a big NBC press day tomorrow.

It was a long five-hour flight made immeasurably worse by the fact that I was incarcerated with Sharon Osbourne in a confined space—it was a private jet—and she was in a "frisky" mood after a couple of glasses of red wine.

Every time I tried to sleep, I was woken by a shrieking Sharon, either poking my nose, pulling my ears, or laughing hysterically inches from my face. All dutifully recorded on a video camera by Nick Cannon.

Finally, I got to sleep and was in a deep slumber when I was woken yet again.

My eyes opened wide, to be met with Sharon's naked right breast dangling literally two inches away.

FRIDAY, APRIL 15, 2011

Had dinner at Cut tonight, and met Arnold Schwarzenegger and his wife, Maria Shriver, on the way in.

"Congratulations on the show!" he boomed. "I liked Larry a lot, but you're growing on me!"

We chatted for a few minutes, and I was struck once again by what a happy marriage they seem to have—they celebrate their twenty-fifth wedding anniversary on April 26. Particularly remarkable given the industries he's worked in (body-building, movies, politics) and the Kennedy family she comes from.

WEDNESDAY, APRIL 20, 2011

It's the first anniversary of the BP oil spill today, and we devoted the whole show to it last night. Mainly because there's nothing else actually happening in the world.

Big mistake.

Ratings were horrific—a 77 (that means seventy-seven thousand viewers watched the first U.S. airing of the show at 9 P.M. ET) in the crucial, younger twenty-five-to-fifty-four age demo number, the lowest since I've been on air.

I didn't think anything could affect my mood quite as badly as the vagaries of daily newspaper circulation figures in Britain.

But this is just as bad, if not worse.

The stage, and stakes, are both way bigger.

Jonathan sensed my misery.

"Don't be depressed. One shitty night. Monday was strong. We won't do an anniversary oil spill again. And next week is the start of a big event."

Ah yes, the royal wedding. That should get us back on track, but *will* it? My confidence is dented.

SATURDAY, APRIL 23, 2011

I've flown into London, where I am doing a week of shows on the royal wedding of Prince William and Kate Middleton.

The city is basking in unseasonal sunshine, and buzzing with excitement for the big day.

Well, most of the city anyway.

You can divide the British public into two types at the moment: the cynics who loudly and proudly proclaim their hatred for the royal wedding and everything it stands for, and those who see it for what it is—a harmless bit of romantic fun that has cheered us all up when much of the world is besieged by misery, famine, financial crisis, natural disaster, and war.

I readily confess to getting caught up in all the hype. My family has always been monarchists. Mum even camped on the Mall overnight with my sister Charlotte and brother Rupert before Diana and Charles's wedding.

I believe that whatever the royal family cost us, they more than make up for it financially in tourism and global PR for Britain.

CNN's studio was part of a specially erected media center outside Buckingham Palace, and I could tell how big a deal this is by the fact that every major U.S. TV news star is here—led by Katie Couric, Barbara Walters, Diane Sawyer, and Matt Lauer.

TUESDAY, APRIL 26, 2011

I finally got to actually interview Sir David Frost today, and asked him all the things that I had always wanted to ask him.

"What are your personal career highlights?"

"Well, there are odd lines with some people. Desmond Tutu, for instance. I said to him once, 'I always think of you as an optimist.' And he said, 'I'm not an optimist, I'm a prisoner of hope.' Great phrase."

"And Nelson Mandela. I asked him, 'How did you get through twenty-eight years, wrongly incarcerated, and you're not bitter?' And instead of basking in the tribute, he said, 'David, I would like to be bitter, but there is no time to be bitter. There is work to be done.'

"That was just before the election of ninety-three, which of course he won."

"Who would you most like to have interviewed from history?" I asked.

"Cyrus the Great—the founder of Persia. Because he was the first man ever who used power to alleviate and improve the human condition and not make it worse."

"You've interviewed seven U.S. presidents. If you could choose one of them to head the country you were living in, who would it be?"

"George H. W. Bush. He was wise, and cautious, a man of compassion and sincerity, and knew what he was determined to do, and he was a man of his word, as I discovered from personal experience."

But what I really wanted to know was how he felt after Richard Nixon finally buckled under his relentless questioning and made his historic apology to the American people.

"I felt a sense of euphoria or a joy, I guess. And at the same time—quite a bit of exhaustion, because that last two and a half hours, pushing him to go further, him finding being pushed further very difficult to deal with. Coming face to face and I was saying to him at one point, if you don't say that, you'll regret it for the rest of your life. And the last twenty minutes built into that, and so on. By the end of it, we were both drained, actually, so we didn't instantly jump for joy afterward because it had been such a draining and worthwhile and historic experience."

WEDNESDAY, APRIL 27, 2011

I interviewed missing toddler Madeleine McCann's parents, Kate and Gerry, this morning. Madeleine was snatched from a holiday resort villa in

Portugal as her parents dined with friends in a nearby restaurant within the complex.

It's the first TV interview they've given to promote Kate's book on their daughter, and will air on CNN next month.

I'll admit to having had mixed feelings about the couple. Not because I thought they had anything to do with Madeleine's disappearance, because I don't. But because, like most parents, I felt uneasy about the way they left three children under five years old on their own while they went out for dinner with friends.

I would never have done that with the boys.

But seeing the horrific grief still etched on Kate McCann's face for myself, and hearing her and Gerry tell their awful story of four years of desperate, fruitless searching for Madeleine, I felt an increasing surge of intense sympathy.

The truth is that no parent is perfect when it comes to keeping an eye on their children.

I can still remember vividly a day in the summer of 1999 when I was attending a cricket match on the private Oxfordshire grounds of a former newspaper boss of mine.

As I sat in the open-sided tent having lunch—with my then-wife, Marion—Spencer, seven, and Stanley, two, played with other children a few yards outside.

Every few minutes, I'd flick an eye toward them and check that they were OK. It seemed like the safest scenario imaginable.

Then Stanley vanished.

For half an hour, I ran around those grounds in an increasingly desperate search.

To my horror, I discovered a small creek that I hadn't noticed before, running around the back of the tent.

I can picture now the security guards, walkie-talkies in hand, actually trawling the water.

And I can remember my feelings as the clock ticked on—horror, fear, nausea, and an impending sense of utter doom.

Then, suddenly, he was found. Inside the tent, standing patiently by the bar waiting for someone to give him a Coke. He was so small that his head was lower than the tables, so he couldn't be seen from any distance.

I ran toward him, plucked him up, and ran out of the tent in sheer, unbridled ecstasy. My nightmare, one that has been shared in some form by every parent, was over.

The McCanns' nightmare continues, and may never end.

THURSDAY, APRIL 28, 2011

A series of devastatingly powerful tornadoes have swept through the south of America, killing more than three hundred people and injuring many more.

Entire neighborhoods have been wiped out in places like Alabama, and the scenes are apocalyptic.

It's the worst tornado damage to human life and property in over forty years. It puts the comparatively frivolous events here in London into a new perspective.

Brian Williams flew into Heathrow this morning, heard the severity of the news as he was coming from the airport to the city, instructed the driver to turn back, and flew straight home to anchor the *NBC Nightly News*.

Jonathan said we'd devote half of tonight's show to the disaster, the second half to the royal wedding. Our coverage has been getting us big ratings all week, so this seems a sensible compromise.

The reality is that there are so many natural disasters in America, where the weather hits every extreme with alarming regularity, that this will pass through quickly as just another terrible storm-related incident. There are more than a thousand tornadoes a year, more than everywhere else in the world. In Britain, if three hundred people were killed by a tornado, it would be one of the biggest news stories for decades.

FRIDAY, APRIL 29, 2011

What a fabulous day. I loved every minute of the royal wedding, a sumptuous feast of great British pageantry, pomp, and ceremony.

Everything was perfect, from the weather to Pippa Middleton's now world-famous derriere.

Watching from my CNN studio balcony vantage point as first the magnificent Household Cavalry, and then a million ecstatic people, marched up the Mall to the palace was one of the most stirring experiences of my career.

Though my expert British royal credentials took a bit of a battering when I assured Anderson Cooper, as the crowd chanted for William to give Kate an unprecedented second kiss on the balcony: "Trust me, it will never happen."

Only for it to then immediately happen.

SUNDAY, MAY 1, 2011

Flew back to New York and landed to find an urgent email from Meghan.

"LAND! The prez making a big statement soon. We don't know why."

Obama was addressing the nation late on a Sunday night? This must be huge.

I called Jonathan as my car sped back into Manhattan.

"What is it? Something Libya-related, do you think?"

"No clue. Maybe we've caught Gaddafi or something."

Twitter had reached the same conclusion. But then I read a solitary tweet that suggested a much bigger story. "Bet it's bin Laden."

Wow. Could it be?

It's hard to think of a single human being's death right now that would cause more of a global tremor.

Around 10:30 P.M., Jonathan called back. "It's Osama!"

As I neared central Manhattan, people were on the streets cheering.

And by the time Obama made his speech—declaring proudly: "Justice has been done"—word had spread so fast that huge crowds began gathering at Ground Zero in New York and the White House in D.C., all chanting, "USA, USA," and singing "The Star-Spangled Banner."

It was a profoundly moving sight.

Details of bin Laden's death were as startling as the news itself.

He'd been shot dead in a firefight with Navy SEALs at a luxury compound in Pakistan. The SEALs then grabbed the al-Qaeda chief's dead body and whisked it away on a helicopter.

Finally, America had exacted revenge on the man responsible for 9/11.

Just as being in London this week was to share something special and uniquely British, so being in New York when this news broke evoked similar emotions.

I remember coming here three weeks after 9/11 and finding a city in collective trauma.

Tonight, there was jubilation. The waiter at the Mandarin brought me some coffee with a massive grin on his face, and said, "We got him! Finally some good news!"

By an amazing coincidence, Adolf Hitler's death in 1945 was also announced to the world on May 1.

But unlike with Hitler's death, bin Laden's demise is not the end of this particular war. It is a huge step forward toward defeating al-Qaeda, though.

To quote Churchill after the Second Battle of El Alamein in 1942: "Now this is not the end. It is not even the beginning of the end. But it is, perhaps, the end of the beginning."

MONDAY, MAY 2, 2011

I couldn't think of anyone I'd rather interview about bin Laden's death than Rudy Giuliani, who'd been mayor of New York on 9/11 and did a heroic job fortifying his city's broken spirit.

I asked him where he was when he heard the news. "I was at home, reading a book. And I saw a little banner on the television that the president was going to hold a news conference, or give a statement. And I thought to myself, well, there has to be something terrible for it to be on a Sunday night. And then of course it developed within about fifteen minutes that it was bin Laden. And I felt very relieved because I thought maybe there was some kind of new terrorist plot. I had a good feeling and a bad feeling. The bad feeling was, I hope they don't think it's over because it isn't. The good feeling was, they still remember. I mean it was really very, very heartwarming to see so many people just spontaneously go out on the street in Washington and New York. And a lot of young people. It means they still remember and they still have an understanding of what happened on September 11."

"How do you think history will judge him [bin Laden]?"

"I think he's going to be viewed as one of the great monsters of history. I mean, maybe the numbers aren't as great as a Hitler or a Stalin, but the viciousness and the horror of his attacks are just as bad."

I also interviewed Andy Card, the former White House chief of staff who was the man seen on television whispering in George Bush's ear as he spoke to a classroom of schoolchildren when the 9/11 attacks happened.

And he pointed out the power of national events in unifying disparate factions.

"Two things happened over the course of the last few days," he said. "The British all rallied together and were very proud to be British for the royal wedding. And the United States broke into spontaneous cheers of 'USA, USA, USA' yesterday—there was no 'GOP, GOP, GOP' or 'Democrat, Democrat, Democrat.'

"We were all Americans, just like the Brits were all Brits. And we've demonstrated that yes, there are times that we can all come together for what is good."

WEDNESDAY, MAY 4, 2011
Donald Trump's unofficial presidential campaign continues unabated.

Today he gave his views on gay marriage.

"It's like in golf. A lot of people—I don't want this to sound trivial—but a lot of people are switching to these really long putters, very unattractive. It's weird. You see these great players with these really long putters, because they can't sink three-footers anymore. And I hate it. I am a traditionalist. I have so many fabulous friends who happen to be gay, but I am a traditionalist."

The gay rights debate reminds me of the civil rights movement.

It's surely not a question of if America will change its cultural position, but when.

Older people, of Trump's and my parents' generation, find it hard to accept two gay people getting married.

Younger people don't give a damn.

It's as simple as that.

Less predictable is the guns issue. Guns are simply so embedded in the fabric of American life, it's hard to see how it will ever be any different.

But that doesn't mean sensible, lifesaving new controls won't be brought in.

Drunk driving killed a lot of Americans until the famous Mothers Against Drunk Driving campaign in the eighties forced through tighter regulations and saved a lot of lives.

It may take the mothers of America to rise up again against assault weapons.

TUESDAY, MAY 10, 2011
Shocking news.

Arnold Schwarzenegger and Maria Shriver have announced they're splitting up.

In a joint statement, they said: "This has been a time of great personal and professional transition for each of us. After a great deal of thought, reflection, discussion, and prayer, we came to this decision together. At this time, we are living apart while we work on the future of our relationship."

What on earth has happened?

WEDNESDAY, MAY 11, 2011
Christopher Hitchens is battling cancer, and has been writing and talking about his ordeal with typical courage, belligerence, and humor.

I got to know him during my newspaper days, employing him to write for *The Daily Mirror,* and enjoying a few quite magnificently debauched lunches. After one of these he sent me a thank-you letter, ending with the following advice: "The four most overrated things in life are champagne, lobster, anal sex, and picnics."

THURSDAY, MAY 12, 2011

Stanley took a hat trick today—three batsmen out with three consecutive balls—while playing cricket for his school in a tournament at the Oval, one of England's great sporting stadiums.

The nearest American equivalent would be pitching a perfect game at Yankee Stadium.

And I'll sadly add it to the growing list of great things I've missed my sons achieving since working in America.

FRIDAY, MAY 13, 2011

Chaz Bono, formerly Cher's daughter, Chastity, until his recent gender reassignment surgery, appeared on my show last night with his bisexual girlfriend, Jennifer—and hesitated when I pressed him, live on air, to set a date for their marriage.

As he hemmed and hawed, and steadfastly avoided any concrete commitment, I laughed and told Jennifer:

"Right—he's now behaving like a typical man!"

TUESDAY, MAY 17, 2011

Wow. Arnold Schwarzenegger has confirmed the rumors behind his marriage split—he impregnated his housekeeper.

His statement read: "After leaving the governor's office I told my wife about this event, which occurred over a decade ago. I understand and deserve the feelings of anger and disappointment among my friends and family. There are no excuses and I take full responsibility for the hurt I have caused."

I'm shocked, like everyone is.

But I also feel sorry for him, which very few other people seem to.

This afternoon, I went to the White House for a meeting with Dan Pfeiffer and Jay Carney, the president's press secretary.

We cleared the air over "Maya-gate," and they made encouraging noises about an Obama interview.

"You're a card we definitely want to play," Dan said. "We just don't know yet exactly when we want to play it."

WEDNESDAY, MAY 18, 2011

Locked horns tonight with Ted Nugent, the self-styled "Motor City Madman" rock musician and ardent gun lover.

"Anybody that wants to disarm me can drop dead," he snarled. "Anybody that wants to make me unarmed and helpless, people that want to literally create the proven places where more innocents are killed, called gun-free zones, we're going to beat you.

"We're going to vote you out of office or you can suck on my machine gun."

Of course, it's precisely this kind of violent rhetoric that makes me so worried about people like Ted Nugent having guns.

THURSDAY, MAY 26, 2011

Back on the *Tonight Show* this evening, and Jay Leno came into my dressing room for a coffee.

I asked him what he'd learned from forty years in show business.

"That there are two types of people in the world," he said with a chuckle. "Those who when it's cold in a room say politely, 'Hey, it's a bit chilly in here, isn't it?' And those who scream, 'Someone shut the fucking window!' "

I sped to CNN afterward to interview Paris Hilton with her mother, Kathy, expecting a lighthearted romp through Paris's comparatively trivial celebrity life. But it turned into something much more dramatic.

The catalyst came when I brought up the subject of the infamous sex tape that catapulted Paris into global stardom.

When I asked Kathy what the tape had done to her family, she broke down and wept.

"It was awful," she sobbed.

As Paris tried to comfort her, Kathy's crying became so intense that I had to actually ask for the floor manager to bring her some tissues.

"The worst thing," she said afterward, "is that the Internet means it will always be there, so Paris's children, my grandchildren, will be able to see it one day. And there's nothing we can do to stop it."

TUESDAY, MAY 31, 2011

The weirdest day of my TV career so far. The sixth season of *America's Got Talent* started up tonight on NBC, airing at exactly the same time as my CNN show (with the Hiltons).

This will be the case, twice a week, for the next four months. So I will be quite literally competing with myself.

"So, what is the smart way to live-promote *AGT* and *PMT* on Twitter when they clash?" I asked Jonathan. "I'm struggling!"

He replied: "Torn between two lovers, feelin' like a fool. Lovin' you both is breakin' all the rules."

WEDNESDAY, JUNE 1, 2011

Celia went for her three-month sonogram in Los Angeles today, and everything's fine.

"Do you want to know what you're having?" asked the doctor.

We nodded.

"A baby girl."

Wow.

I called the boys to break the news they were going to have a little sister.

"Oh, thank God," said Stanley. "We've been discussing this and decided it wouldn't be good to have a rival brother living with you!"

I hadn't even thought of it like that.

THURSDAY, JUNE 2, 2011

Made my debut on Jimmy Kimmel's show, and he played me a clip from my Paris Hilton interview, featuring me saying the following words: "I could type in 'Paris Hilton sex tape' and up it comes."

The audience roared with laughter. Jimmy didn't have to say anything.

FRIDAY, JUNE 3, 2011

My ratings are getting decimated by a trial involving an alleged baby killer called Casey Anthony.

A lot of our younger viewers are migrating to watch Nancy Grace cover this disturbing case on HLN.

The big question is, what the hell do we do about it?

Larry got into ratings trouble overdoing coverage of hot tabloid stories like the deaths of Anna Nicole Smith and Michael Jackson, because it alienated his core CNN audience.

Jonathan and I discussed it with Ken, and we all agreed that we should pretty much leave the Casey Anthony story to HLN.

But it's going to hurt us until the trial ends, no question.

MONDAY, JUNE 6, 2011

America is reeling from a series of extraordinary political sex scandals.

First, Arnold Schwarzenegger impregnating his housekeeper.

Then, French politician Dominique Strauss-Kahn is accused of attacking a hotel chambermaid.

And just when you thought you'd heard it all, along comes a congressman named Anthony Weiner, who's been caught sending photos of his wiener to random women on the Internet.

I had the offender on my show a few weeks ago, and he was a bombastic, arrogant, quick-witted, and undeniably entertaining character—who got into a splendidly vicious debate with Donald Trump.

Then I watched him bring the house down at a Washington political dinner. After which I emailed him my congratulations. "Brilliant speech, made me laugh out loud."

He responded, "I have a newfound respect for guys who make funny for a living. It's hard."

In fact, as he's now discovering, it's not that hard to make people laugh. You just have to be a sex-scandalized politician by the name of Weiner.

Tea Party darling Christine O'Donnell about to exit stage left from our interview, after I had the effrontery to ask her about revelations in her own book . . .

5

Mitt Romney is emerging as the clear early favorite in the race to be the Republican presidential nominee.

In person, as I've discovered firsthand over several interviews now, Romney's a polite, friendly, and solicitous man.

He's a great father and grandfather, according to his five devoted sons, and a great husband, according to his wife, Ann, the woman who was his teenage sweetheart and whom he's helped nurse with deep compassion through her ongoing battle with multiple sclerosis.

But there's barely a big issue on which Romney hasn't switched his position, earning him the nickname "Mr. Flip-Flop."

In fact, it's hard to even recognize the new Mitt from the one who was a successful and popular governor of Massachusetts.

On abortion, he was then firmly prochoice, now he's equally firmly prolife. On guns, he outlawed lethal assault weapons. Now he says they're fine, despite a rash of horrific recent mass gun killings. On health care, he was the first governor to bring in a compulsory "mandate" health insurance scheme. But when Obama did the same thing, he lambasted it as a "terrible idea." He was also a huge fan of stem cell research, but now he says he's "been persuaded the stem cell debate was grounded in a false premise."

Each switch was dictated by the need to make him more electable—not to the wider public, but to his own party members, particularly the far-right

Tea Party element, so he could win the Republican nomination during the primary race, and it seems to be working.

I asked him tonight why he'd done a U-turn on something as emotive as abortion.

"Ronald Reagan was also prochoice and then became prolife. And George W. Bush was prochoice and became prolife."

He's right, they were. And it raises an interesting question. Are politicians who change their minds on big issues doing it purely for political expediency, as Romney's accusers claim, or because they've genuinely changed their minds?

On gay rights, he was more evasive, saying he opposed gay marriage but was in favor of ending discrimination against gays.

When I asked if he believed homosexuality was a sin, as his Mormon church says it is, he refused to answer.

"Nice try, but I'm not going to get into this."

"That's a valid question, isn't it?"

"It's a valid question and my answer is 'nice try' . . ."

"There are people watching you saying 'nice try' repeatedly, saying, well, why doesn't he just answer the question?"

"I'm not here in a religious context. I'm here as a candidate for president. It's hard for me to imagine describing something as a sin in a political sense. You can talk about something being wrong, or evil. There are murderers—that's evil, and that's wrong. It also happens to be a sin according to most religions.

"But the terminology is religious terminology, that's probably not something which would figure into public policy."

This is the purest illustration of the separation of church and state imaginable, and it will be interesting to see if he can get away with sustaining that distinction if he does end up as the nominee.

One thing Republicans won't have to worry about with Romney is any skeletons rattling in his closet.

"Have you ever drunk alcohol?" I asked.

"No. Well, I tested it once, but it was not a good experience."

"Taken drugs?"

"No."

"And presumably you've never had an affair?"

"Of course not!"

I think Romney would be a serious challenge to Obama. He's smart, experienced, politically savvy, and not too right wing.

And his strength is the economy, which may well turn out to be what settles this election.

WEDNESDAY, JUNE 8, 2011

Spent the morning with Chris Christie, the giant—in every sense—governor of New Jersey.

He's a budget-slashing, tough-talking, former U.S. attorney whom Republicans love and Democrats fear.

I took him back to his old school, then drove with him to his house. It gave me a fascinating insight into one of the most charismatic politicians in the country.

"America right now is in the fight of its life as a nation, particularly economically," I said. "Do you think America needs somebody like you who's going to be tough?"

"I think America needs lots of tough people. Not just me. I think America needs to get tougher, all of us. We need to understand that it's time to step up and pay for what we want. And you know, we haven't been doing that for a long time, and both parties have been guilty of it."

I liked that answer.

During the drive to the house, I asked him how many cases he fought as a federal prosecutor.

"A hundred and thirty."

"How many did you win?"

He smiled. "Ask me how many I lost . . ."

"How many did you lose?"

"None. Zero."

Christie's a Catholic, like me.

So I asked the same question I asked Mitt Romney.

"Is homosexuality a sin?"

"Well, my religion says it's a sin. But I've always believed that people are born with the predisposition to be homosexual. And so I think if someone is born that way, it's very difficult to say then that that's a sin. I understand that my church says that. But for me personally, I don't look upon someone who is homosexual as a sinner."

I liked that answer a lot more than Romney's equivocating.

"Part of being a Catholic is you confess sins," I continued. "In light of Weiner-gate, Schwarzenegger-gate, and so on, is there anything you want to get off your chest?"

"You don't look like a priest to me, Piers. So, no."

"Well, should we be worried about any skeletons tumbling out of the Christie closet?"

"Listen, any confessions I need to make, I'll make to my wife and to my priest, not on CNN to you, pal!"

I liked that answer too.

"The other thing about being a Catholic is feeling guilty. Do you feel guilty about stuff?"

"My weight," he said. "Because I'm really struggling, been struggling for a long time with it. And I know that it would be better for my kids if I got it more under control."

"Why do you think you've had a battle with your weight?"

"If I could figure it out, I'd fix it."

"You don't know what it is?" I said.

"I don't."

"Do you ever get help for it?"

"Sure, plenty of times."

"Where do you fall down in terms of dealing with it?"

"I eat too much," he said. "I mean, it's not a complicated thing. And you know, it's one of the things, everybody has faults."

"Is it the one jibe about you that really stings?"

"No, because I know the people who jibe me about that are just ignorant. Because, in the end, it doesn't have any effect on the way I can do my job. And so, if they're commentating about me as governor and decide they want to do that, you know what I conclude? I must be doing a damn good job, because if that's all they got to jibe me about, amen, man, I'm having a good day."

At the house, his wife said something on-camera about his extraordinary record as a prosecutor, which shed an interesting light.

"His overriding focus was to never prosecute the wrong person. People will never know how hard Chris worked at not prosecuting someone when he wasn't absolutely confident they were guilty."

I liked that answer too.

If he ever decides to run for president, Christie would be a formidable candidate.

TUESDAY, JUNE 14, 2011

I watched *AGT* tonight, and saw myself judging a man who blows up water bottles until they explode, and a talking trash can.

Then I flicked over to CNN, to see myself interviewing Chris Christie—a man I suspect will be president of the United States one day.

The absurdity of my double TV life was laid bare.

WEDNESDAY, JUNE 15, 2011

New York's state assembly today approved same-sex marriage.

This bandwagon is well and truly off and running.

WEDNESDAY, JUNE 29, 2011

Charlize Theron, whom I interviewed tonight, suffered a terrible tragedy as a sixteen-year-old teenager when her alcoholic father came home drunk to their South African home and started shooting at her and her mother. To save their lives, her mother grabbed a gun and shot back, killing her father.

South Africa, like America, has a huge gun culture, and many home-owners have guns in the house.

In this case, the gun that Charlize's mother grabbed to defend them both probably saved their lives.

She was never prosecuted on the grounds of self-defense, and they now live close to each other in Los Angeles.

It's hard to argue against a citizen's right to possess a gun for that purpose in countries where there are so many guns in circulation.

But, as Charlize said: "I obviously had an experience in my life where, in the wrong circumstances, a gun could be used in a very tragic way. But I also understand people's feelings about wanting to protect themselves. I just don't think anyone should ever have a semiautomatic or automatic weapon for anything."

SATURDAY, JULY 2, 2011

I'm back in Britain for a week's holiday.

Elisabeth Murdoch and her PR tycoon husband, Matthew Freud, threw a lavish *Great Gatsby*–style party at their stunning new Oxfordshire home, attended by all the great, good, and slightly dubious of British society.

At midnight, I found myself by the bar with Rebekah Brooks and James Murdoch, two old friends.

They are currently running News International, the UK newspaper division of Rupert Murdoch's News Corporation empire. Rebekah is chief executive, and James is chairman.

They're selling lots of papers, and making lots of money, but the company's been dogged by an ongoing phone-hacking scandal that keeps popping back into the headlines.

Both seemed to think the worst was over.

MONDAY, JULY 4, 2011

The phone-hacking scandal exploded today after *The Guardian* newspaper made the most serious accusation yet.

They asserted that the *News of the World* hacked into the voice mail of a murdered schoolgirl called Milly Dowler after she went missing in 2002.

And worse, it alleged they deleted messages that had been left for her, thus giving her parents false hope that she might still be alive.

Turrets are now being aimed at Rebekah, who was editor of the paper at the time.

She's the most powerful woman in British media, and has inevitably made a few enemies along the way. They're all queuing up to attack her, and the coverage is already absolutely vicious.

I've been on the receiving end of this kind of dog-eat-dog assault in Britain a few times, and it's horrible.

WEDNESDAY, JULY 6, 2011

Eliot Spitzer's CNN show has been canceled.

I sent him a note: "I'm really sorry. You gave it everything you've got and I enjoyed your show a lot, and working with you. Good luck with your next venture. Get back into politics, I'd vote for you."

"Thanks," he replied. "Where are you registered to vote?"

THURSDAY, JULY 7, 2011

Casey Anthony was found not guilty of killing her daughter, though guilty of lesser charges of providing false information to the police. Today, she was sentenced to four years in prison, but with time already served, she will spend just six more days inside.

I went to the CNN bureau tonight to tape a show on this shocking development.

As I sat in the makeup room, I suddenly saw a banner shoot up on the TV saying: "BREAKING NEWS: *News of the World* to close."

I scrambled my phone out of my pocket and began furiously flicking through Twitter to see what the hell was going on.

Sure enough, there was confirmation from James Murdoch that the paper was shutting down in the wake of the hacking scandal.

I couldn't believe it.

Britain's oldest and most popular newspaper was gone.

A place I'd devoted eighteen months of my life to.

Once I'd gotten over the shock and sadness, I tried to work out why on earth the Murdochs would have taken such drastic action.

I can only assume that this scandal is far, far worse than everyone thinks.

The BBC's *Question Time* TV current affairs show became a huge inquest into the breaking news, and panelist Hugh Grant stomped on the *News of the World*'s grave with predictable gusto.

He's never forgiven the paper for paying Divine Brown for her story. The hooker with whom he cavorted and was caught by police in Hollywood in 1994. Nor has he forgiven me, as I was the editor at the time.

It seems like war has been declared on the British tabloids, and anyone connected with them.

I was surprised nobody in the American media made a big deal out of my tabloid past when I got the job.

This will give them all the encouragement they need.

FRIDAY, JULY 8, 2011

Andy Coulson has been arrested over alleged phone hacking and illegal payments to police.

Andy's another of my oldest friends in journalism. He lost his job as *News of the World* editor a few years ago in the wake of the first phone-hacking scandal, when the paper's royal editor, Clive Goodman, was jailed in 2006 for hacking royal employees' phones.

Andy then became David Cameron's communications chief, doing a brilliant job in helping him become prime minister. But he quit in January, as the heat from the new hacking allegations became too hot for Downing Street to handle.

Cameron has reacted to the news of the last few days by announcing a full judge-led inquiry into the scandal. This is clearly going to be an absolute shit-fest.

I hope I can stay out of it all, but I fear anyone who has been involved in running a tabloid in the last decade is going to be dragged into the melee.

SATURDAY, JULY 9, 2011

William and Kate, or the Duke and Duchess of Cambridge as they've now been formally renamed, have come to L.A., and I was invited to a BAFTA dinner tonight to welcome them.

I spied Barbra Streisand, my singing heroine.

"Ms. Streisand, how do you do? I'm Piers Morgan . . ."

"I know," she said. "I watch your show."

"Really? Would you come on it?"

"Maybe. But only if you learn how to pronounce my name properly. It's Strei-*sand,* not Strei-*sund.*"

It was fascinating to see celebrities looking so starstruck themselves around the royal couple—proof to me that William and Kate have quickly become the biggest celebrities on the planet.

Only Tom Hanks seemed in control of his senses.

"I don't normally go to many parties," he admitted to me. "But when this event was announced, my wife said we had to go."

Hanks recently pulled out of a planned CNN interview with me at the last minute.

"What happened?" I asked.

"Honestly? I was tired."

"That's it?"

"Yep. That's it. I had a ridiculous schedule and decided something had to give . . ." Then he looked straight into my eyes and smirked. "And that something was you, Piers."

SUNDAY, JULY 10, 2011

Caught up with the sad scenes outside News International in East London last night, as *News of the World* staff all came out brandishing copies of the final edition of the paper.

I recognized a few old faces from the production team that worked for me there in the midnineties, and the shock and dismay on their faces was really upsetting to see.

They'll have had nothing to do with the news-gathering process, and will now really struggle to find other work in national newspapers.

Very few people will give a damn what happens to them now, but I do.

THURSDAY, JULY 14, 2011

Hugh Hefner's been stood up almost at the altar by his twenty-five-year-old fiancée, Crystal Harris, and I landed the first interview with him about it tonight.

Hef, eighty-five, was philosophical.

"I was for a moment potentially devastated," he admitted. "But I got such remarkable emotional support from friends . . ."

Our cameras cut to the green room where two sexy young blondes lay preening on a sofa.

He departed by clambering into a brand-new Bentley with the license plate HEF 1—clutching his new Playmates on each arm, and sporting a massively smug grin.

The healing process seems to be going well.

FRIDAY, JULY 15, 2011

Rebekah has resigned after a week of unrelenting pressure.

"I feel a deep sense of responsibility for the people we have hurt," she said in a statement.

I feel so sorry for her. She's one of the hardest-working people I know, and has given her life to the Murdochs. She's also been an incredibly loyal friend to me over the years, way beyond the call of normal friendly duty.

I always say you can work out who your real friends are by asking yourself who would get out of bed at 4 A.M. and come and help you if you were in trouble.

Rebekah's one of those people for me.

This will hit her hard.

Rupert Murdoch himself met with Milly Dowler's family in London today, and made a fulsome personal apology.

I've never seen him look so shaken.

A further indication of the severity of what is happening here.

MONDAY, JULY 18, 2011

Rebekah has been arrested on suspicion of phone hacking and making illegal payments to public officials. And Britain's two top policemen have now also quit over the hacking scandal. This is ripping apart the whole fabric of the British establishment.

The media, police, and politicians are all trying to kill each other in a real-life game of *Reservoir Dogs*. It's ugly and nasty, and it's going to get uglier and nastier.

TUESDAY, JULY 19, 2011

Rupert Murdoch appeared before members of Parliament today to be quizzed over the scandal.

"This is the most humble day of my life," was his opening line.

Extraordinary.

But not quite as extraordinary as what happened next.

As he was giving evidence, a protester ran forward and tried to hit him with a custard pie. Rupert's young wife, Wendi, sprang from her chair and punched the guy. It was a magnificently quick, gutsy reaction.

I was still laughing about it an hour later when I heard one of the parliamentary members, a Conservative called Louise Mensch, claim at the hearing that I had boasted about using phone hacking to get stories about newspapers in my book *The Insider*.

This was complete nonsense.

I never wrote any such thing.

The only reference I made to phone hacking in the book was when I revealed how I had once been warned about the practice, by someone who feared my own phone may have been hacked.

I was incensed.

And even more so when the story suddenly blew up on the Internet.

"British member of Parliament says Piers Morgan boasted of being phone hacker!" screamed tweets, Facebook posts, and media blogs.

Meghan rang.

"I'm getting inundated with calls, what do you want me to say?"

"That I've never hacked a phone, told anyone to hack a phone, nor to my knowledge published any stories based on the hacking of a phone."

This seemed to have little effect in quelling the rising storm.

I spoke to Jonathan, who suggested I go on CNN, live, to make my position clear.

By chance, Wolf Blitzer had already booked Louise Mensch, so I offered to appear at the same time.

It made for an explosive encounter.

I went straight on the attack, angrily branding her a liar, and challenging her to repeat the allegations on air—without the legally privileged protection she had in a parliamentary committee room.

She declined to do so.

Mensch was insistent: "I said what I said in the committee. To repeat something outside of Parliament doesn't give me the cloak of privilege. Mr. Morgan is a very rich man."

She added: "I'm sure that the ferocious investigative journalists at CNN and across the news media in the United States will take careful note at what was said in the committee, and look into it."

I couldn't believe what I was hearing.

She was now urging journalists all over the world to dig into completely false allegations she'd made about me, simply because she hadn't read my book properly.

I was still seething when I got home tonight.

This is going to be used as an excuse to rub my nose right in the mire of this scandal, and there's nothing I can do about it.

Rebekah also gave evidence today, and I tweeted my support to a "great and loyal friend."

Christa Robinson called: "Please think twice, this was a bad idea. You are your own man—you don't need to come to anyone's defense today."

"I don't ditch my friends in a crisis," I replied. "Sorry, Christa, but she's been there for me for twenty years through heavy shit. Time for me to support her in her hour of need."

"The world doesn't know your friendship," Christa responded. "And maybe today's not the day you want to highlight that. I would just think about it."

Of course, she's trying to protect me and CNN. I get that.

But I'm not throwing Rebekah to the wolves like everyone else seems to be doing.

Simple as that.

WEDNESDAY, JULY 20, 2011

Jim Walton called and we had a long chat about the phone-hacking stuff. He couldn't have been more supportive, and I greatly appreciated it.

But I can't pretend this isn't all massively annoying now.

Journalists are rummaging over every word I've ever written or said, desperate for any semblance of ambiguity about phone hacking or any other unethical journalistic activity.

I can almost taste their blood lust.

SATURDAY, JULY 23, 2011

Tom Watson, MP, one of the leading UK parliamentary investigators into the scandal, tweeted this afternoon: "I've not seen any evidence linking Piers Morgan to hacking, and I've seen a lot of documentation these last two years."

This should keep at least some of the dogs at bay.

But I'm getting besieged with calls from media everywhere, and it's both agitating and unnerving.

Later, news broke that Amy Winehouse is dead, from a suspected overdose. What a senseless waste of a fabulous talent.

Fran, Celia's brother, plays saxophone in her band, so knows only too well the hellish journey to oblivion that she's been headed down for a while now.

This was not entirely shocking news to anyone who knew what Amy was doing in her private life.

But it's an utter tragedy, nevertheless.

SUNDAY, JULY 24, 2011

Louise Mensch is still in full-on attack mode, hurling all sorts of wild allegations at me.

She's obviously desperate to vindicate herself, but I'm having none of it—and firing back at every outlandish tweet claim she's making.

This probably isn't the most sensible PR strategy.

Meghan keeps urging me to say nothing, and let it blow over.

She sent me a hilarious email from her mother:

I saw all of the stuff online about Piers. I wish they would leave him the hell alone. Who the hell cares? Didn't this happen fifteen years ago? Why don't they pick on something legit like Casey Anthony?

Coincidentally, Jonathan then forwarded me an email from his dad, containing a quote from the poet Humbert Wolfe:

You cannot hope to bribe or twist
(Thank God) the British journalist!
But seeing what the man will do
Unbribed, there's no occasion to.

Both made me laugh. And, God, I need a laugh or two right now.

TUESDAY, JULY 26, 2011

Spencer's eighteen today.

He's never been arrested, suspended from school, nor stomach-pumped.

And like his brothers, he makes me laugh every time I speak to him.

Not sure you can wish for much better than that from a son.

THURSDAY, JULY 28, 2011

Larry King was asked by *GQ* magazine today: "Would you rather spoon Piers Morgan for three nights in a row, or put your iPhone in a blender and drink it?"

He replied: "What does 'spoon' mean?"

GQ: "It's when you lie in bed and cuddle, both facing the same direction. You'd be the back spoon."

Larry: "I'd do the phone thing."

FRIDAY, JULY 29, 2011

Woke up in L.A. at 5 A.M. this morning to discover a ridiculous rumor exploding on Twitter that I have been suspended by CNN because of the phone-hacking scandal.

It was all complete nonsense, started, as I quickly worked out, by a fake tweet from a fake account, masquerading as a well-known Fleet Street journalist.

But to my astonishment, *Channel 4 News* host Jon Snow, one of the most respected news broadcasters in Britain, fell for it, and tweeted the news himself, with what can only be described as undisguised glee.

"Piers Morgan suspended by CNN," he wrote. "The rise and rise, and fall and rise, and fall of Piers Morgan!"

I could almost picture the spittle of foaming delight spilling from his lips.

He was quickly followed by senior journalists from *The Guardian* and Reuters, as the Twitterverse celebrated with collective joyous delirium.

Meghan called. "I'm getting hundreds of calls saying you've been suspended. What the hell's going on?"

"It's complete nonsense, started by a fake tweet."

"So why are so many journalists tweeting it too?"

"Because they're idiots who haven't even bothered to check. Let me
deal with it."

I tweeted my statement: "Sorry to disappoint you all, but I'm afraid poor
old Jon Snow got duped by a fake Twitter account."

Suitably chastened, Snow responded: "Retraction ahoy! Jon Snow
suspended from Tweeting Piers Morgan henceforth . . . dupe was duped
alas . . . apologies old chap . . . Sorry, I mean young man!"

"Ironically," I replied, "we've now seen the rise and rise, and fall and
rise, and fall of Jon Snow's credibility. Back to the naughty chair for you,
Snowy."

I had to laugh.

When I was fired from *The Daily Mirror*, Mr. Snow was one of the
more censorious of my critics for me allowing myself to be so dreadfully
duped.

In a strange way, his screwup seemed to calm everyone down.

Particularly when Louise Mensch finally issued a public apology for
defaming me.

In a letter to her own committee, she said she had "wrongly stated" that
I had boasted of hacking phones.

"I must apologize to Mr. Morgan for the error," she concluded.

Jim Walton rang.

"That's great news. Be gracious in your response."

He was right. There was nothing to be gained by continuing to be
churlish.

I tweeted the following: "Apology accepted, Louise Mensch—
thank you."

MONDAY, AUGUST 1, 2011

Meghan didn't receive any media calls today. First time since the phone-
hacking scandal blew up.

"Think we're over the worst now?" she asked.

"Yes," I replied.

WEDNESDAY, AUGUST 3, 2011

A nice email came in overnight from an old *Mirror* colleague, James Steen, who wrote a gossip column for me at the paper.

> Piers, I've been watching the saga unfold, and it is particularly odd when I think back to my times with you.
>
> I remember you saying, "Be mischievous as hell, but don't break the law." And something like, "Infuriate, irritate and go to all the bars. But never do anything that'll get you behind bars."
>
> In short, I am utterly astonished that your integrity is being questioned. It's ludicrous.
>
> Though I notice those who are now dishing out the questions are people who are best known for avoiding answers.
>
> All the best,
>
> James

THURSDAY, AUGUST 4, 2011

I spoke too soon about the hacking saga calming down.

Harriet Harman, the deputy leader of the Labour Party, and one of the world's most crashing political bores, has demanded I return to Britain immediately to "answer serious questions."

Of all the reasons to go back to Britain right now, I think doing so at the behest of Ms. Harman has to rank lowest on my list.

Late tonight, a story broke that David Leigh, chief investigations editor of *The Guardian*—who first broke the hacking scandal story—admitted himself to phone hacking a suspected arms dealer a few years ago, in an article he wrote for the paper after Clive Goodman's conviction.

I'm sure nothing will happen to him, though. This is a tabloid witch-hunt, and all dodgy things a "serious" newspaper has done will be ignored or put down to being "in the public interest."

It's the same hypocrisy that plays out when they report tabloid scoops, run acres of material from them, and then write editorials condemning the tabloid for publishing the story in the first place.

SATURDAY, AUGUST 6, 2011
A bad day for America.

Its credit rating has been downgraded—something that would have been unthinkable ten years ago.

And thirty Special Forces soldiers have died in a helicopter crash in Afghanistan.

Many of the victims were members of SEAL Team 6, the elite unit that captured and killed Osama bin Laden. Though none are thought to have been on that particular operation.

Both these blows will further damage the country's confidence when it can least afford to be timid.

WEDNESDAY, AUGUST 17, 2011
One of the more remarkable aspects of my interviewing career, in print and on TV, is that nobody has EVER walked out on me. I must have done more than five thousand interviews in various forms over twenty-five years, but despite the occasional deeply awkward encounter, I've escaped the ultimate badge of interviewing disrespect.

And then came Christine O'Donnell.

Ms. O'Donnell became an American political star during the country's midterm elections last November—despite eventually losing her bid to become a senator.

She's a leading member of the Tea Party—the populist conservative movement named after the original Boston Tea Party incident in 1773, when colonists boarded British ships and chucked a huge quantity of tea cargo into the sea. A senseless waste of our great national drink, which helped trigger the full-scale American Revolution.

Tonight, O'Donnell came on my CNN show to promote her new autobiography, aptly named *Troublemaker*, in which she openly discusses the many controversies in her career to date. She's admitted to dabbling in witchcraft, has publicly espoused views on "sexual purity" so severely puritanical they make Mitt Romney look racy, and thinks gay people have an "identity disorder."

It all started friendly enough, but then I began to detect a certain frisson of tension entering the conversation as I quizzed her over the aforementioned controversies. "I address it all in the book," she kept saying, bizarrely refusing to actually make any further comment.

Eventually I asked her what her view was of gay marriage.

"I address that stuff in the book," she sniffed.

"Yes, you're here to promote your damn book!"

"You're borderline being a little rude," she fumed.

"I'm baffled why you think I'm being rude—I'm just asking you questions based on your own public statements and what you've written in your book. Why are you being so weird about this?"

"I'm not being weird. You're being a little rude. I'm promoting the policies that I lay out in the book that are mostly fiscal, constitutional. That's what I want to talk about. Don't you think as a host that if I say this is what I want to talk about, that's what we should address?"

"Not really, no, you're a politician."

At which point O'Donnell looked to someone off camera before saying: "OK, I'm being pulled away here." Her publicist then jumped up and blocked the camera, creating a sinister and yet deeply comical, big black shadow across the screen.

"Where are you going?" I asked. "You're leaving?"

"I was supposed to be speaking at the Republican women's club at six P.M., and I chose to be a little late for that—not to endure rude talk show hosts, but to talk to you about my book and to talk about the issues that I address in my book. Have you read the book?"

"Yes, but these issues I raised are in your book. That's my point. You talk about them."

"OK, all right. Are we off? Are we done?" she snapped.

"I'm not, I'm still here . . ." I replied.

But she wasn't, and marched out of the studio.

"It would appear," I informed the viewers, "that the interview has just ended because I had the audacity to ask questions about stuff that's in this book. Anyway, it's a good book. It's called *Troublemaker,* and I think we all now know why!"

Within a few hours the walkout had become a hot news story.

FRIDAY, AUGUST 19, 2011

Christine O'Donnell appeared on various media outlets including the *Today Show* and decided that attack was the best form of defense over an incident that's been dominating the headlines for thirty-six hours now.

She claimed her walkout had nothing to do with me asking her about gay marriage but happened because I was "obsessed with sex." Furthermore, I was a "little creepy," a "cheeky bugger," and my questions had been "borderline sexual harassment."

All of which was completely baffling to anyone who had actually watched the interview, as I'd demonstrably been none of those things. Well, possibly the "cheeky bugger" bit. Even hosts and commentators on Fox News, the unofficial mouthpiece for the Tea Party, lambasted her for making a bad situation even worse.

But hey, who's complaining? The walkout attracted big ratings and everyone's talking about my show.

Tonight, music producer David Foster threw a dinner party at his sumptuous Malibu beachside house for Barbra Streisand and me to meet each other properly, as he promised a few weeks ago when I interviewed him.

There were fourteen other guests, including Donna Summer, Regis Philbin, and Dr. Phil McGraw.

Barbra and I were seated next to each other at the dinner table, and for two hours, we barely exchanged a word with anyone else. It's so rare to meet a personal hero who lives up to expectation, but Barbra was if anything even more impressive than I imagined: smart, funny, warm, engaging, and politically astute.

Halfway through the meal, David suggested I sing to the group.

He was joking, but the wine had flowed and I seized the moment, dropping on bended knee, grasping Barbra's hand, and crooning a quite spectacularly bad rendition of "The Way We Were" to her as he raced to the piano and accompanied me.

As I wailed away, I caught sight of Donna Summer actually grimacing.

"That was very . . . nice, thank you," said Barbra, who then exploded into fits of giggles.

"Will you sing for us later?" I asked.

"Nooooo," she replied, firmly. "I never sing at parties."

"Why not?"

"I feel uncomfortable performing to an audience where I can see the faces looking at me. I've always suffered from stage fright, but as long as I can't see the faces, I'm usually OK. Singing at a dinner party like this would freak me out!"

SUNDAY, AUGUST 21, 2011

Celia and I spent the afternoon musing about possible names for our little girl.

"I think Delphine is a lovely name," she suggested.

I Googled it.

"It means 'to look or act like a dolphin.' "

"Jeez. Well, how about Elise? I think that's beautiful."

I checked its origin. It's a French name, meaning "God's promise."

I said it out loud a few times. I like it.

THURSDAY, AUGUST 25, 2011

A large hurricane, named Irene, has clattered along the East Coast, causing huge damage.

It also sparked a heated debate between Jonathan and me tonight over how to pronounce the word "hurricane."

The English way is "*hurri*-cun"; the American way is "*hurri*-cain."

"You're in America, so you should say it how we say it," he said, after I used my own version at the top of the show.

"But I'm not American, and nowhere in my contract does it say I have to speak American."

"You're talking to an American audience, why say words in a way they don't say them?"

"It's our language, you just changed it."

"For the better."

"How many schools teach American in America?"

"What do you mean?"

"I mean, the answer is zero. They teach English. Do the maths."

"It's 'math.' "

THURSDAY, SEPTEMBER 8, 2011

Seven years ago, I was frog-marched out of my office at *The Daily Mirror* after being fired for publishing what were claimed to be "fake" photos of British troops from the Queen's Lancashire Regiment abusing Iraqi civilians in 2003.

I've never fully accepted the pictures were necessarily faked, mainly because the incident depicted in them was never denied, and the soldiers who brought them to us were credible. And also because the people crying "fake" were the government (which had just led us into a war insisting, falsely, that Saddam Hussein had weapons of mass destruction) and the QLR itself, which had a vested interest in discrediting *The Mirror*'s revelations.

Today, the long-awaited investigation into the activities of the QLR was published. It focused on the appalling torture and murder of Iraqi hotel receptionist Baha Mousa. But it also covered the wider malpractice of QLR soldiers in Iraq following the supposed end of the war in 2003. The findings were devastating.

Civilian detainees had been beaten with metal bars, had lighter fuel poured over them, toilets flushed over their heads. They were kept handcuffed, hooded, and in stress positions in "extreme heat and squalid conditions."

In the most disgusting of all revelations, one soldier, a corporal called

Donald Payne, had played "choir" with his victims, kicking and punching them in sequence to create musical tunes from their groans.

Oh, and the report confirmed that "trophy photographs" were taken of the beatings.

Sir William Gage, the retired judge who presided over the inquiry, described it as an "appalling episode of serious, gratuitous violence . . . cowardly assaults and abuse." And further, that there had been a "loss of discipline and moral courage" by officers and soldiers alike.

General Sir Peter Wall, head of the British Army, said the report "cast a dark shadow on the reputation of the army and must not happen again."

I still don't know for sure if those pictures *The Mirror* published were genuine. I've never seen conclusive evidence they weren't.

But what we all now know from this report is that rogue elements of the Queen's Lancashire Regiment did indeed commit a series of atrocities against Iraqi civilians, many far worse than *The Mirror* ever alleged, and took celebratory photographs (like the ones we published) as they did so.

It's not contradictory to be 100 percent supportive of our magnificent armed forces—of which many of my family are, and have been, members—and detest this kind of shameful behavior from a few bad apples.

I remain proud of *The Mirror*'s role in exposing it.

FRIDAY, SEPTEMBER 9, 2011

The tenth anniversary of 9/11 is on Sunday, and tonight I recorded a quite extraordinary interview with a man called Howard Lutnick.

He's the boss of the Wall Street firm Cantor Fitzgerald, which had its corporate headquarters on the 101st to 105th floors of One World Trade Center.

On the morning of the terrorist attack, Lutnick would have been at his desk as normal, but was otherwise engaged taking his young son Kyle to his first day at kindergarten.

Lutnick heard the news of the first plane hitting, and raced down to see what was happening. He arrived just after the second plane struck, and ran for his life, ending up facedown in the street, covered in thick, smoldering ash, in pitch black.

He lost six hundred and fifty-eight of his New York–based employees that day, including his brother and most of his closest friends. It was the single greatest loss by one firm in the atrocity.

Lutnick admitted that as he stumbled away from the carnage, all he could think was: "I'm done. That's it. There's nothing left."

But then another instinct kicked in. Lutnick was orphaned, and never forgot how his extended family wasn't there for him. "I wasn't going to let that happen to these people," he told me.

The challenge was extraordinary. His company had been decimated, and was losing $1 million a day. He had to stop all paychecks to grieving widows, a decision that inspired fury from many of them.

He burst into tears in an interview with Larry King, crying, "I don't have any money to pay their salaries."

But what he did have was resolve. He announced that he would donate 25 percent of all the profits Cantor Fitzgerald made over the next five years to the dependents of those who died, plus ten years of free health care.

"Their immediate reaction was 'Twenty-five percent of zero is zero, that's no good to us.' "

They underestimated Howard Lutnick.

Lutnick has rebuilt Cantor Fitzgerald, literally from the ashes of Ground Zero, and it is now nearly twice as big as it was on 9/11.

To date, the company has paid over $180 million to the families, way more than they could have ever hoped for or dreamed of.

The families that doubted him now adore him.

The interview was without any doubt the most moving, emotional, and inspiring I've ever done.

By a strange coincidence, BBC1 aired the finale of the American version of the U.S. show *Celebrity Apprentice* this week, three years after it happened. Viewers will have seen a thickset balding guy in glasses make two sensational hundred-thousand-dollar bids in the charity auction to help me win Donald Trump's competition, and raise money for the Intrepid Fallen

Heroes Fund, which aids severely wounded American, and sometimes British, soldiers.

I didn't know the man personally. I'd just asked Sarah, Duchess of York, who was the most generous person she knew in America when I was trying to find high-roller bidders, and she hadn't hesitated.

"Oh, Howard Lutnick. He's the most generous person in the world, never mind America."

WEDNESDAY, SEPTEMBER 14, 2011

Tonight was the finale of *America's Got Talent*, which was won by a brilliant young dreadlocked black Sinatra–style crooner called Landau Eugene Murphy Jr., who was homeless at nineteen and washed cars for a living.

He's a sublimely talented, charming, and humble guy who perfectly personifies the ethos of this kind of show—someone with a true natural gift who'd never had the chance to realize his potential.

Now he'll headline in Las Vegas.

I went to the wrap party afterward, and everyone was asking me if I'd be back next season.

The honest answer is that I don't know.

I'd like to be released from my contract, which still has another two years to run, but the show is one of NBC's biggest hits and it's entirely up to them.

Simon Cowell knows how I feel, because I asked to be released last summer when I first got offered the CNN job.

He agreed, because he knew how difficult it would be for me to juggle both shows, but NBC overruled him.

Now the company has new management though, so it may be possible.

FRIDAY, SEPTEMBER 16, 2011

I've had shockingly awful food poisoning all week, prompting an equally severe sense of humor failure.

Tonight I had rehydrating fluids dripped into my veins for an hour, then large amounts of blood sucked out by an Eastern European nurse.

"Where are you from?" I asked.

"Transylvania."

"Ha—no, seriously."

She looked bemused.

"I'm seriously from Transylvania."

SATURDAY, SEPTEMBER 17, 2011

It's Emmy Awards weekend in Hollywood.

I've got zero interest in going to the event itself tomorrow.

But wild horses wouldn't have kept me away from attending Jeffrey Katzenberg's celebrated "Evening Before" party tonight.

The first person I saw was Hugh Laurie.

"Ah, Hugh, how are you?"

"I'm fine, thank you, Morgan."

Laurie, star of the brilliant hospital drama *House,* usually gives one interview a year to a British newspaper or magazine in which he moans about everything in his glamorous Hollywood life: L.A., the weather, his workload, press intrusion—you name it, he whines about it.

"Have you ever thought about doing an interview where you *don't* sound like such an inherently miserable git?" I asked.

He laughed. "That's true—I always do, don't I?"

"How about coming on my CNN show and being, well, happy?" I suggested.

"Let's not get ahead of ourselves here, Morgan . . ."

I walked on, and someone barged into me, sending my vodka tonic flying.

"Hey . . ." I began to complain. Then realized it was Tom Cruise, dashing to the side of his wife, Katie Holmes.

He's as small, and extraordinarily youthful looking, as I'd imagined him to be.

"Tom—Piers Morgan. Nice to meet you."

He smiled, shook my hand, said, "Hello, Piers"—then turned around to speak to someone else. My audience was over. I didn't even get the chance to say I'd seen *Top Gun* at the cinema twelve times as a trainee reporter on the *Wimbledon News*.

Fortunately, Katie stayed behind to chat. "I'd love to have you on my show," I said.

"We'll see," she replied.

"That's not a no," I noted. "But I would have to insist on one thing."

"Oh? What's that?"

"That under absolutely no circumstances are you allowed to bring him with you."

Katie's eyes turned to where I was looking, and she pointed at Tom. "Him?"

"*Him.*"

She giggled. "OK, understood."

MONDAY, SEPTEMBER 19, 2011

I conducted a fiery interview tonight with a journalist called Joe McGinniss, who's written an explosive new book about Sarah Palin.

One of his many lurid, and often unsubstantiated, claims is that Palin had a one-night stand with a black NBA basketball star called Glen Rice, supposedly contradicting other allegations that she was a racist in her younger days.

But his evidence for this rests on a phone call he had with Rice, in which he didn't ask him directly if they had sex, but skirted around the issue, before slyly saying, "So you never had the feeling she felt bad about having sex with a black guy?" To which Rice answered, "No, no, no, nothing like that."

"He's thinking about the racism part of the question, when you slip in the sex part," I suggested to McGinniss.

"There's nothing to slip in," he replied.

"Well, that's another question altogether," I said.

McGinniss didn't react.

But my phone, sitting on my desk in front of me, did, with an instant email from Rod Stewart—watching live at his Beverly Hills mansion.

"Dear Piers, 'There's nothing to slip in' went right over his head. Rod."

But not Rod's, unsurprisingly.

TUESDAY, SEPTEMBER 20, 2011

I interviewed Morgan Freeman.

He was startlingly, deliciously open and indiscreet.

"I don't think I've ever had an affair with an actress," he announced soon into the chat.

"Why not?"

"If I'm supposed to be in love with an actress, I don't have to fall in love with her to play the part. I don't think it's a good idea."

"I always thought you were a natural ladies' man in the sense that women really love you?"

"I absolutely adore women. But I'm not a real big skirt-chaser. There's a secret."

"What's the secret?"

"Don't chase women, they'll chase you. I'm going to get into trouble for saying this, but it works very well for me. You meet a lady, express how wonderful she looks, and then go on about your business. They are curious. They're like horses in a pasture. You walk into a pasture, and the horse sees you. He's coming over to investigate. And if you see a lady and you don't go drooling over her, she's going to want to know why."

We turned to politics, where he was equally incendiary about the Tea Party.

"Has Obama's election helped the process of eradicating racism in America?"

"No, it's made it worse. Look at the Tea Partiers, who are controlling the Republican Party. Their stated policy, publicly stated, is to do whatever it takes to see to it that Obama only serves one term.

"What underlines that? Screw the country. We're going to do whatever we need to do to get this black man out of here."

"But it's not necessarily a racist thing . . ."

"It *is* a racist thing."

"Does it unnerve you that the Tea Party is gaining such traction?"

"Yes, it shows the weak, dark underside of America. We're supposed to be better than that. That's why people were in tears when Obama was elected. This is America, you know? And then it started turning, because these [Tea Partiers] surfaced, stirring up muddy water."

The last tense seconds before I go head-to-head with America's
public enemy number one, Iranian President Ahmadinejad.

6

Iranian president Mahmoud Ahmadinejad wins most polls in America for "Most Dangerous Man Alive" now that Osama bin Laden has been killed.

His annual visit to the United Nations General Assembly in New York follows a familiar pattern: he makes a long, ranting speech about how dreadful America is, a load of delegates walk out, and the U.S. media goes crazy.

Ahmadinejad's outrageous outbursts in the past have included claims that the Holocaust never happened, 9/11 was an inside job, and there are no gays in Iran.

Today I was invited to meet him after his speech, along with a small group of twenty or so other U.S. media figures. It was originally going to be off the record, then they changed their minds and allowed in cameras.

It was an extraordinary ninety minutes.

Ahmadinejad is a small, unassuming-looking man. He arrived, flashed a sheepish grin, praised God liberally, thanked us all for coming, and then invited questions.

His answers were detailed, forceful, provocative, defiant, and occasionally downright offensive.

Asked by my CNN colleague Wolf Blitzer if he still thought there were no gays in Iran, Ahmadinejad fired off a lengthy homophobic tirade about "this ugly deed."

But he was also, to my surprise, quick-witted and at times—like many dictators—disarmingly charming.

I kept my own question simple. "Mr. President, could you tell me what your biggest mistakes have been in your presidency?"

He smirked. "I will make a list and make it available to you at the end of the meeting."

"Well, how about giving me the top three now?" I persisted.

He stared straight into my eyes. "One of them is that I got to meet you quite late in the game," he said, and chuckled.

"Maybe we should have met earlier," I replied. "The reason I'm asking is that former Vice President Dick Cheney recently wrote a book about his eight years running America and didn't admit to any mistakes. I'm curious as to whether you're prepared to admit you're not so perfect."

He dropped his smile. "I never pretend to be completely free of errors. See, there are a limited number of people who make no mistakes, and those are people like the Prophet of Islam, Jesus Christ, Moses, and some of their followers and successors. Everyone else makes mistakes. I'm just one of those many. But I will certainly make a list, for you specifically—my memoirs for when my service is over . . ."

The room broke into laughter (a remarkable thing when hard-bitten journalists were trying very hard not to even smile in his presence with cameras watching).

From that moment on, I became, rather disconcertingly, his go-to man for a quick laugh. Ahmadinejad answered several other questions with, "As I was saying to my good friend Piers Morgan, I'm not perfect . . ."

I came away from the meeting with a much better understanding of the man, though, which was useful.

I'd say that Ahmadinejad's not as mad as people think, and that he says everything in America, however controversial, for deliberate effect, and to rally support with his own people back home. He was also better briefed than I expected on world affairs, albeit slanting his responses to suit his own political agenda.

When asked about Iran's political prisoners, he replied that at least he didn't have anything like Guantanamo Bay. And when someone quizzed him about "Iran's economic crisis," he mockingly replied: "I don't think I'll take lectures on the economy from Americans right now, thank you."

But on balance, given the intensity of his hateful remarks about the United States and Israel in particular, I'd remain very concerned about Ahmadinejad if I were President Obama or Prime Minister Netanyahu.

Not a man you'd trust with the family silver, as they'd say on *Downton Abbey*.

MONDAY, SEPTEMBER 26, 2011

I was having a quiet drink with John tonight at the Mandarin when a woman approached our table and said, "Mr. Morgan, there's a man over there who would like to meet you."

I looked over to see an old guy sitting nearby. He caught my eye and gave a slight wave of his hand. There was something about him that commanded attention. "Sure, of course," I replied.

She led me over, and introduced us. His name, Clint Hill, meant nothing to me.

"You may be interested in interviewing me sometime," he said.

"Oh, really? Why?"

"Because I was on President John F. Kennedy's Secret Service detail team."

"You were?"

"Yes. On the day he died in Dallas."

I stepped back and took a long hard look at this guy. He was rugged-faced, steely-eyed, straight-backed.

"Were you with him when he got shot?"

"I was."

"Where?"

"I was in the car traveling behind the president."

Now he had my full, transfixed attention.

"What did you do when the bullets were fired?"

"I ran to the presidential car."

I suddenly knew exactly who he was.

It is immortalized in one of the most famous, notorious, iconic pieces of video footage in history.

As JFK is shot, a solitary Secret Service agent leaps from the car behind and charges toward his president's car. He's seen scrambling aboard the car as the first lady, Jackie Kennedy, starts to throw herself back on the trunk, desperate and screaming, reaching out to him.

The agent tries to comfort her, then stands aboard the back of the car as it races at high speed to the nearest hospital.

I stared at this man again; he looked both proud and sad-eyed now.

"You were that agent?"

"I was that agent."

I felt goose bumps. This man was a piece of history.

"That must have been a terrible day for you."

"It was the worst day of my life."

"Do you feel guilty?"

"The president died on my watch. Of course I feel guilty."

"How often do you think about it?"

"Every day."

"Could you have saved him?"

"I don't think there's anything we could have done to stop what happened from happening. I wish there had been. If I'd gotten there a second before, maybe I could have taken the third bullet."

A tear appeared in his eye.

"Do you believe in any of the conspiracy theories?"

"No. I think the president was shot by Lee Harvey Oswald, who acted alone."

He spent four years protecting Jackie Kennedy (she had been Hill's specific charge that day) before and after the assassination, and is now writing a book about his extraordinary experience.

"What was Jackie like?"

"She was a wonderful woman, I loved her."

Another tear.

MONDAY, OCTOBER 3, 2011

Amanda Knox has been dramatically freed by an Italian court, after successfully appealing her conviction for murdering British student Meredith Kercher.

I knew Meredith's journalist father, John, when I worked at *The Mirror*.

He used to file foreign desk stories with us, and was a thoroughly decent man. I can only imagine the new emotional torment he and his family are enduring since the verdict came in.

Bad enough having your daughter killed in such a brutal fashion, let alone not knowing who did it.

I can't decide what to make of this case, other than noting that most Americans, driven by their partisan media coverage about it, believe Knox to be completely innocent.

And most Brits, driven by our own equally partisan media coverage, believe she either had something to do with the killing or had knowledge of how it happened.

I suspect if Amanda had been British, and Meredith an American, both these viewpoints would have been reversed.

TUESDAY, OCTOBER 18, 2011

I've flown to Las Vegas to interview Herman Cain, the surprise new front-runner in the Republican presidential race.

He's a flamboyant character, a former CEO of the Godfather's Pizza chain, and the only black face amid all the candidates.

We soon got into a heated debate about social issues.

After he declared homosexuality a "sin" and inferred that gay people aren't born gay, I said: "You genuinely believe millions of Americans wake up in their late teens and go, 'You know what, I quite fancy being a homosexual'?"

"You haven't given me any evidence to convince me otherwise, and nor has anyone else," he replied in all seriousness.

"My gut instinct tells me it has to be a natural thing."

"OK, so it's your gut instinct against my gut instinct. That being said, I respect their right to make that choice. You don't see me bashing them or anything. I just don't have to agree with it."

"It would be like a gay person saying, Herman, you made a choice to be black?"

"We know that's not the case. I was born black. Piers, this doesn't wash off, I hate to burst your bubble!"

"I don't think being a homosexual washes off."

"Well, maybe. This is just my opinion."

We moved on to abortion.

"I believe that life begins at conception, and abortion under no circumstances."

"No circumstances?"

"No circumstances."

But when I asked him if he'd force his own daughter or granddaughter to have a baby in such circumstances, he retorted: "You're mixing two things here, Piers. It's not the government's role or anybody else's role to make that decision. It gets down to a choice that the family or that mother has to make. I can have an opinion on an issue without it being a directive on the nation," he continued. "The government shouldn't be trying to tell people everything to do, especially when it comes to social decisions they need to make."

So he's prolife and prochoice.

Got it.

THURSDAY, OCTOBER 20, 2011

Colonel Gaddafi is dead.

Libyan rebels found him hiding in a sewer pipe, and brutally killed him in a ferocious gunfight.

With sublime irony, the aging despot's last words to the rebels were reported to be: "What you're doing is wrong, guys. Do you know what is right or wrong?"

He'd ruled his country since I was four years old, and is the latest victim of this extraordinary despot-deposing Arab Spring.

Exciting though it is to see young oppressed people rising up to kick out these tyrannical leaders, it's also very unclear what will follow next.

Nobody really seems to know.

SATURDAY, OCTOBER 22, 2011

A beautiful sunny day in New York, so I decided to go for a coffee in Central Park.

After half an hour or so reading the papers in a delightful café buried in the bowels of the park, I heard a small commotion going on a few yards away from me.

A middle-aged woman with a strong New York accent was berating some guy standing with his son.

"Do *not* do that!" she shrieked.

I looked closer to see what the grave offense could be.

"Mr. Morgan is entitled to his *privacy*!" she yelled.

What? The man, who was carrying a camera, looked completely bemused, as did his young son.

So the woman clarified the situation, very loudly: "I saw you taking his photo—you shouldn't do that without asking permission!"

My heart instantly swelled with admiration. This brave, heroic lady had rushed to protect me from a sneaky tourist paparazzo.

Or had she?

The man, who looked and sounded Scandinavian, was shaking his head violently. Then he looked toward me, threw his arms in the air, and exclaimed: "Who *is* he?"

I realized this act of valor was about to turn very embarrassing, very fast.

"Who *is* he?" shouted my savior. "Don't give me that, you *know who he is*!"

The man stared closer at me, still shaking his head.

"No, no, I do not."

"He's Piers Morgan from CNN!"

"Who?"

"Don't pretend! You were taking his picture, I saw you!"

The man sighed. "No, I was taking photographs of the tree behind him. It is very pretty."

We all turned to where he was pointing, and sure enough, there was a very attractive tree.

An uncomfortable silence ensued.

And then came the words that typified the never-say-die philosophy of New Yorkers: "Well, if you *are* thinking of taking Mr. Morgan's picture, don't! OK?"

With that, my heroine stomped off with her yapping terrier. The Scandinavian continued to shake his head, more slowly now. And I sank back in my seat, behind my copy of the *New York Times,* feeling a slight reddening of humiliation creeping up my neck.

WEDNESDAY, NOVEMBER 2, 2011

I first interviewed Condoleezza Rice for my launch week at CNN back in January, and to say it's been a busy news year since then is a stunning understatement.

"Dr. Rice," I began our second interview tonight. "Since we last spoke, we've had the Arab Spring uprisings, bin Laden has been killed, Gaddafi has been killed, and Mubarak overthrown. There has been the biggest financial crisis we've ever seen, and a guy who used to sell pizzas leading your party's chance to take on the president."

She nodded. "It's been a busy several months, that's right!"

Of all the U.S. politicians I've met this year, I'd rate Dr. Rice near the top in terms of intellect. She also has a warm charm that wasn't always obvious from her usually stern appearances as secretary of state under President George W. Bush.

Hardly surprising, then, that she attracted many male admirers. Unfortunately, one of the most ardent turned out to be Colonel Gaddafi.

After he fled his compound, soldiers found a scrapbook he'd kept on his beloved Condoleezza. And she confirmed today that when she once paid an official visit to him in Libya, he played her a video featuring a staggeringly inappropriate song called "Black Flower in the White House."

"I had actually known that he had this fixation on me," she admitted. "A couple of foreign ministers had told me. It was all weird and a bit creepy."

MONDAY, NOVEMBER 7, 2011

Dr. Conrad Murray has been convicted of the involuntary manslaughter of Michael Jackson.

It was the right verdict.

Murray didn't mean to kill Jackson, but he was grossly negligent in the way he administered drugs to him.

One of the jurors explained afterward that they found him guilty for three reasons: 1) he took way too long to call emergency services; 2) he had no backup equipment at the house for such an emergency; and 3) he left Jackson alone in a room after pumping him with the superstrong sedative Propofol.

The truth is that Jackson's life probably could have been saved if Murray had not committed these three cardinal sins of medical practice.

And for that, he must now pay the price.

TUESDAY, NOVEMBER 8, 2011

A fascinating day in D.C., during which I interviewed two iconic American political figures—Newt Gingrich and Colin Powell.

Gingrich, the former Republican speaker of the House, is now running for president and gaining momentum in the polls. He's a real political bruiser, and doesn't suffer fools. When I tried suggesting that the reality of politics is that he's being perceived as the "anti-Mitt" candidate, he scoffed: "I've been involved with politics since 1958, I helped grow the modern Republican Party of Georgia, and you're explaining to me the reality of politics!"

But we bonded well after that, and he gave me one of the more memorable answers to one of my favorite questions, "What's been the greatest moment of your life?"

"Oh, on the Serengeti Plain. Watching two cheetahs that have just finished eating an antelope, sitting up on this rock, sunning themselves. An extraordinary thing."

"Extending the metaphor, you seeing antelope, Barack Obama, cheetah, Newt Gingrich?"

He smirked.

General Powell is a beloved figure in America—his military service alone would qualify him for that, as he was one of the country's great modern generals.

But his time serving as secretary of state under George W. Bush propelled him into global superstardom.

It was Powell, of course, who was tasked with selling to a skeptical world the "proof" about Saddam Hussein's WMD arsenal to justify war in Iraq—something he now admits was based on completely false information.

"Did you feel you were used in some way?" I asked.

He thought for several seconds.

"No. But when I realized that a considerable part of the intelligence was wrong, and we should have known it was wrong, I felt terrible."

Powell is a good man. And I think he *was* used.

WEDNESDAY, NOVEMBER 9, 2011

We've spent the last few weeks negotiating with Mickey Rourke's "people"—trying to fix an interview with him.

Mickey doesn't care for the normal behavioral niceties of Hollywood. This was a city that built him up, then spat him out and left him to fend, almost literally, with the wolves. He owes it nothing, and cares not for its hypocrisy and self-pretense.

As a result he is delightfully politically incorrect.

The problem is that his ex-wife, Carré Otis, has written an explosive book detailing all sorts of abuse Mickey supposedly dished out to her during their chaotic and mutually self-destructive marriage.

His management, lawyers, and PR people have been desperately trying to get him *not* to react to it during his promotional tour for his new movie, *The Immortals*.

Tonight we finally got him to the studio. But his publicist was adamant: "Don't mention Carré's book, or he'll walk."

Fortunately, Mickey himself desired no such censorship.

"You want to ask me about Carré's book, right?" he whispered as we met in his dressing room.

"Well, yes," I replied.

"Do it," he nodded, "I've got a lot I want to say."

Excellent.

When the moment came during the actual interview, Mickey went off like a freshly stoked steam train, accusing Carré of being "delusional," "narcissistic," "self-centered," and "buck-chasing."

I looked at his publicist, who didn't know whether to laugh or cry.

THURSDAY, NOVEMBER 10, 2011

Simon Cowell rang this morning to say I can leave *America's Got Talent*.

NBC's new management is OK with letting me out of my contract.

It's a huge relief.

I think everyone involved with the show knows my heart's not in it anymore. Especially with election year coming up.

It's always good to go out on a high from these things, and I'll be bowing out after *AGT*'s just enjoyed its strongest season in terms of ratings.

It's been America's number-one summer TV show since the day it started back in 2006—something that seemed utterly fanciful when Simon first invited me to do it.

And I feel very proud to have been involved in something that's become as much a part of the average American family's summer as apple pie and baseball.

"I do believe you've finally grown up," chuckled Simon.

I thanked him genuinely for the amazing break he gave me.

When I was struggling to find a new career after getting fired from *The Mirror*, it was Simon who stuck his neck out and took a massive gamble on me in the States.

I won't forget it.

After the news broke tonight, a random tweet from a member of the public made me laugh out loud: "BREAKING: Piers Morgan leaves *America's Got Talent* after finally accepting he has no talent and is not even American."

SATURDAY, NOVEMBER 12, 2011

It is the historical tradition that TV anchors take a big-name guest to the White House Correspondents' Dinner, so I thought I'd get in early—it's next April—and try to land the biggest Hollywood fish of them all, George Clooney.

I confidently expected a rejection note from either his publicist or a manager.

Instead, I received a personal response from George, almost immediately:

> Piers, always good to hear from you. Listen, I agreed to sit with the Time magazine folks, maybe that's the same table come to think of it. I'll be just coming back from Sudan, so hopefully will have a good reason to come on your show and catch people up on what's going on over there. Until then, I hope you're well and enjoying your gig.
>
> All the best,
>
> George

I'm beginning to sense that George Clooney's just a really classy guy.

WEDNESDAY, NOVEMBER 23, 2011

I became a father tonight, for the fourth time, to a beautiful baby girl called Elise Margaux.

She's tiny (five pounds, seven ounces), utterly adorable, and I already feel murderous toward her first boyfriend.

Her arrival wasn't without its drama, though.

Twice in the space of a few hours, Elise's heart rate plummeted and the emergency team all ran in to stabilize her.

It was terrifying to watch, but they were all extraordinarily calm, professional, and reassuring.

Celia, through it all, was unbelievably strong.

It's Thanksgiving tomorrow, and I couldn't be more thankful.

THURSDAY, NOVEMBER 24, 2011

News broke today that I've been asked to give evidence on December 20 to the Leveson inquiry, set up by David Cameron to investigate the phonehacking scandal.

Because of Elise's arrival, I have requested, and been granted, permission to give evidence via satellite from Los Angeles—as Celia can't fly with the baby for the rest of the year.

The inquiry, presided over by Lord Justice Brian Leveson, has already turned into a predictable smackdown of angry celebrities ranting about tabloids, and defensive tabloids coming under ferocious attack from the lawyers.

One thing's for sure. This is now effectively an inquest into tabloid journalism in Britain over the last twenty years. And it's not very edifying.

TUESDAY, NOVEMBER 29, 2011

One of the minor miracles of my tenure at CNN in America has been the avoidance of any major live on-air blunder.

Until tonight.

My research cards for an interview with a comedian called Dane Cook had been amended close to airtime to include the fact that another comedian, Patrice O'Neal, had sadly died today.

I didn't know this person, but was told that Dane Cook did, and it would therefore be appropriate to ask him to comment.

Unfortunately, one rather important fact had not been made clear to me, and I hadn't thought to clarify it, leading to a disastrous assumption on my part.

"It's a sad day for comedy with the death of Patrice O'Neal," I said, halfway through the interview, "who I know you knew well. She died of a stroke today."

Dane nodded, seriously, but said nothing, so I continued. "I want to take a look at a clip of Patrice on the Jimmy Fallon show, just to remind everyone how funny she was . . ."

The video began playing, and I was bemused because it featured a large *man* talking to Jimmy, not a woman.

I immediately assumed we were playing the wrong clip.

But then Jonathan whispered in my ear: "Um. Patrice was a man."

My heart sank, but I decided to just plow on and hope that nobody noticed.

So when the clip ended, I said, "Patrice O'Neal died today, very funny guy," and hoped no one would notice.

They did, obviously. And I got the kicking on social media that I deserved.

WEDNESDAY, NOVEMBER 30, 2011

Tonight, I attended a special British Academy of Film and Television Arts "Britannia Awards" honoring five Hollywood stars, including Warren Beatty.

I boasted details of my "special relationship" with Warren to a skeptical-looking group of strangers at my table.

Then the man himself walked over.

"Hi, Piers!"

Pause.

"That guy . . ." he announced, pointing at me, "sleeps in my old bed!"

Sadly, this is no longer true. My hand forced by Elise's arrival, I've finally moved out of the Beverly Wilshire and bought a house in Beverly Hills. Celia and I have also leased an apartment in Manhattan for when I'm in New York, which is where I will be a lot more now that I'm no longer doing *America's Got Talent*.

As I left, I bumped into Morgan Freeman, who chuckled: "Since our interview, I've had a lot of women asking if they're the horse in my pasture."

SATURDAY, DECEMBER 3, 2011

Herman Cain has quit the presidential race after allegations of various sexual dalliances emerged, derailing his hopes.

At a press conference today, he exclaimed: "I am at peace with my God! I am at peace with my wife! And she is at peace with me!"

I'll miss the old devil. What a character.

THURSDAY, DECEMBER 8, 2011

Jeff Bewkes, Time Warner chairman and CEO, told a UBS media conference today that CNN ratings were up 25 to 30 percent, and added: "Piers Morgan at nine o'clock is working well."

I'm nearing the end of my first year at the network, and this is about as good as I could have hoped for.

WEDNESDAY, DECEMBER 14, 2011

A fascinating interview with Tom Brokaw tonight about the modern media and news world.

"Tom, for me, who's a new boy to this news anchoring game, it seems like it's been the most incredible year for news."

"Well, it's been a chaotic year. And I think part of the reason that we see it in the way that we do is that it never stops coming at us because of the new instrumentation. It's not just on cable television or broadcast television or talk radio. It's now all over the Internet, at all times. All over the social media at all times. So there is really no escaping it.

"In the old days, when there were big events, you'd hear something in the morning, you'd spend the day at work, and come home in the evening. And then you'd take it in again and maybe read the morning paper the next day. Now it goes on all day long. You can't escape it, even at work. If you go online, you're likely to get some kind of a news site that will pop up as well."

This is so true.

Even when I first started working in newspapers twenty-five years ago, there was no Internet, email, social media, or cell phones. And barely any cable TV.

If you wanted to know what had happened in the world, you bought a newspaper or watched the network news.

Now news has become one long, relentless, streaming invasion on our consciousness.

Brokaw was also damning about the way America has gone from the great producer to the great consumer.

"After World War Two, the United States was a colossus in the world. Europe had been destroyed, Japan had been destroyed. China was one of those blank spots on the map that might as well have said, 'Beyond here serpents lie.' We didn't know what was going on there.

"So we were able to have this great industrial economy that enriched the middle class. I think what has happened since then is that we're playing too much by the old rules and not enough by the new rules.

"We did lose our manufacturing base in this country. And we've not yet caught up to the reality of that when it comes to job creation. Forty percent of the GDP now is made up of financial services. They don't make anything. They trade money. I mean it's not a dishonorable profession, but it is not in the best interest in a broad sweep of America to have so much concentration in financial services without having high-tech manufacturing, without having job opportunities that used to exist in the agriculture sector.

"When you had smaller farms you had more people working on them. Now it's big agribusiness and more mechanized harvesting procedures.

"And so we have reduced our job foundation in this country to a perilous point. And we need to think carefully about how we get out of that."

MONDAY, DECEMBER 19, 2011
Interviewed Dr. Henry Kissinger today, and all I could think of, as he sagely debated the merits of North Korea's new leader in that slow, unbeliev-ably gravelly, four-octaves-lower-than-Barry-White baritone voice, was that Kissinger would have been the greatest movie announcer ever.

TUESDAY, DECEMBER 20, 2011

I gave evidence to the Leveson inquiry today, and it went exactly as I assumed it would.

The inquiry's top attorney, Robert Jay, basically beat me up over every ethical, moral, and legal offense I'd ever committed, or he hoped I'd committed, in the history of my editing career.

Almost all of which I had myself put into the public domain through books, articles, and interviews.

It was like going back to school and being lectured by my old headmaster.

There's an absurd double standard going on with this inquiry.

All the celebrities they're wheeling in—many of whom have used the press for commercial gain when it suited them—are being treated like Mother Teresa.

And all the tabloid editors and executives are treated like Hannibal Lecter.

The script for this play has been written, and it's not going to change much.

I was just pleased I didn't lose my cool, because that was clearly what they were trying to force me to do.

General verdict after I'd finished was that it was a hard-fought score-draw, with no damaging knockout blow against me.

I just wish the whole damn thing would go away. It's such a distraction.

FRIDAY, DECEMBER 23, 2011

My official first-year ratings are in, and they're pretty good—up 8 percent in total viewers on the 9 P.M. hour in 2010, but crucially, up 24 percent in the demo.

Jim Walton, in a note to staff, wrote: "This was the year that the CNN/U.S. prime-time schedule regained its footing."

TUESDAY, JANUARY 3, 2012

The American election race kicked off properly in Iowa tonight, with the first actual vote for Republican candidates, to see who will be their official nominee to challenge Barack Obama in November.

The electoral process is unbelievably long, involving nearly two years of debates, votes, and conventions.

But as an outsider, I rather like the laborious procedure. You get to know the character and record of each candidate in such extraordinary depth and detail that by the time the race is over, it's almost impossible to imagine any major shocks emerging to surprise everyone about their president.

I've interviewed all the major players during the Republican campaign so far, and found it a fascinating experience.

There's the radical libertarian Ron Paul—the oldest man in the race, but also probably the one with the most energy, and definitely the one with the biggest youth and social-media following, thanks to his antiwar, pro-Constitution, pro-legalizing-drugs views.

Then you have the social conservatives, led by Rick Santorum—a strict Catholic who abhors abortion (even in cases of rape or incest), gay marriage, and stem-cell research, and thinks global warming is "junk science," and a "beautifully concocted scheme."

The third type are the moderate conservatives, Mitt Romney and Jon Huntsman. Both are very smart businessmen, with good economic records as governors, great families, and markedly more tolerant positions on social issues.

The problem for all of them is that the Republican vote is split among all three camps. The party doesn't seem to have any firm idea of what it wants to be going forward, or the candidate who can best deliver it.

I was part of the CNN on-screen election team tonight at the network's HQ in Atlanta—a vast, high-tech colossus of a building that we dub "the Mothership."

And the first night turned into an absolute thriller.

At 1:35 A.M., with 99 percent of the votes cast, Romney led Santorum— who had incredibly attended 360 town hall meetings in all ninety-nine Iowa counties!—by *one* vote, before the two switched places.

In the end, Romney edged it by just eight votes—the closest-ever Iowa caucus result in history.

We finally came off air at 3:30 A.M., and I found every second utterly enthralling.

I've enjoyed many exciting moments in journalism. But I don't think anything can quite beat being a prime-time anchor at an American news network during a U.S. presidential race.

It's going to be a riveting year.

TUESDAY, JANUARY 10, 2012

I'm anchoring live CNN midnight shows after each Republican primary, and we've recruited a regular panel including Andrew Breitbart, a firebrand Republican blogger.

He's a controversial character who spews venom at all and sundry, but has sharp, incisive political antennae beneath all the bellicose rhetoric.

Unfortunately, as I discovered tonight, he also has very thin skin.

Opening a debate about Republicans attacking fellow Republicans, I joked: "Andrew, you're notoriously evil about almost everybody; what do you think about the new politics where everyone whacks everyone else?"

"I don't think you know me, Piers Morgan," he snarled out of the screen (he was appearing by satellite). "We've maybe spent eight seconds together."

"It was a long eight seconds," I replied, assuming he was kidding with me.

He wasn't.

"I honestly don't know what you mean by that."

Breitbart was unshaven, his hair was long and ragged, and he looked furious.

"I've gone out there with a snarl on my face because I'm defending good and decent people. Sarah Palin was attacked mercilessly a year ago for the Gabby Giffords thing. She had nothing to do with that."

"Come on, Andrew, give me a smile," I teased. "Force yourself."

He half grimaced.

"On second thought," I said, laughing, "I think I preferred the snarl."

He stared at me, clearly enraged.

All a bit baffling given he'd fired off a battle-cry tweet in the afternoon, urging people to tune in to our showdown.

Afterward, I sent him an email:

Andrew, I was trying to be funny earlier, after reading your combative tweet, and thought you'd see the joke and respond in kind. But it didn't quite work, and I'm sorry if it pissed you off. You're always a great guest, and I'll telegraph my weird British humor more obviously next time.

Kind regards, Piers

He replied immediately:

Don't sweat it. I appreciate your promptly reaching out. As to the tweet, it was my way of getting my following to watch your show. Next time, like many on Twitter, perhaps go after my "neck beard" and wild-man hair ensemble. I'd deserve it.

Andrew

WEDNESDAY, JANUARY 11, 2012

Interviewed Newt Gingrich again at a small science museum in South Carolina, full of stuffed animals.

"What animal would you like to be if you had the choice?" I asked him.

"An elephant," he replied, "because they have one hundred and five thousand muscles in their trunks, they're big, they live a long time, they're smart, and they're social animals. And very few things can attack them . . ."

I suspect he'd predicted my question and planned that answer, since he knew the venue for our interview.

Which is why I'd never underestimate Newt Gingrich.

WEDNESDAY, JANUARY 18, 2012

There are only two exclusive men-only clubs that really matter anymore in the world—those who've played James Bond in a movie, and those who have been president of the United States. The six men who've been 007 are all still alive—Sean Connery, George Lazenby, Roger Moore, Timothy Dalton, Pierce Brosnan, and Daniel Craig.

And there are just five living U.S. presidents—Jimmy Carter, Bill Clinton, George H. W. Bush, George W. Bush, and Barack Obama.

I've never interviewed any member of either group—a nagging stain on my talk show career.

But today, President Carter invited me to spend a morning with him at his presidential center in Atlanta.

As we chatted in his office beforehand, I asked if he'd seen the new Margaret Thatcher movie, *Iron Lady*.

"No, but I'd like to. I was president for her first year as prime minister; she was a tough person."

"Did you like her?"

"Yes, but let's just say she thought she knew more about America than I did, and more about Germany than Helmut Schmidt did . . ."

His voice trailed off and he chuckled. The point was made.

Carter's one-term presidency has been oft criticized.

But as he pointed out, he didn't go to war with anyone, brought lasting peace between Egypt and Israel, reconciled China's relations with America, and kept the country's budget balanced.

Since leaving office, he's been an outstandingly industrious world statesman, and still bursts with energy at eighty-seven.

He also has one of the great marriages in political history, to his childhood sweetheart, Rosalynn.

They wed sixty-six years ago, and I was intrigued by how they'd managed to stay so happy together for so long.

"Compromise," he chuckled.

Carter revealed he forgot both Rosalynn's birthday and her Christmas present in recent years—but resolved both fiascos by making lifetime pledges.

"I gave her a certificate in writing, and I signed it, vowing that I would never again criticize her for being late."

"He's stuck to it pretty good!" she said with a laugh. "And when he forgot my Christmas present, he said he would do anything I wanted him to do. So I told him I wanted him to bring me coffee in the mornings. And every morning since, he's brought me coffee."

Carter sighed. "From now on, I'm going to buy some earrings or a necklace. It would be a lot easier on me!"

THURSDAY, JANUARY 19, 2012

Attention on Rick Santorum has exploded in this Republican nominee race since Iowa, and I sat down with him and his large family today in South Carolina.

His key selling point seems to be that whether you agree with him or not, at least he's been consistent on his political views.

And it's a fair point. As Romney has flip-flopped all over the place on social issues, Santorum has remained steadfastly hard-line.

I don't agree with almost any of his views, but I can admire the fact that he's true to his beliefs.

He doubled down tonight on gay marriage, suggesting he would actually try to make it illegal throughout America again.

"I would change the law to make a uniform definition of marriage. And that is between a man and a woman. It's something that reflects nature and God's will for us."

He also insisted there should be no exceptions for abortion.

"If you have a daughter," I asked, "who came to you who had been raped and made pregnant, and was begging you to let her have an abortion, would you really be able to look her in the eye and say no, as her father?"

"If she kills the child, that too could ruin her life. As horrible as the way that son or daughter was created, it's still her child. I believe the right approach is to accept this horribly created—in the sense of rape—but nevertheless a gift in a very broken way, the gift of human life, what God has given you."

FRIDAY, JANUARY 20, 2012

I've got a stinking cold, hardly surprising given I've already taken nine flights since the start of this year—from L.A. to Atlanta, to L.A., to New York, to Atlanta, to South Carolina, to New York, to Atlanta, to South Carolina, and now back to L.A.

This afternoon, I had to fly again, this time by helicopter, to Camp Pendleton in California, one of the largest American marine bases in the country, to interview Jill Biden—wife of Vice President Joe Biden.

Their son, Beau, served in Iraq, and she does a lot of work with Michelle Obama promoting a charity called Joining Forces that helps military families.

She perfectly encapsulated the kind of help needed most.

"It's the simple things. My daughter-in-law was by herself and we had a big snowstorm, and one of her neighbors just came by and quietly shoveled the snow out. He never said a word, never went to the door."

Just as Mrs. Biden began to tear up, a large plane flew overhead and interrupted filming.

This is always the interviewer's curse. A crucial moment ruined by extraneous noise.

"I'm so sorry," I said. "We're going to have to wait for it to pass."

"I quite understand," she replied.

We both looked up—to see Air Force Two coming in to land.

"Oh dear, I'm so sorry—it's my husband!" she exclaimed, as the whole crew collapsed laughing.

SATURDAY, JANUARY 21, 2012

John rang.

"Congratulations, you've been offered your first movie cameo role."

"Great! What is it?"

"A new Jim Carrey film called *The Incredible Burt Wonderstone*."

"Are you serious? That's fantastic."

"You may not like the script," John replied, trying to stifle a laugh.

"I don't care what the script says, this is my Hollywood breakout moment."

"Read it before you agree to anything," John insisted. "It's not very long."

He emailed it over.

In the scene, I am interviewing Jim's character, Steve Gray, on my CNN set.

"For me, it's about the power of the mind," he says. "I consider myself more shaman than showman."

I then reply: "What's going through your mind?"

Steve Gray ponders for a moment before saying: "I really have to pee, Piers."

And that's exactly what he then does, all over me.

I rang John back. "Pass!"

TUESDAY, JANUARY 24, 2012

Tonight was President Obama's annual State of the Union address.

At his side was Vice President Joe Biden, who commentators noted was suffering from a heavy cold.

A surge of guilt suddenly hit me.

It would appear that I may have indirectly infected the man a heartbeat from the presidency with acute nasopharyngitis.

WEDNESDAY, JANUARY 25, 2012

My signature CNN question, "How many times have you been properly in love?" has now become so cemented in guests' minds that they've started coming prepared for it.

The reason I like it so much is that it always elicits a great response. Either guests start revealing the truthful answer in often extraordinarily emotional detail, or they sit like startled deer in headlights wondering how truthful they *should* be, or they're diplomatic and start naming all sorts of people they probably weren't properly in love with, or they simply refuse to answer and berate me for my impertinence.

Last night, Alec Baldwin went one further and got in first.

"I must ask you, Piers," he began, mimicking an English accent that sounded like a cross between Prince Charles and the Earl of Grantham from *Downton Abbey*. "Have you ever been *properly* in love?"

"I have indeed been properly in love," I replied. "But I was about to ask you, Alec, how many times have *you* been properly in love?"

"The past is just a blur," he retorted, deadpan, still in the thick English accent.

"The woman I'm with now is really the only woman I've ever been in love with. Everything else was just child's play before now. I wasn't *properly* in love."

He smiled, and winked.

FRIDAY, JANUARY 27, 2012

Mum and Dad are on their first trip to Los Angeles, and I took them to dinner tonight with Jackie and Joan Collins.

Both sisters tell the most fantastically entertaining gossip-laden stories about the rich and famous.

Joan excelled herself tonight.

"I tried cocaine once, but I sneezed, and blew it all over Sammy Davis Jr."

TUESDAY, JANUARY 31, 2012

Before tonight's Florida primary midnight show, Julie Zann sent me a warning note: "Completely unintentionally, you gave Andrew Breitbart the finger after his answer on his last appearance while you were scratching your face. I talked him off the ledge after he sent me the screen grab his fans were sending him."

What?

I had no recollection of doing anything of the sort, and would certainly have never done it deliberately.

He's a strangely sensitive guy.

FRIDAY, FEBRUARY 3, 2012

My crazy road trip continued today when I flew to Vegas to interview Ron Paul.

He's a true maverick, and it was an engaging hour.

But when I asked him—as a doctor who has delivered thousands of babies—about Rick Santorum's hypothetical "I'd make my daughter have the rapist's baby" statement, he stunned me by responding: "If it's an honest rape, that individual should go immediately to the emergency room and I'd give them a shot of estrogen."

An "honest" rape?

What on earth is that?

He tried to clarify what he meant. "An hour after intercourse, or a day afterward, there is no legal or medical problem. But if you're talking about somebody coming in and saying, 'I was raped and I'm seven months pregnant,' then that's a little bit of a different story."

Paul's moral/ethical assessment of where abortion is permissible or not just confirmed to me again how twisted this whole debate is.

Almost every politician I speak to in America has a different interpretation of where precisely "conception" occurs, or at what stage, and in what circumstances, a woman has the right to choose what to do with her body.

SATURDAY, FEBRUARY 11, 2012

I was driving home through Beverly Hills late this afternoon when I looked up to see three choppers circling the Beverly Hilton Hotel, venue for music impresario Clive Davis's big pre-Grammys party tonight.

I assumed they were for the early arrivals on the red carpet.

But by 5 P.M., there were more than a dozen of them buzzing around, police sirens were blaring everywhere, and all hell was breaking loose.

Then Jonathan called: "Whitney Houston's dead. Suspected overdose. Go straight to the bureau—you're coanchoring."

Wow.

I showered, changed, and drove at high speed up Sunset Boulevard to the studio.

There was only one problem—nobody from the makeup department was at the bureau when I arrived. They don't usually work Saturday nights, when taped shows tend to air on CNN.

As I waited for someone to arrive, I toyed with the idea of just going on air without any makeup.

But it's a bit like appearing without any clothes. You look weird, and it makes the viewer uncomfortable.

Fortunately, one of our terrific makeup team raced in from home a few minutes later, and performed an instant miraculous repair job.

At moments like this on a major international news network, you desperately want to book guests who preferably a) knew the person, b) work in the same business, and c) can speak both eloquently and informatively without any preparation.

Simon Cowell ticked every box.

But it was now 6 P.M. in Los Angeles, 2 A.M. in the UK.

However, he's a night owl.

And I knew he was in Scotland filming *Britain's Got Talent,* so would be bored and sleepless in his room as he always is after shows.

I texted him: "Any chance of calling in to my CNN show to talk about Whitney?"

"Yes," he replied instantly. "Give me the number."

Our ensuing half-hour conversation on air was about as good a tribute and analysis as you could wish for.

"This is one of those days that will always be horrible to remember," he said. "Like when Lennon died, or Elvis, or Michael Jackson, or Amy Winehouse."

His voice slightly choking up, he added: "Whitney had her issues, that was obvious to anyone who saw her in the last few years. But the fact remains that she was one of the greatest superstars the world's ever seen, and had one of the greatest voices I've ever heard."

For the next four hours, coanchor Don Lemon and I interviewed a string of other guests including Lionel Richie, Smokey Robinson, and Jermaine Jackson—all making the same point that modern-day superstardom of the kind Michael Jackson or Whitney had is much harder to endure with the new, ever-more-intense, triple-pronged prying eyes of the Internet, twenty-four-hour media, and a paparazzi public armed with camera phones.

Add drug addiction, illegal or prescription, to the mix and it's a disastrous, life-ruining cocktail.

But they were also keen to remember her extraordinary talent.

I asked Lionel how he'd rank Whitney as a singer.

"Oh, she was the best."

Oddly, Clive Davis's party went ahead, with Whitney's body still a few floors above.

To some, it seemed an astonishingly inappropriate decision.

To others, it was the only thing to do. The show must go on, as Whitney would have understood better than anyone.

But it did feel very odd when I drove back home around 11 P.M., passed the Beverly Hilton, and heard the sound of revelers, knowing they were all partying a few floors below where Whitney's dead body still lay.

Jonathan congratulated me on a solid job.

"By the way," he added, "something many anchors do. Keep a small compact of makeup in your briefcase and/or office so if you need to go on in a pinch like tonight you can slap some on until the makeup department arrives."

"Good idea," I replied, "but what happens if I get stopped at customs with my *compact*?"

"Give it to them. It's like five dollars," he replied, missing my point.

"Er, I meant from the 'what's with the compact, Piersy darling?' standpoint."

"Oh, I see. Well, I assume the heels will be a bigger tipoff . . ."

TUESDAY, FEBRUARY 14, 2012

Juliana sent me an e-card this morning, which summed up today's meaning perfectly: "No woman will ever be truly satisfied on Valentine's Day because no man will ever have a chocolate penis that ejaculates money."

Later, she sent me a photo of herself looking shell-shocked with her head in an ice pack.

"What's this about?" I asked.

"I fell at home, smacked my head on the wall heater. Went unconscious. Woke up to lift my head but my ear was stuck in the heater, and when I snapped my head it pulled all the earrings out and ripped the bottom of my earlobe from my head. 1) Stitches. 2) CAT scan. I think it's from all the anxiety of working for you."

WEDNESDAY, FEBRUARY 15, 2012

Rick Santorum, who is still surging in the polls, was back on my show tonight, and said an interesting thing about Whitney Houston's death.

"In a sense, celebrities are the aristocracy of America. They're the kings and the queens and the princes of our society. And they have a huge impact on the rest of society, much more than any other group, certainly much more than a politician does.

"And that's why this is so disturbing that you see, in a sense, the royalty of America setting such a poor example and being troubled by these things.

"And obviously, that's going to have a downstream effect and a very harmful downstream effect."

Not many politicians would say this kind of thing about a hugely popular entertainer who's just died. Again, I admire Santorum's courage to say what he really thinks.

SATURDAY, FEBRUARY 18, 2012

I coanchored CNN's coverage of Whitney Houston's funeral from New Jersey today, with Soledad O'Brien, and it was an extraordinarily uplifting experience.

As a Catholic, I'm conditioned to funerals being very sad, often miserably serious affairs.

But the Baptists celebrate death as much as they mourn it, and I found the joyous laughter and singing that rang out around the church where Whitney sang as a young girl profoundly moving.

A fact that I tweeted during the service, from CNN's vantage point five hundred yards away from the church.

This prompted Ricky Gervais to tweet back: "Hey, Piers, you can come to my funeral if you promise not to tweet during it."

SATURDAY, FEBRUARY 25, 2012

At the annual pre-Oscars "Night Before" party, Meryl Streep and I discussed *The Iron Lady,* for which she's been Oscar-nominated.

"I felt in *awe* of Margaret Thatcher," she said. "Whether you agreed with her politics or not, she was a remarkable woman. To do what she did, when she did it, in a world dominated by men, was quite extraordinary."

Thatcher, like Blair, is still much more popular in the States than in Britain.

"Why is that?" asked Meryl. "I've never understood it."

"They both ruled as prime minister for over a decade—do any big political job that long, and everyone ends up hating you."

"I guess so, yes!"

I ended our conversation with a stern warning: "The fact you haven't appeared on my show yet will probably cost you the Oscar tomorrow night."

Meryl nodded: "Of course, I realize this."

SUNDAY, FEBRUARY 26, 2012

Meryl Streep won Best Actress.

Soon after I arrived at the *Vanity Fair* party, a strikingly tall, slim woman appeared right in front of me, barefoot. Then, very slowly, put two absurdly high-heeled shoes on, one by one, without once using her hands.

She rose back up to her full, imperious six-foot, four-inch heel-clad stature, winked, and walked away.

It was Karolina Kurkova, the Czech supermodel.

Jon Hamm, who witnessed the same scene, looked at me, raised an eyebrow, and grinned.

Cameron Diaz was being harangued by two drooling young British men, so I intervened.

"Guys, she's so *way* out of your league."

"My hero!" she laughed.

"Anything for a damsel in distress."

"I'll come on your show soon. I just need something serious and intelligent to talk about."

"The *Something About Mary* sequel?" I suggested.

At which point I felt a sharply pointed shoe connect with my ankle.

As I moved on, a firm arm gripped my shoulder.

"I'll do your show if you pay me forty dollars," said Chevy Chase.

MONDAY, FEBRUARY 27, 2012

There was another horrific school shooting today.

A young man called Thomas Lane randomly shot six students at Chardon High School in Ohio.

Three died, three were wounded—one of them left paralyzed.

My special guest tonight was Bill Maher, who tried to explain America's relationship with guns.

"We love guns. I'd love someone to make a speech and say, 'OK, we're never going to get rid of all the guns. But do we have to adore them, do we have to love them so much?'

"I look at guns like antibiotics. Sometimes you need them, but I don't kiss my antibiotics, I don't polish them, I don't worship my amoxicillin. If I need it, it's there. You know? But this country just has a very bad relationship with guns.

"Rick Santorum likes to talk about theology. This is a theology in this country. Guns are a religion. They're next to godliness for a lot of people. And you wonder what they're doing with them. I know they love to blow the brains out of innocent animals for fun, I guess that's one thing. But they also have this fantasy in their head, if you talk to a lot of right-wingers, that somehow they read the Second Amendment as necessary because we might have a tyranny in this country. Some sort of alien totalitarian menace might take over, and they're not saying who specifically, but then they will have to rise and take this country back.

"They really have this fantasy in their head that they can take over the government. I mean this may have made sense when the Second Amendment was written, when maybe you could defeat the government when everybody had muskets.

"But now the government has, you know, nuclear weapons, the F-22, and the Marine Corps, and it's probably unlikely that Vern and Earl are going to be able to take over the government no matter how much they dislike it."

I asked him how he countered the argument that many Americans see it as their constitutional right to have guns.

"Well, of course, it's in the Constitution—but where does that end? The Constitution could not foresee assault weapons, or bazookas. Should we be able to have those? What about a tank? What about a nuclear weapon if you could afford it?

"I mean it's ridiculous. No one is saying that we're attempting to create a gun-free society. We know that's impossible. Just reasonable limits. Make sure that the mentally ill people don't get them. Make sure you can't get them at these gun shows, these loopholes.

"And by the way, there's nothing wrong with saying we could rewrite the Constitution. The Constitution itself was rewritten. After all, it is the Second Amendment."

Everything Maher said makes complete sense to me.

Why doesn't it to so many Americans?

TUESDAY, FEBRUARY 28, 2012

Another live midnight show, after the Arizona/Michigan primaries.

Andrew Breitbart was on the panel again, this time in the studio with me in L.A.

We had a laugh before going on air about the alleged "raised finger" incident.

"Honestly, I would never do that," I protested. And I wouldn't; well, not on air anyway.

"I believe you," he replied, his face etched in disbelief.

I think these political bloggers are so immersed in spinning conspiracy theories that they see them everywhere.

But Breitbart's good TV, and I like having him on the show.

He's smartened up his act too, appearing in my L.A. studio tonight in a suit, and clean-shaven.

"Is this whole new image for me?" I joked.

"Yes! I cleaned up and got my aerodynamic fashion for you!"

I thanked him afterward.

"See you at the next primary night?"

"Definitely."

THURSDAY, MARCH 1, 2012

Andrew Breitbart is dead.

He collapsed of a suspected heart attack while walking in Brentwood, a neighborhood in L.A. He was forty-three, and married with four children.

His appearance on my show on Tuesday was the last time he was seen on television.

I feel strangely very sad for someone I didn't know that well, had clashed with a few times, and with whom I disagreed about almost everything.

But I loved his passion, for politics and for life.

FRIDAY, MARCH 2, 2012

The issue of gay rights, and gay marriage in particular, is getting hotter by the day. Seven states have now legalized it, with more set to follow.

And a new poll released this week by NBC/*Wall Street Journal* shows that public opinion is moving incredibly fast in the U.S.

Overall, 49 percent of Americans now support gay marriage, with 40 percent opposed. This is almost a direct reversal of the same poll results in 2009, when support was at just 41 percent and opposition at 49 percent.

The debate has sparked fury on both sides, and as someone who was brought up a Catholic, I understand how people with strong religious conviction feel about it, and respect their Bible-based beliefs.

BUT—and it's a big "but," as far as I'm concerned—being opposed to something doesn't give you the right to be a bigot. And some of the vile, abusive rhetoric being spat out by so-called Christians about gays and gay marriage is disgustingly indefensible.

Particularly when many of those spitting it out also claim to laughably stand for "freedom."

Yesterday afternoon, I taped an interview with an actor called Kirk Cameron.

He was the heartthrob young star of a smash hit sitcom in the eighties about unruly teenagers called *Growing Pains*. But he hasn't done much since.

I'd never heard of him, and wasn't keen to do the interview.

But Jonathan persuaded me by saying: "He's become a fervent born-again Christian in recent years, so he may be quite vocal about social issues."

"But who cares what some ex–child star thinks of anything?"

"Just try it. It may be better than you think."

I still didn't think it was worth it, but Jonathan's instincts are very good, so I agreed to do it anyway.

Cameron seemed a very respectful, polite man when he walked out on set, and we exchanged the usual niceties.

Then we started the interview, and fairly soon into it, I asked him: "What is your view of gay marriage?"

He smiled. "I feel like I just got imported into the Christine O'Donnell interview you did back in August . . . I believe that marriage was defined by God a long time ago. Marriage is almost as old as dirt. And it was defined in the garden between Adam and Eve, one man, one woman, for life, till death do you part. So I would never attempt to try to redefine marriage. I don't think anyone else should either. So do I support the idea of gay marriage? No, I don't."

"Do you think homosexuality is a sin?"

"I think that it's unnatural. I think that it's detrimental and ultimately destructive to so many of the foundations of civilization."

Good grief. Had he really just said that? What an astonishing comment.

Jonathan was right—this was already turning into great television.

"What do you do if one of your six kids says, 'Dad, I'm gay'?"

"I'd sit down and have a heart-to-heart with them just like you would with your kids."

"If one of my sons said that, I'd say, 'That's great, son. As long as you're happy.' What would you say?"

"Well, I wouldn't say, 'That's great, son, as long as you're happy.' I'm going to say, 'You know, there's all sorts of issues that we need to wrestle through in our life. Just because you feel one way doesn't mean we should act on everything that we feel.' "

I then said, "Some people would say that telling kids that being gay is a sin is in itself incredibly destructive and damaging in a country where eight states now have legalized gay marriage."

"Yes, but you have to understand that you yourself are using a standard of morality to make that statement, telling people such-and-such of a behavior is sinful, and *that* is terribly destructive."

"What's your view of abortion?" I asked.

"I think that it's wrong."

"Under any circumstances?"

"Under any circumstances."

"Even rape and incest?"

"I think someone who is ultimately willing to murder a child, even to fix another tragic end, a devastating situation like rape or incest, is not taking the moral high road. I think that we're compounding the problem by also murdering a little child."

"Could you honestly look a daughter in the eye if she was raped and say you have got to have that child?"

It's become a preferred question of mine in this debate because I'm genuinely fascinated by the answer, to see if private reality overrides public position.

"Yes. Because I love my daughter. I love that little child. This is a little creature made in God's image. Imagine if you were the result of that and you had been aborted. We wouldn't be here having this conversation. So I value life above all things."

The discussion moved on to freedoms.

"I'm concerned that we're losing what we want to hang on to," Cameron said. "I want to understand, where do we get these freedoms from? If the government gives them to us, they can take them away. But if they're given to us by God, they cannot be taken away."

"When you talk about freedom," I replied, "a lot of what we talked about before is about stopping people having freedom, isn't it? About stopping them getting married if they're gay, about stopping them having an abortion if they get raped. That's not freedom. That is stopping people having the right to do things they want to do."

"Well, you have to understand that there are those of us who hold values very dear and precious to us."

"Freedom is fine as long as we subscribe to your values."

"Or your values."

It was a fascinating conversation. And one that I suspect many Americans are having with each other as the Republican primary race becomes more focused on social issues.

But I suspect Mr. Cameron will regret some of his remarks. I can't remember any celebrity being so overtly, publicly homophobic like this for a long time.

Sure enough, within minutes of the interview airing tonight, he began trending worldwide on Twitter. Most of the tweets expressed blind fury, though some also defended his right to freedom of speech.

I was asked by a paparazzi camera crew in Beverly Hills tonight for my reaction to Cameron's comments, and tried to be as fair-minded as I could.

"I think he was pretty brave," I said. "He was honest about what he believes. And I don't think he was expecting the furor it created. But many will find his views antiquated."

Incredibly, my own comments also started getting a negative reaction—from people appalled that I had used the word "brave" to describe Cameron.

Yet surely that's exactly what he was.

The dictionary definition of brave, after all, is "ready to endure pain and danger." You don't have to agree with someone to think he's brave—and saying what Cameron said, on national television, in a country as divided on the issue as America, was indisputably indicative of someone "ready to endure pain and danger."

I don't agree with what he said, but I know one thing for certain—there are many Americans who do.

SUNDAY, MARCH 4, 2012

Skyped Bertie this morning, and he was wearing a bandanna and listening to Eminem.

He's eleven.

MONDAY, MARCH 5, 2012

Kirk Cameron has now been trending on Twitter for nearly three days.

Something even his death wouldn't have achieved.

By fortuitous coincidence, my guest tonight was Michele Bachmann—recent presidential candidate, and infamous in American politics for espousing some of the most antigay statements ever heard. (Example: "Being gay is a very sad life. It's part of Satan. If you're gay, it's a lifestyle of personal bondage, despair, and enslavement—and therefore so dangerous.")

But, bizarrely, when I asked her for her reaction to Cameron's comments, she replied: "I'm not here to be anyone's judge."

I laughed. "Well, you've been pretty judgmental in the past."

Her eyes widened. "Me? Hardly, hardly, hardly."

I laughed louder. "Probably one of the most judgmental people in American politics! Come on."

"Well, that's *rude!*" she retorted. "That's absolutely rude. I'm not a judgmental person."

I then read her the Satan quote above to jog her memory. But she still persisted in her preposterous "I'm not judgmental" line of defense.

After the show, I asked her why she'd been so reticent to say anything about Cameron, and she revealed that since she ran for president she and her family had been subjected to a year of death threats and horrific abuse over her antigay statements.

"It's been outrageous," she said.

"Yes, and inexcusable," I replied. "But are you surprised people would be angry about what you said about the gay community?"

"They should respect my views, which are based on my faith."

"But why, when you don't respect theirs?"

And that is the crux of the debate.

With the extraordinary pace of change on gay rights, both in America and Britain, there is bound to be this period of confusion, acrimony, and mutual disrespect. But in the end, tolerance will win the day. It has to, and it should.

Hating gays, like hating people with black skin, is bigotry, plain and simple.

A politician or church leader who used phrases like "unnatural, detrimental, and destructive to society" about a black man or woman would instantly lose his job and be rightly reviled.

The same rules should apply to those who use inflammatory language about people born gay.

Because, and I hate to break this to the homophobes, gay people really are born, not made.

THURSDAY, MARCH 8, 2012

A new seventeen-minute movie lauding the achievements of Barack Obama as president has been released by his election campaign this week—directed by Davis Guggenheim, the Oscar winner behind Al Gore's remarkable *An Inconvenient Truth* documentary.

"Most documentary makers balance their movies with the negative as well as the positive," I told Guggenheim when I interviewed him tonight. "What are the negatives in your movie about Barack Obama?"

"Well, I mean the negative for me was there were too many accomplishments," Guggenheim replied. "I had seventeen minutes to put them all in there."

I laughed. "Oh, come off it! You can't say that with a straight face. Come on. The only negative about Barack Obama is there are too many positives?"

He didn't laugh, replying simply: "That was the negative for me."

"But where do you find fault in him, personally?"

Guggenheim paused for thought. "I don't, frankly."

Highly amused by now, I asked how much he'd been paid to make it, and he replied: "I took a pay cut."

I laughed even louder.

"I'm only surprised you weren't paying him, by the sound of it, for the sheer honor and joy!"

Not a flicker of a smile passed his lips.

THURSDAY, MARCH 15, 2012

Hackers have broken into Syrian leader President Bashir Assad's email account and revealed that he was a fan of *America's Got Talent*.

Assad shared a YouTube video with his wife of an *AGT* magic act audition in which a man gets sawed in half.

I remembered the act well. It was a particularly bloodthirsty illusion.

No wonder Assad liked it.

TUESDAY, MARCH 20, 2012

Kirk Cameron appeared on the *Today Show* this morning, and accused me of unfairly editing him—which is complete nonsense.

"I love all people, I hate no one," he said. "When you take a subject and reduce it to a four-second sound bite, I think that's inappropriate and insensitive. It certainly didn't reflect my full heart on the matter."

What a load of guff!

I responded by tweeting: "Kirk Cameron is moaning I stitched him up by releasing a four-second sound bite re his comments on gay marriage. These are the four seconds: 'Homosexuality is unnatural, detrimental, and ultimately destructive to so many foundations of civilization.'

"I'll let others decide if he was stitched up, or just a bigot."

Got to admire his chutzpah. He's probably basking in all the attention he's been getting this past week after years in the show business wilderness.

The Dalai Lama blesses me with a Tibetan scarf after
our interview. An extraordinarily happy man.

7

WEDNESDAY, MARCH 21, 2012

For the past few months, I've been getting increasingly annoyed on my show by the fact that Apple, now America's richest and most successful company, continues to give jobs to ten times more people in China than it does in the United States.

I'm a huge Apple fan and a regular customer. But it just seems utterly perverse to me that 8.1 percent of Americans remain jobless, while America's number-one innovating firm prefers cheap labor factories in places like Shenzhen to somewhere like Ohio.

Apple's bosses, of course, argue they have a responsibility to shareholders to make the maximum profit. But I believe the financial hit they'd take by bringing jobs home would be offset by an increase in sales from grateful, patriotic Americans.

Today, I finally found someone who agrees with me.

Howard Schultz, chairman and CEO of Starbucks, told me it was time for a new kind of "moral capitalism" to kick in, where the best American companies look after their own.

To back up his point, Schultz—who, never mind the coffee beans, probably makes more cardboard cups than anyone in history—revealed he's opening a new factory in Georgia, rather than overseas. "It's the right thing to do," he explained.

I bet all the tea in China that Starbucks makes even more money with this strategy.

MONDAY, MARCH 26, 2012

Today, I heard the greatest excuse of my life.

I was due to meet Felipe Calderón, the president of Mexico, in Puerto Vallarta, but he was running late. His aides kept apologizing, and stressing that he is a stickler for punctuality. "It must be something very important," they assured me.

Calderón eventually rushed in, an hour after our appointed time.

"I'm so sorry for keeping you waiting," he said, "but I've been with the pope."

TUESDAY, MARCH 27, 2012

America is raging over the killing of a young black teenager called Trayvon Martin by a local Neighborhood Watch coordinator called George Zimmerman in Florida.

It's a highly emotive case because Martin, seventeen, was unarmed and simply picking up sweets from a store before walking back to his father's house when a passing, suspicious Zimmerman decided to report him to police, then apparently follow him against police instructions.

The exact details of what happened next remain debatable. Zimmerman claims he was walking back to his car when Martin appeared from nowhere and attacked him.

Martin's family says Trayvon was hunted down, a confrontation ensued, and Zimmerman shot him.

Zimmerman claimed self-defense immediately after the shooting, and because the police had no evidence to prove otherwise, he was allowed to go home without even being arrested.

It was only weeks later, after huge media pressure, that he was finally held, and then charged with second-degree murder.

What's most perplexing to me is the new law in Florida called "Stand Your Ground"—which may or may not be used as an actual defense in this case—that basically allows anyone to shoot anyone else if they believe their life's in imminent danger, and unlike with "self-defense," there is no need to even attempt a retreat.

The "Stand Your Ground" law is already being used and abused in

Florida, and the numerous other states where it has also been introduced, by drug dealers and gang leaders to avoid prosecution.

There is much to be admired about the American justice system, but "Stand Your Ground" is dangerous nonsense—especially in a country with more than three hundred million guns in circulation.

THURSDAY, MARCH 29, 2012

Mike Tyson was my guest tonight, and I asked him how much of his wild behavior could be attributed to his dreadful upbringing in Brooklyn, New York.

"A great deal of it, but that same emotion, that crudeness and stuff, is the same fire that everybody else liked too. I couldn't just separate the two at the time, it fed off one another."

And that's so true, isn't it? Tyson the barbarian appalled us outside of the ring, but enthralled us inside it.

"Are you at peace with yourself now?" I asked.

"I don't know if I'm ever at peace with myself."

When I questioned why he felt he was still so popular, he smiled: "People call it luck. Napoleon said greatness masters the artistry of luck. I'm not saying I'm great, I'm just saying what a great man said about luck."

SATURDAY, APRIL 7, 2012

Gordon Brown is in L.A. to make some speeches, so Celia and I had dinner with him and his wife, Sarah, tonight.

"Where are you watching the soccer tomorrow?" he asked as the check arrived. Arsenal, the team I've supported since I was a boy, was playing a big match.

"My place, want to join me?"

"That would be great."

SUNDAY, APRIL 8, 2012

I woke at 7 A.M., and went to shake the boys, who are here on vacation, out of their stupor.

"You'd better get up, we've got a prime minister coming to watch the game."

As the game finished, with a magnificent Arsenal win in the bag, my Skype began ringing, and I saw it was my mother in Sussex, where the rest of the family was gathered for Easter.

Chance for some amusement.

"Hi, Mum, I've got someone who wants to say hello."

I turned the laptop to face Gordon, who went straight into politician mode.

"Mrs. Morgan, this is Gordon Brown, how are you?"

I could see various members of my family's jaws drop open with shock in the background. Though Mum never missed a beat, as if this whole scene was perfectly normal, and went straight into maternal mode: "Hello, Gordon, how are your boys?"

TUESDAY, APRIL 10, 2012

Bubba Watson won the Masters golf tournament, and the American media's been desperate to land the first big interview with this wonderfully eccentric character.

To my amazement, he insisted on giving it to me.

When I asked him why tonight, he explained: "Honestly? It's because I loved what a prick you were on *America's Got Talent!*"

SUNDAY, APRIL 15, 2012

Saw Bill Cosby on CNN talking about guns and the Trayvon Martin case.

Of George Zimmerman, he said: "It doesn't make any difference if he's a racist or not, if he's scared to death and not a racist, it's still a confrontational provoking of something."

Cosby said he used to own a gun himself, to protect his family, but gave it up.

His own son Ennis was shot and killed by an armed robber in 1997.

"When a person has a gun," he said, "sometimes their mind clicks that this thing . . . will win arguments and straighten people out."

This surely is the key point.

Gun rights lobbyists say that you need a gun to deter aggressors and make yourself safer.

But as Cosby says, often the mere presence of a gun has the complete opposite effect, and merely serves to escalate the violence into a deadly conclusion.

"When you tell me that you're going to protect the neighborhood that I live in, I don't want you to have a gun," he said. "I want you to be able to see something, report it, and get out of the way."

MONDAY, APRIL 16, 2012

Robert De Niro is reputed to be the hardest star to interview. I've heard endless stories of how tricky he can be—monosyllabic, humorless, gruff, irritated, or just plain bored.

One of his aides even warned me before our encounter today:

"Don't ask Bob any questions that can be answered with yes or no, because that's exactly how he will answer."

To complicate matters, I was in Los Angeles and he was in New York, so we were doing the interview via satellite, with a slight time delay.

I spoke to him briefly before we began the interview.

"Hi, Robert, it's Piers here, how are you?"

"Fine," he replied. "Thank you."

To try to lighten things from the start, we thought it would be amusing to break the ice with that hilarious clip from *Meet the Fockers* where De Niro wears fake breasts.

His face, as he watched, never flickered.

"Now, Robert," I began, "when we have dozens of great movies to choose from for a trailer, and we choose the one of you wearing false mammary glands, does your heart swell with pride or does part of you think, 'Why the hell couldn't you have done something a little bit more serious for me?' "

His brow furrowed.

"My heart"—he grimaced—"swells with pride."

And that was about the only real answer I got out of him.

For the next ten minutes, he responded to virtually all my questions about the economy, politics, gun control, and the American Dream with phrases like "I don't really know," "I can't really say," "That's a big question," or—the ultimate death knell for interviewers—prolonged silence, and a shrug of the shoulders.

As we approached a commercial break, I announced: "I want to come back and talk about news with you because I hear you're a bit of a news junkie . . ."

Silence.

". . . So I'm hoping that includes this show . . ."

Silence.

". . . let's leave viewers on this gigantic cliff-hanger, Robert . . ."

Silence.

"Don't give it away yet . . . your facial expressions aren't telling me any good news here . . ."

Silence.

We went to the break. My mouth was dry, small beads of sweat had formed on my neck, and I glugged from an emergency bottle of cold water at the side of my desk.

"I think he likes you," chuckled Jonathan.

After the break, I asked De Niro to name his favorite actor.

"How can I answer that?" he said with a sigh.

Rather easily, I thought.

"What's the trick to great acting?"

"I don't know . . . It's hard for me to answer. I don't know if I can give it . . ."

I gave up on the acting questions.

"We have something in common, Robert."

"Really?"

"Yes, we both became fathers to baby girls four months ago."

"I didn't know that, congratulations."

"Number four for me, number six for you. How's fatherhood going the sixth time around?"

"Well, as any parent will tell you . . . it's an . . . experience."

Unfortunately, not an experience he wished to share in any further detail with me!

It was time to admit defeat.

"Well, congratulations on the baby, and indeed on surviving this interview, because I know you can't stand doing them."

He nodded. There was no denial.

"For my part, I've loved every second and it's been a great honor."

And finally, Robert De Niro laughed. Loudly.

"Oh, you're just saying that."

And maybe I was.

TUESDAY, APRIL 24, 2012

The Dalai Lama, who became ruler of Tibet in 1950, is the world's second longest serving leader of any kind—religious, political, or royal. Only King Rama IX of Thailand, who was crowned in 1946, beats him. Britain's own Queen Elizabeth II comes third, with sixty years on the throne, and Cuban dictator Fidel Castro fourth, with forty-nine years in power.

I flew to the world-famous Mayo Clinic in Minnesota today to interview him. He was there for his annual health checkup, and unsurprisingly, given his abstemious lifestyle, he'd been given a very positive report.

"Do you ever drink alcohol?" I asked.

"Never."

"Have you ever smoked a cigarette?"

"No."

"Ever taken a drug?"

"No. My mind quite peaceful. So no need these things."

"Let's move on to other issues. As a monk, you obviously subscribe to a vow of celibacy."

"Yes."

"Is that hard?"

"No. If you just see physical experience, then you may find a certain desire. But when I go to England, and watch people who have families, sometimes I notice on my first visit, another woman, another wife. Second visit, another woman, another wife. Previous wife, some children. Then another occasion, third wife.

"Children suffer much when parents divorce. Married people, their mental state, their emotional state, too much ups and downs!

"Compare that with celibate people, mind more steady. So, long run, we have some advantage."

He roared with laughter as he said this.

"Do you ever feel temptation when you see a woman?" I asked.

"Oh, yes, sometimes I see people and think, 'Oh, this is very nice.'

"But I'm Dalai Lama. I always remember. I am monk, always monk." He said he hadn't watched TV in two years, and never uses email, computers, or cell phones.

Nor does he listen to music, or go to the movies.

"Not even to see your friend Richard Gere?"

He chuckled. "No!"

"Have you heard of Simon Cowell?"

Bemused, he turned to his interpreter, and muttered: "What IS that?"

I'd been warned that if the Dalai Lama sat back in the interview, it meant he was bored.

"I'm encouraged to see you've been sitting forward, Your Holiness," I told him toward the end. "Does this mean you've been enjoying the interview?"

"It seems you are talking with certain feeling," he replied, "and I love your accent!"

Perhaps the most surprising revelation came when I asked him to name the most impressive world leader he's ever met.

"I like President Bush."

"Which one?"

"The younger one. His policies were not very successful. But as a person, I found him a very nice person. I love him."

This is the curious contradiction about George W. Bush. He was one of the most divisive, war-mongering U.S. presidents in modern history—yet numerous people who met him have said exactly the same thing to me about his personal likability.

When the interview was over, the Dalai Lama presented me with a magnificent white Tibetan khata ceremonial scarf.

"I wish you great peace and happiness!" he said.

"I feel happier for just meeting you, Your Holiness," I replied.

He exudes such warmth and serenity that it's impossible not to.

WEDNESDAY, APRIL 25, 2012

Tom Repicci, John's excellent deputy, emailed: "Hi Piers, please see attached offer for a free top-of-the-range toilet from Kohler. Let me know if you'd like to accept it."

I passed.

I'm not going to be beholden to anyone for my bowel movements.

SATURDAY, APRIL 28, 2012

Goldie Hawn was my guest at the White House Correspondents' Dinner in Washington tonight.

"Coming down. Drink. Bar," she texted as I drove over to pick her up from her hotel.

Goldie arrived wearing a dazzling black Dolce & Gabbana dress, a white fur wrap, and enough large sparkling jewels to light Capitol Hill for the night.

We ordered champagne and talked about our daughters. Goldie's, of course, is superstar actress Kate Hudson. Mine is Elise Morgan, only five months old but no less of a superstar to me.

"You will be the most important man in her life forever," she warned. "Don't ever forget that."

We drove to the Hilton. "This is where Reagan was shot," Goldie noted as we walked inside.

"Well, I'm sure our evening will go better," I reassured her.

President Obama made a very funny speech, mocking all and sundry. This time last year, at the same event, he made a similar speech having just ordered SEAL Team 6 to take out Osama bin Laden.

His favorite target that night was Donald Trump, who'd been loudly questioning the veracity of Obama's birth certificate.

Tonight, his opening line was: "Last year, we finally delivered justice to one of the world's most notorious individuals . . ."

As the audience broke into applause, the big screens suddenly switched to a photo of Trump. Cue mass hilarity.

At the *Vanity Fair* party inside the French Embassy afterward, I got drunk with George Clooney.

As in properly, delightfully, head-damagingly intoxicated.

We stood together in the center of the lobby from 2 A.M. to 3 A.M., drinking a lot of vodka, discussing everything from phone hacking to the Sudan, and exchanging regular bear hugs.

He's hilarious.

THURSDAY, MAY 3, 2012

I interviewed Ted Turner tonight.

"Are you still proud of CNN?"

"Absolutely."

"Do you still watch CNN?"

"You bet!"

"Do you like what you see?"

"I like most of what I see . . ."

I was curious as to how he would have responded to the new competition from Fox News and MSNBC.

"Should CNN still remain the impartial observer of news?"

"Yes, and cover the substantial news. That doesn't mean you don't cover Hollywood, kidnappings, and the sensational too. But the emphasis should be on hard news. I wanted CNN to be the *New York Times* for the news business, not the *Daily News,* even if the ratings weren't the greatest.

"If you had the most prestige and you were the network that everybody turned to in times of a crisis, that was the most important position in the news business to hold."

Ted singled out the rescue of a baby called Jessica from a well in 1987, the first Gulf War in 1991, and the 9/11 attacks as the three biggest stories in his CNN tenure.

And as he spoke about them, I could see the fire burning again inside his news-obsessed body.

We spoke about Jane Fonda.

"Was she the great love of your life?"

"Probably."

"Have you ever gotten over her?"

"No."

"Think you ever will?"

"No. When you love somebody and you really love them, you never stop loving them, no matter how hard you try. You can't, and there's nothing wrong with that. That's good."

"You're a man used to winning, and you lost Jane . . ."

"I lost Jane, I lost my job here, I lost my fortune, most of it, got a billion or two left. You can get by if you economize!"

"Which upset you the most?"

"They all broke my heart. But I rallied. Winners never quit and quitters never win."

Ted now has four girlfriends, who all know about each other.

"How do you get away with that?"

"With great difficulty!"

"What would you like written on your tombstone?"

"I'd like, 'I have nothing more to say!' "

A CNN staffer later sent me a hilarious Ted Turner anecdote, after watching the show.

"I was at his table for a lunch hosting the winners and finalists of the CNN African journalist of the year competition.

"Ted told them, 'You know, fellas, this year I have lost my company, billions of dollars, and my wife . . .'

"Quick as a shot, one of the African lads said, 'But as I understand it,

Mr. Turner, you are still a billionaire, and according to the papers, you are fucking Bo Derek.° Where I come from, that would not be considered such a bad year.'

"Ted laughed his ass off."

SUNDAY, MAY 6, 2012

Vice President Joe Biden today publicly backed gay marriage.

On NBC's *Meet the Press,* he said: "I am absolutely comfortable with the fact that men marrying men, women marrying one another, and heterosexual men and women marrying one another are entitled to the exact same rights, all the civil rights, all the civil liberties."

He called the debate surrounding the issue a simple question of "who do you love? And will you be loyal to the person you love?"

Within minutes, Biden was being accused of dropping a huge gaffe, because he had said all this before the president had said it.

But I think he knew exactly what he was doing.

The VP was basically telling his boss to get on with it, and endorse gay marriage himself.

Good for him.

MONDAY, MAY 7, 2012

I interviewed David Axelrod tonight, and pressed him on when the president would endorse gay marriage.

He insisted that Obama and Biden were on the same page.

"He believes that couples, heterosexual couples and gay couples, should have exactly the same legal rights."

"Right," I replied, "but is there an inconsistency between saying 'I am supportive of all gay rights and gay equality' whilst not saying that you believe in gay marriage? Particularly when eight states have now legalized it."

"The whole country has gone through an evolution," he said, "and the president has gone through that as well. He is very much in accord with

—————————

°Bo Derek later denied any romance with Ted Turner.

the rights of the states and the people in those states to do it. And he wants to make sure that if people are legally married in those states, that these marriages are recognized, just as marriages between men and women are recognized."

"So why doesn't he just go one step further and say he supports gay marriage?"

"I'm not going to make news for the president here. He speaks very well for himself, Piers!"

WEDNESDAY, MAY 9, 2012

Well, that didn't take long.

President Obama today endorsed gay marriage.

In an interview with Robin Roberts for ABC, he said: "I've concluded that for me personally it's important for me to go ahead and affirm that I think same-sex couples should be able to get married."

He revealed that his change of heart had come in part from prodding by gay friends, and by conversations with his wife and daughters.

"I had hesitated on gay marriage in part because I thought civil unions would be sufficient," he said. "And I was sensitive to the fact that for a lot of people, the word *marriage* was something that invokes very powerful traditions and religious beliefs."

Yet, ironically, it was his own religious Christian beliefs that finally triggered his U-turn.

"The thing at the root that we think about is not only Christ sacrificing himself on our behalf, but it's also the golden rule—treat others the way you would want to be treated. I think that's what we try and impart to our kids, and that's what motivates me as president."

It's a big, bold, risky move by Obama, and I applaud him for it.

He knows gay marriage is a very divisive issue, but he also knows that he would never have become president if people before him hadn't also taken big political risks on civil rights.

MONDAY, MAY 14, 2012

I've flown to Dallas to interview an array of American Olympic stars.

And today, I came face to face with the man who is on the verge of becoming officially the greatest Olympian of them all—swimming phenomenon Michael Phelps.

He needs just three medals in London to surpass former Soviet gymnast Larisa Latynina's all-time record of eighteen Olympic medals.

And considering he won gold in all eight swimming events he competed in during the last Beijing games, this is almost a certainty.

Physically, he's an extraordinary sight—six feet, four inches tall, but with a surprisingly skinny torso, especially his sticklike legs. Then you see these enormous size fourteen feet, massive hands, and quite startlingly long arms, giving him an eighty-inch albatross-like wingspan.

Add double-jointed ankles, and you begin to understand why Phelps has been described as a "unique physical freak."

He sat down and promptly delivered an enormous yawn.

"Are you tired, or bored?" I asked.

"Maybe both . . ." he smirked, again.

"Do you enjoy doing interviews?"

"It's OK, if I'm not in a grumpy mood."

"Are you today?"

"Not yet."

He stared at me defiantly.

And I saw in that moment just why Michael Phelps is such a formidable competitor. He doesn't even like losing at interviews.

But really, all you need to know about Michael Phelps is something he told me halfway through our encounter: "I once trained for five years without a break—three hundred sixty-five days a year, for at least four or five hours a day in the pool."

"Why would anyone do that?" I said with a laugh.

"Because I wanted to be the best there had ever been, and that's what it takes."

WEDNESDAY, MAY 16, 2012

It's been a very slow few weeks for news, and our ratings have softened as a result to dangerously low levels.

It doesn't help that May is a huge "sweeps" month for the major TV networks, where they unleash all their big-gun finales to get high numbers they can use to ramp up advertising rates.

But nothing quite prepared me for the shock of what happened at 4:30 P.M. today.

I was sitting in my New York studio, about to start a taped interview with Billy Bob Thornton, when Jonathan emailed me last night's ratings, as he always does around this time.

The overnight figure had looked worryingly low, but can often be misleading. Not this time.

The first thing I read was Jonathan's comment: "No words."

This was not a good sign.

My eyes raced down the figures for CNN prime time, and alighted on the 9 P.M.-hour younger-viewer demo number: "Thirty-nine."

My whole body literally arched in shock.

It couldn't be right.

That would be almost 50 percent lower than any rating I'd had before.

It meant that just 39,000 people in that age range had watched my show last night. A complete and utter catastrophe.

The total viewer number, including all viewers, was 284,000. Another record low number in that category too.

Cold sweat appeared on the palms of my hands.

It made no sense. The show had been a regular one, no different from most nights. We'd started with good breaking news developments surrounding the Trayvon Martin case, and the investigation into disgraced Senator John Edwards, plus exclusive interviews with *Glee* star Jane Lynch, and a homeless guy called Ted Williams with an extraordinary golden voice.

Oddly, the Lynch interview was the moment we plunged to our lowest rating, of just twenty-three in the demo. Meaning almost nobody at all was watching.

Later this afternoon we worked out why we may have had such a calamity—*Glee* had been extended to a special two-hour episode last night, meaning we had scheduled the Lynch interview to clash with her appearing in her own smash hit show on another channel.

Anyone who likes her, or *Glee*, would have been watching NBC, not CNN.

This was pure suicidal idiocy on our part, and one of us should have realized in advance.

Ken Jautz sent a supportive "don't jump, tomorrow's another day" email, which was good of him.

"Thanks Ken," I replied. "I don't know what the fuck is going on with these numbers but obviously we will be doing everything we can to get out of it as fast as possible. I can only apologize for last night. Horrific."

I felt physically sick. Genuinely. I wanted to go to my office, lock the door, and puke in the trash can.

But I had to get through the Billy Bob Thornton interview first, which I managed to do without displaying too much of the misery I was feeling inside.

Afterward, I slinked back to my office, feeling utterly wretched.

Jonathan walked in, shut the door, and sighed.

"Every good show has brushes with death. Now we'll see who our friends are!"

"We could get canceled for this," I replied.

"That's not going to happen. This was unique, the ratings will bounce back tomorrow. We were up against three big reality show finales last night, and we fucked up the *Glee* thing."

I finished the rest of tonight's show, and went home in a semidaze. The media critics and bloggers have been brutal about the ratings—even the Drudge Report screamed LOWEST EVER RATINGS FOR PIERS MORGAN! on its home page.

This was picked up on Twitter, and I was gleefully abused by all and sundry.

Around midnight, after I'd sunk a bottle of wine, Jonathan emailed: "Cock of walk or feather duster?"

"Feel pretty dustery, have to be honest," I replied. "Brutal reaction everywhere."

"Get some sleep, we'll get 'em tomorrow."

THURSDAY, MAY 17, 2012

Woke at 5 A.M., feeling hungover and exhausted from the sheer mental anguish of that thirty-nine demo number.

The Internet was full of more vitriol in my direction, mostly along the lines of "when will CNN fire this clown?"

It's been particularly vicious back in Britain, where many of my old media "friends" would like nothing better than seeing me fall flat on my face again.

Unfortunately, I'm flying to London tonight to spend a week taping my *Life Stories* show. Perfectly awful timing.

As I was driven to JFK, Jonathan sent me last night's ratings, which were three times higher than Tuesday's.

Nobody back home will see or care about this recovery, as they continue to delight in the horror of that record low number.

FRIDAY, MAY 18, 2012

Jonathan sent me the ratings for last night, which showed we did a 175 in the demo, over four times the disastrous thirty-nine, and comfortably the highest on CNN all day and night.

We had bounced back strongly.

Jesus, what a scary week.

Bill Clinton, the world's greatest politician.

8

CNN has announced that I will be anchoring the network's coverage of Queen Elizabeth's Diamond Jubilee, marking the sixtieth anniversary of her accession to the throne.

I've had quite a ride with the royals over the years.

"Ah," said Princess Diana, the first time we met. "The man who thinks he knows me *so* well."

I always chuckle when I remember that encounter.

Because it said it all, didn't it?

The royal family is the most discussed, debated, adored, and derided collection of relatives in the world—yet how well do we really know any of them?

I've met most of them at some stage, and am still none the wiser, although my own firsthand experiences suggest the caricatures are not a million miles off the truth.

Prince Philip was quite splendidly rude at a Buckingham Palace reception to mark his son Charles's fiftieth birthday in 1998—refusing to utter a single word when I introduced myself as the editor of *The Daily Mirror*, and snarling to a friend of mine as he shot off, "God, you can't tell from the outside, can you?"

I loved him for his brutal honesty.

Charles himself oozed ostentatious charm and politeness that day, as he always does in public. Say what you like about the man, I think he'll make a brilliant king—he has extraordinarily good manners.

Camilla's warm, earthy, and funny. A minute spent in her company and you instantly understand why she was so much better suited to Charles than Diana.

Andrew, Edward, and Anne, by contrast, were stiff, formal, and . . . well, how can I put this gently . . . a tad on the dull side.

Harry, I've never met. Which is probably best for both of us given that he once asked my actress friend Amanda Holden: "Is Piers Morgan as big a prat in real life as he seems on TV?"

William, I know better. I once had a quite extraordinary lunch with just him and Diana at Kensington Palace, when he was thirteen years old, wearing braces, and heading into the perils of royal adulthood.

We discussed everything from Cindy Crawford and James Hewitt to paparazzi and kissing girls in discos. All of it agonizingly off the record.

But I thought then that William had a much older head on his shoulders than his age dictated. And I still do. He's a man who grew up to loathe the press for the way they harassed his mother and despised them even more after she died. Yet he understands his "duty" and the need to engage the media in his life to fulfill that duty properly.

William has a sharp sense of humor. I once ribbed him about the size of his feet and he smacked me in the stomach, crying, "What about the size of your six-pack . . . or should I say keg?"

My brother-in-law Patrick, a former army colonel, trained both princes at Sandhurst, and said they were both terrific soldiers. He also said that neither of them ever made any attempt to be treated any differently from other cadets. "They just mucked in like the others."

As for Diana—she was a beautiful, complicated woman who struggled endlessly with the intolerable pressure of being the biggest celebrity on planet Earth. She was great company, as mischievous and provocative as she could be, serious, fiery, and contrary. We all miss her, whether we loved her (as I did) or not.

But the biggest star of them all in the royal firmament is the queen. She always has been. And what a magnificent queen she is.

I've met her three times.

She is smaller than you think, always perfectly groomed, and deploys that famous fixed grin to cover myriad emotions. But don't be fooled by that benign appearance. Beneath the smile lurks a formidably sharp brain and a waspish sense of humor.

"Do you enjoy hosting your garden parties?" I once asked her at a Windsor Castle party thrown for the British media in 2002—as we looked out over the magnificently tended green fields.

"Well, Mr. Morgan," she replied, "let me put it this way: How would *you* like twelve thousand complete strangers trampling on *your* lawn?"

I've only seen the queen rattled on one other occasion, and that was in the days after the death of Princess Diana.

The royals decamped to Balmoral in Scotland as the nation descended into grief, and Her Majesty was personally attacked for the first time anyone could remember for refusing to lower the flag at Buckingham Palace and for making no personal address to the nation.

I spoke to one of her press chiefs at the time, and he said she was like the proverbial deer trapped in headlights—unable to rid herself of the rigid formality the royals had always been taught to practice in such times of crisis and personal grief.

I remember approving the headline on *The Daily Mirror* front page: SPEAK TO US, MA'AM, YOUR PEOPLE ARE SUFFERING. It may seem impertinent now, but in the moment it accurately reflected the mood of the country.

The next morning, the queen came back to London, lowered the flag, and spoke to the nation on TV without her famous tiara.

She spoke "as your queen and as a grandmother" and made one of the greatest speeches I've ever heard—sincere, eloquent, moving, and direct.

The mood changed instantly, from anger to respect and affection.

And there, right there, I understood the primary purpose of the queen— to console, celebrate, encourage, and stabilize Britain.

The ongoing debate of why taxpayers should pay for the royals has always struck me as utterly fatuous—they more than pay for themselves with the incredible tourism they attract. In America alone, millions of people see them as almost their own royal family—such is the deep-rooted affection I encounter for them on my travels around the U.S.

But if you ask me what the queen's most important "point" is, I would say it's the weekly meeting she has with her prime minister.

I spoke to three of them—Margaret Thatcher, Tony Blair, and Gordon Brown—about those encounters. All attested to her extraordinary wisdom, based on unparalleled experience of world affairs. The queen, after all, has met every leader for the last sixty years and surveyed every world crisis in that time.

"There was no problem I encountered that she hadn't seen before, in some form," Blair told me once. "I found that very comforting."

"She's so intelligent," agreed Brown, "and never hesitated to challenge me about something if she didn't agree."

"I trusted her instincts better than almost anyone else's," said Thatcher.

I suspect a lot more British government policy is decided over a cup of tea in those meetings than in any cabinet meeting.

In 1992, during the making of an official royal documentary about her life entitled *Elizabeth R,* she told the director: "One feels the buck stops here, so to speak. I had a letter this morning. It said: 'I've been going round and round in circles but you are the only person who can stop the circle.' I thought that was rather nice."

In the end, the buck does indeed stop with her. And she stops a multitude of circles on a daily basis.

And for that, I remain her grateful, if occasionally disobedient, servant.

SUNDAY, JUNE 3, 2012

I've been very excited about coanchoring CNN's coverage of the Diamond Jubilee from London.

But I arrived at Tower Bridge this morning—our location for the thousand-boat river pageant—to find a slight problem. My coanchor, Brooke Baldwin, ate a dodgy oyster last night and is suffering from wretched food poisoning.

I went to see her in one of our makeshift tents, and found poor Brooke sitting in a chair, eating a small cracker, and looking deathly pale.

"You OK?"

"I'll be fine," she groaned.

I could see she was about to be sick again.

There really is nothing worse for anyone doing a live broadcast than food poisoning. Almost any other ailment can be concealed with a variety of tricks and potions.

But acute vomiting is the ultimate nightmare.

I felt so sorry for Brooke. She's a rising young star at CNN, and was so thrilled to land this assignment.

We sat in the chairs an hour later, and prepared to begin the simultaneous live broadcast to the world on CNN International and CNN America.

"If I suddenly tap you on the leg, it means I have to leave urgently," Brooke said.

"OK, got it. Don't worry—if it happens, it happens. I will cover for you."

She looked terrible. But she gritted her teeth, and we started as if nothing was wrong.

Then, half an hour into the two-hour show, ferocious rain swept over the whole area.

It transpired, pretty quickly, that we were partially exposed to the skies, thus causing the rain to lash into our backs.

It also turned suddenly very, very cold.

Within an hour, we were sitting in pools of cold water, our clothes soaked through. These were the most shocking conditions I'd ever tried to film in, and Brooke began to deteriorate badly.

"Are you all right?" I asked during a commercial break.

She was ashen white and shaking. "Not really."

To liven the tension, members of the huge crowd were peeling off to shout things up at me. Most of it very nice.

Then I heard the words: "Piers Morgan! You are a *war criminal*!" Which, of all the charges leveled at me, seemed a little perverse, given that *The Daily Mirror*, under my editorship, had opposed the Iraq War so vociferously.

About ninety minutes in, Brooke tapped me on the knee.

She was about to keel over.

I called for help, and some of the CNN crew rushed forward to take her out.

The only solace was that we didn't have much actual anchoring left to do, as attention was now focused on the actual parade of boats and musical performances.

So viewers were none the wiser about what was going on.

But I was very worried about Brooke.

As soon as we wrapped, I unhooked my microphone and raced off to see how she was—just in time to see her being carried on a stretcher into an ambulance.

"Is she OK?" I asked her producer.

"Yes, she's just got hypothermia, and they want to get her to hospital as a precaution."

Fortunately, she made a quick recovery, and within a few hours we were exchanging cheery emails.

"Like you promised, my friend, this is a day I will *never* forget!" she quipped.

WEDNESDAY, JUNE 6, 2012

For politicians, a reputation can be made or broken on a single decision. Or, as in the case of former American Defense Secretary Donald Rumsfeld, a whole welter of charges from waging illegal wars to endorsing torture. He remains one of the most divisive characters in modern American politics.

"Why do you think you've attracted the reputation you have?" I asked him tonight.

He thought for a few seconds, then smirked.

"Dogs don't bark at parked cars."

TUESDAY, JUNE 12, 2012

We booked Casey Anthony's lawyer, Cheney Mason, today, to get an update on how his client has been doing since her dramatic acquittal over the alleged murder of her baby.

He came to my office before we went on air, and I asked him what the chances were of landing the first interview with his client.

"Do you want to speak to her now?" he replied.

"For the show?"

"No, on the telephone. Then we can see down the line about a proper interview."

Cheney called her on his cell phone, then passed it to me.

"How are you doing?" I asked.

"I'm trying to adjust the best that I possibly can," she replied. "You know, given everything that continues to be thrown at me every day. So I mean I have good days and bad days and I'm trying to take the best out of everything."

Her voice was calm and ordinary.

"What do you think your public perception is?"

"Oh, it's bad, it's absolutely horrible. And a lot of that has to do with the constant media scrutiny, even today. I mean even reputable media, like the *New York Times* and the *Boston Herald,* report the same rumors about me as tabloids like the *Enquirer*.

"So I know that the perception out there is not the best and could absolutely be improved and that's obviously something that we'd like to try to improve, because the perception of me that's out there couldn't be further from the truth. I don't know where people got these ideas from, it's so far out of even my own comprehension at this point, I don't even know where any of this stuff came from."

"What do you think is the biggest misconception about you?" I asked.

"Well, there are several misconceptions. Obviously I didn't kill my daughter. If anything, there's nothing in this world that I've ever been more proud of, there's no one that I love more, than my daughter, and this still remains the same thing. She's my greatest accomplishment.

"I've never been the quote unquote 'party girl.' I don't drink now. I've probably had a handful of beers since I've been on probation, which is being completely honest. I've never done drugs. Smoking a little bit of marijuana in my early twenties, that was as far as that went.

"There are so many things out there that aren't even remotely true, that there isn't even the slightest bit of truth to."

"Like what?"

"I don't weigh five hundred pounds now. I'm not moving to Costa Rica. I'm not making gazillions of dollars at the hands of other people or trying to sell myself to anyone that is willing to throw a couple of dollars at me. I don't give a shit about money. I may have in the past for other reasons, before any of this stuff started, because I was a stupid kid.

"But I'm twenty-six now and I've gone through hell. And even I know the situation isn't what it should have been when my life totally changed almost a year ago. This isn't the situation that I should be in right now but I'm dealing with it."

"Where do you think you personally went wrong?" I asked.

"By not being honest. I didn't trust law enforcement because of my relationship with my father, who was ex–law enforcement. And I didn't give them the benefit of the doubt, which is part of the reason that they didn't give me the benefit of the doubt.

"People are critical of me and the thirty-one days of my lying to law enforcement, and my not being forthcoming, but what they don't understand is the reason why. And I totally get why people look at me and have these opinions, because I look at the things that I said, I look back at some of the interviews and the way that I've come across, and it's horrible, it looks absolutely horrible.

"And I'm ashamed in many ways of the person that I was because even then that wasn't who I was. I wouldn't even have been able to begin to tell you the person that I was outside of being a mom and, you know, being twenty-two and being scared and confused just with life in general. Not having a direction, or feeling like I had much of a purpose outside of caring for another person. I didn't even know how to care for myself, so that was something . . ."

Cheney Mason stepped forward and ended the conversation.

"OK, that's enough for now."

I thanked him. "Can I use some of those quotes on the show tonight?"

"Yes."

It was quite a scoop, the first interview of any kind that Casey Anthony has given any journalist.

Tonight I had dinner with Jonathan and Conor.

For reasons almost certainly connected to mutual exhaustion, stress over softening ratings, and copious quantities of alcohol (especially on my part), a convivial conversation escalated into an angry midnight argument between me and Jonathan.

Eventually, I stormed out, marching the ten blocks home in a fit of blind fury.

WEDNESDAY, JUNE 13, 2012

Woke at 6 A.M., feeling horrendous.

Had an instant flashback of last night's farce, and groaned.

Then I checked my phone and saw an email Jonathan had sent at 1 A.M., after I'd crashed into a stupor.

"I don't know what we were arguing about or why we kept at it, but I meant no disrespect and I certainly don't want you angry. Apologies."

I replied in kind: "I think we should just get married and be done with it. Silly end to a fun evening. Apologies my end too. Let's forget it."

The reality is that we see more of each other than we do our wives most weeks, and live, eat, and breathe the stresses and strains of a rolling nightly news show together.

I couldn't do it with anyone else, and I suspect/hope he feels the same way.

Letting off steam occasionally like last night is no bad thing. It clears the air of any simmering tension.

And on a nightly cable news show, just as there was on a daily newspaper, there's always a lot of simmering tension. But you only get that kind of passion from people who really care about what they're doing.

SATURDAY, JUNE 16, 2012

Sir Roger Bannister was the first person to break the four-minute mile—a milestone that many "experts" had said would never be achieved.

It was an astonishing feat of willpower, and sheer bloody-minded British grit.

Sir Roger, now eighty-three, quit athletics a few months after smashing the world record, and became a neurologist.

I met him at a party in London tonight, and asked him if he ever got bored of having to talk about the four-minute mile to every breathless fan (like me) he meets. He smiled. "No, no, I remain very proud of it. But I only ran for seven years—I'm much prouder of my work in neurology, to which I devoted the next fifty years of my life."

As for what drove him, Sir Roger—a charming, razor-sharp man who still looks fit enough to beat me over a mile—once came out with this great quote about competitiveness: "Every morning in Africa, a gazelle wakes up. It knows it must outrun the fastest lion or it will be killed. Every morning in Africa, a lion wakes up. It knows it must run faster than the slowest gazelle, or it will starve. It doesn't matter whether you're a lion or a gazelle—when the sun comes up, you'd better be running."

A perfect metaphor for life in the cable news business!

SUNDAY, JUNE 17, 2012

The boys sent me a joint Father's Day card this morning:

"Dear @piersmorgan, #HappyFathersDay love, your three best follow-ers, Spencer, Stanley, Bertie."

MONDAY, JUNE 18, 2012

Flew back into New York today, and attended the premiere of Aaron Sor-kin's eagerly anticipated new HBO drama, *The Newsroom,* about a cable news show not dissimilar to my own. It stars Jeff Daniels as a bored, iras-cible old TV anchorman called Will McAvoy who has a reputation for being too lightweight—a reputation he then decimates by suddenly transforming himself into an enraged, passionate, hard-news assassin.

The trigger for this metamorphosis comes early in the first episode we watched, during a tedious college panel debate, when the moderator goads him into answering a question posed by a student: "What makes America the greatest country in the world?"

McAvoy pauses for a few seconds, then goes on an almighty rant about why America is *not* the world's greatest country.

"We're seventh in literacy, twenty-seventh in math, twenty-second in science, forty-ninth in life expectancy, one hundred seventy-eighth in infant mortality, third in median household income, number four in labor force, and number four in exports. We lead the world in only three categories— number of incarcerated citizens per capita, number of adults who believe angels are real, and defense spending, where we spend more than the next twenty-six countries combined. So when you ask what makes us the greatest country in the world, I don't know what the fuck you're talking about."

As the students look on, stunned, he adds, "We sure used to be. We stood up for what was right. We waged wars on poverty, not poor people. We sacrificed, we cared about our neighbors, we put our money where our mouths were, and we never beat our chest. We built great big things, made ungodly technological advances, explored the universe, cured diseases, and cultivated the world's greatest artists and the world's greatest economy. We reached for the stars, and acted like men. We were able to be all these things and do all these things because we were informed, by great men. The first step in solving any problem is recognizing there is one—America is *not* the greatest country in the world anymore."

Nor, indisputably, is my own country, the previous holder of the title before the United States.

The UK, according to a 2009 study, ranks twenty-third in literacy, twenty-eighth in math, sixteenth in science, thirtieth in life expectancy, thirty-sixth in infant mortality, eighth in household income, twentieth in labor force, and eleventh in exports.

We too used to be all the things McAvoy fondly recalls Americans being in their great past.

What are we Brits still world leaders at? Well, we increase our alcohol consumption over the Christmas holiday more than any other nationality. Cheers!

The Newsroom showed me what's missing from my own show—a voice.

I've had some great interviews, covered the breaking news pretty well, and expressed my opinion over issues like gay marriage. But if I asked my viewers what the show, and I, really stood for—I'm not sure they'd know the answer.

Will McAvoy had that same feeling until he suddenly exploded about the state of modern America. That moment gave him the confidence to push his opinion on air for how America could be better.

I need to find my own voice about something I really care about.

THURSDAY, JUNE 21, 2012

The single worst thing about living abroad is missing the boys' sporting events. I used to attend all of them religiously.

Now, I'm lucky if I get to a handful a year.

I've discussed this with them all many times, and always said that if they wanted me to give up my job and come home, I would.

And I mean it.

But they've always been insistent that they like the work I do, and enjoy coming to see me in America.

And, thanks to new technology, we keep in touch pretty constantly through Skype, BlackBerrys, and iPhones.

Today, though, was a perfect example of when I wish I could have been home.

Bertie, eleven, was taking part in his school summer sports day in South London.

He's a brilliant natural sportsman, so I was expecting him to win something.

I rang him tonight to see how he'd gotten on.

"I did pretty well, Dad," he chuckled.

"How well?"

"Well, I won the hundred meter . . ."

"That's brilliant!"

"And the hundred-meter hurdles . . ."

"Amazing!"

"I won the high jump . . ."

"Seriously?"

"And the long jump . . ."

"Good God . . ."

"And the relay . . . the four-hundred meter . . . and throwing the cricket ball."

I was stunned into total silence for a few seconds.

"You won *everything*?"

"Yes!"

He was giggling.

I, conversely, was on the verge of tears. Of pride and regret.

Having a fancy job in America has many pluses; of course it does. But missing your eleven-year-old son winning every single event on sports day is something I'll never get back, and always wish I had seen for myself.

I wonder on days like today if the sacrifice is really worth it.

"I'm really sorry I missed it, Bertie," I said.

"That's OK, Dad, it doesn't matter."

But it does. We both know it.

FRIDAY, JUNE 22, 2012

There's been a big, scandalous trial in America about a football coach called Jerry Sandusky, who was accused of abusing a large number of young boys at Pennsylvania State University, in the Sports Department run by the legendary Joe Paterno.

The jury began its deliberations yesterday, and is free to go on each night for as long as they like without informing the media until they decide to break.

What this meant in practice today was that although I'd already taped my CNN show by 3 P.M., I then had to sit around for the next six hours twiddling my thumbs in case a verdict was suddenly announced.

My show began to air at 9 P.M., with no sign of any action.

Then, at 9:35 P.M., Jonathan called excitedly: "Go straight to the studio—verdict coming in!"

I raced downstairs, got mic'd up, was live on air by 9:40 P.M., and began talking to a variety of legal experts about the forthcoming verdict.

All the while desperate for the jury to announce its decision in my time slot, as we'd be able to break the news first, and it would attract big ratings, as stuff like this always does at CNN.

The minutes ticked by, and I kept informing viewers, "Any second now, we'll have the verdict."

We got to 9:57 P.M., and still nothing.

"What the hell are they waiting for?" I mused aloud in the final commercial break.

"You to go off air," said one of the cameramen, laughing.

At 9:59 P.M., I did indeed go off air, reluctantly handing the reins to the next anchor, Anderson Cooper.

And at 10:04 P.M., the verdict was duly announced—Sandusky was found guilty, on forty-five of forty-eight counts.

For the next hour, Anderson was able to deliver dramatic live news on all the fallout, and of course, inevitably garner all the huge ratings that would come with it.

To compound my misery, I then had to continue twiddling my very sore thumbs for another two long hours until midnight, when my show reaired, to update it with all the news we'd missed earlier. By which time, most people would have digested the news anyway and gone to bed.

I slumped into bed at 1:30 A.M., broken by the strain of just missing the breaking news.

MONDAY, JUNE 25, 2012

Oliver Stone is arguably the most brilliant, dangerous, unpredictable movie director in the world.

He's also, as I discovered tonight, an exceedingly difficult man to interview.

"Now, you're going to be nice, aren't you, Piers?" he said before we started.

"Of course, Oliver."

"Because I am good friends with both David Frost and Larry King, and they've always been very nice to me."

As we went to the first commercial break, I said: "We'll come back and talk about your new movie, *Savages,* and about politics, and maybe a bit of religion too."

Stone erupted: "I want to talk about the fucking movie!"

I laughed. "I said we'd start with the movie, relax."

During the break, I gently chided him: "Oliver, I think you need to realize that you're not directing this show, I am!"

He smiled. "Of course, of course . . ."

I did indeed come back and talk about *Savages* for several minutes, but he still wasn't happy.

As we went to the second commercial break, I said: "We'll be back to talk more about *Savages,* and also possibly the least savage person in the world—your wife . . ."

He erupted again.

"You've only shown one clip of the fucking movie!"

The good thing about all this pent-up fury over my failure to plug the film enough was that it ignited a really open, frank final segment.

"If you were describing yourself to somebody who had never heard anything about you, what would be the honest description?"

"I'm equally astonished and disappointed by myself," he replied.

"Why disappointed?"

"There are so many things I wish I'd done better."

"How many times have you been properly in love?"

He snorted with derision.

"Only someone from England would ask something like that!"

I pressed on.

"It seems like you've finally found true love with your third wife?"

"It's nice of you to say," he snarled, "but how do *you* know?"

"Well," I persisted, "from the loving way you've talked about her in previous interviews."

He nodded slowly, digesting my riposte like a baby eating a carrot for the first time.

"She's a lovely woman, so beautiful and gracious, it's a different kind of relationship for me—less stormy, calmer."

Afterward, Stone was charm personified. "That was fun, let's do it again sometime."

"I'd like that," I replied truthfully. I wish all guests were as edgy and uncompromising.

As he left, one of my staff asked him how he felt about the interview, and he erupted again: "Astonished and disappointed!"

Then he caught my eye, and guffawed.

THURSDAY, JUNE 28, 2012

The Supreme Court today upheld Obamacare—the president's controversial health plan, which, among other things, will allow more than thirty million uninsured Americans to have health insurance.

It's amazingly unpopular, even among many of the very people it seeks to help.

To us Brits, who enjoy almost universal free health care, this seems an incomprehensible reaction.

Janice Turner, a former journalist colleague of mine, summed it up perfectly by tweeting today: "There's nothing more inexplicably American to a Brit than sick, poor folk who oppose Obamacare. Not even marshmallows served with vegetables."

MONDAY, JULY 2, 2012

Jonathan's been trying for days to persuade me to interview an actor called Robert Blake.

Blake's a scandalous Hollywood figure—a bona fide movie star (he was brilliant in the multiple Oscar-nominated *In Cold Blood*, based on Truman Capote's book), accused of murdering his wife, Bonnie Lee Bakley, in 2001. He was acquitted after a sensational court case, but then found liable for her death in a civil action brought by her family.

Bankrupt and unemployable, he disappeared for the next decade.

Now he's written a book, which reads like the rantings of a madman to me.

I just can't see the point in resurrecting something that was thoroughly dissected by the media ten years ago.

"Why are we doing this guy?" I asked again this morning.

"Because he's a big name accused of murdering his wife," Jonathan replied.

TUESDAY, JULY 10, 2012

Robert Blake arrived in my CNN studio, wild-eyed and aggressive, stared menacingly at me, and snarled: "We're not going to have any problems, right?"

I laughed. "I've no idea. Are we?"

He ignored me, instead checking his face carefully in the camera monitor.

The interview started.

"How are you, Robert?"

"How am I? I'm lonely. The way I always am. I was born lonely, I live lonely, and I'll die lonely."

Blake was fine for a few minutes, then his language began to deteriorate as he ranted about how badly he'd been treated.

I could sense that he was right on the edge, emotionally and psychologically. Hardly surprising, I guess, given what he'd been through.

He never took the stand in his criminal case, so had never been directly challenged in any public forum about the death of his wife.

I'd been warned he might walk off the set if I did, but figured there was nothing to lose. He wasn't making much sense anyway.

"I want to get to the truth, if I can," I said.

His face curled into a fury.

"Tell the truth if you can? Be careful. Does that mean I'm lying to you?"

"I don't know. Are you?"

"If you don't know I'm telling you the truth, then you must have a little scratch in the back of your head about where I'm lying."

He was sitting forward now, in a very confrontational manner. The atmosphere in the studio was electrifying.

"Nobody calls me a fucking liar," he snarled.

"I didn't call you a liar."

"You said I might be telling the truth. What the hell is the difference?"

Then his voice softened.

"My skin is a little bit thin. Which is why I stay away from people mostly. I've never allowed anybody to ask me the questions you're asking. I allowed you to do that because I trust you . . ."

"But you don't know me."

"We're supposed to be talking about the book. Bonnie's not in the book. I chose to allow you to go there and you should deeply, deeply respect that."

Several times up to this point, Blake had jibed about "the man in your ear"—referring to Jonathan, talking to me from the control room.

Now, as I pressed him on details of what happened the night Bonnie died, he snapped.

"What the hell's that guy in your ear telling you? What the hell are you doing?"

"Let me help you," I replied. "Let me take this out of my ear."

I removed the tiny wireless receiver in my ear linking me to Jonathan.

"There's nobody talking to me now, you don't have to worry. These are my questions for you."

"So," he snarled, "tell me about the facts of that night."

"OK. You take your wife for dinner. Your wife goes to the car. You go back to retrieve, as you say, your gun, which is in the restaurant. And when you return, your wife has been shot dead. When they test the gun that you go and retrieve, that is not the same gun that killed her. Am I right so far?"

"Well, it sounds as boring as hell, but go ahead."

"I don't think it's boring—your wife got murdered."

"No, but your questions are boring. Do the people at Tibet give a fuck about this?"

"You've written a book about your life."

"There's a lot more to my life than that night."

"But probably nothing more significant in your life . . ."

"Fuck yes."

"Really. Than the murder of your wife?"

"I didn't murder my wife."

"I didn't say you did."

"Personally it's not the most significant thing in my life."

Blake was now extremely angry, and extremely animated. He stripped off his jacket to reveal muscular bare arms, and his whole demeanor had become so threatening that CNN security guards who'd been watching on monitors outside the studio suddenly came inside, fearing he might do something stupid.

"I would go out to dinner with her to kill her?" he raged. "What the fuck is the matter with you?"

"I didn't say you killed her."

"You didn't say I didn't."

"I'm curious about how you deal with the fact that a civil action was successfully brought against you for killing your wife."

"OK. Here's the bottom line. What you think of me, I don't give a fuck."

"You don't know what I think of you."

"What I care about is what God thinks about me. When I lay on the bed at night and I say, 'God, how are we doing?' I don't include you."

"It's not about me, is it?"

"Yes, it is. Because you opened that door, Charlie Potatoes."

Charlie Potatoes?

What on earth was he on about?

"I'm not going to sit here and let you or anybody else kick the fuck out of me without defending myself. And you can take that to the fucking bank, Charlie!"

"What have I said to you that's factually inaccurate?"

"It's not so much factually inaccurate. It's boring."

"Hasn't it ruined your life?"

"That's another matter, Charlie."

It was time to change tack.

"With all that you've been able to find out since that night, who do you think killed Bonnie?"

"Bonnie had people that she burned. How bad, I don't know. Nobody ever really knew where Bonnie was. She had fifteen ID cards. She had fifteen credit cards. She had different places where she lived and nobody could ever find her, if they were looking for her.

"But one day, somebody opened a paper and said, Bonnie just married Robert Blake. Where does Robert Blake live? And what? A couple of weeks later, she was dead? Now I just want to you to chew on that for a minute with all these facts that you have."

"Robert, how are you going to find peace with yourself? Seriously."

"I'm not looking for peace. I'm seventy-nine years old. I've been this way since I was born. I'd argue with a goddamn rock and then try to beat it up."

At the end of the interview, Blake jumped up and virtually ran out of the studio.

It had been a quite extraordinary hour.

He cursed at me forty-six times, all of which had to be "bleeped"— believed to be an all-time CNN record for one hour of programming.

"Who the hell is Charlie Potatoes?" I asked my team afterward.

Turned out Blake had taken a line from the 1958 Tony Curtis movie, *The Defiant Ones,* about a man called Charlie Potatoes, who struts around like he's the richest, most successful and popular guy in town.

I've been called worse.

MONDAY, JULY 16, 2012

There's nothing more powerful in driving interest in a TV interview than word of mouth.

We re-aired my Robert Blake encounter last night, and it got double the ratings of the original airing.

I suggested to Jonathan that we continue re-airing it three times a week until Christmas, by which time it should be beating *NBC Nightly News.*

WEDNESDAY, JULY 18, 2012

Justice Antonin Scalia is the longest serving, most colorful and divisive member of the current Supreme Court.

He's renowned for believing that American law should be based on the text of the Constitution, "reasonably interpreted." Of course, it's the interpretation of the text of things like the Second Amendment that has led to such deep-seated argument.

I asked him tonight why he had such faith in the Founding Fathers that their words from more than two hundred years ago should still be so rigidly applicable to modern America.

"You have to read the Federalist Papers," he replied. "I don't think anybody in the current Congress could write even one of those numbers. These men were very, very thoughtful. I truly believe that there are times in history when genius bursts forth, like 500 B.C. in Athens, or cinquecento Florence for art. And I think one of those places was eighteenth-century America for political science. Madison said that he told the people assembled at the constitutional convention: 'Gentlemen, we are engaged in the new science of government.' They were brilliant men, and I wish we had a few of them now."

I don't disagree with his assessment that the Founding Fathers were brilliant men.

But they wrote the Constitution when America and the world were very different places.

THURSDAY, JULY 19, 2012

Senator John McCain, who lost to Barack Obama in the last U.S. presidential election, spent nearly six years as a prisoner of war in Vietnam.

He was beaten, abused, and tortured.

Today I finally got to meet and interview him, and afterward, he took me into his Washington office and showed me a few photos and pieces of memorabilia on his walls. In a far corner was a framed citation.

"What's that?" I asked.

He stopped, his cheekbones tweaked hard, and he replied: "Somebody sent me this; it's the original official navy report on my service in Vietnam."

I read it carefully.

It detailed how McCain, often held in solitary confinement, had been exposed to "extreme mental and physical cruelties."

But although "crippled from serious and ill-treated injuries," he refused repeated offers of freedom unless prisoners who'd been held longer than he were released too.

"His selfless action served as an example to others," read the citation, "and his forthright refusal, by giving emphasis to the insidious nature of such releases, may have prevented possibly chaotic deterioration in prisoner discipline."

I turned back to McCain. "How on earth did you find the courage to do that?"

"I had no choice," he said, his eyes welling up with tears. "These men were my friends."

That's not true, of course. He had a choice. He just opted for the one that says all you need to know about the man.

FRIDAY, JULY 20, 2012

My phone rang at 6 A.M., which is never a good thing.

"Turn on your TV," said Juliana.

I switched on CNN, to find that a young man had gone berserk with guns in a movie theater during a midnight screening of the new *Batman* movie—*Dark Knight Rises*—in Aurora, Colorado.

The shooter, a twenty-four-year-old student called James Holmes, shot seventy people, killing twelve, wounding fifty-eight.

It's the single worst civilian mass shooting in American history, in terms of the number of people shot by one person.

Holmes apparently dyed his hair red, told police he modeled himself on the Joker from *Batman,* and used four guns, all of which he bought legally in three local stores a few weeks ago.

As the horrifying details of his senseless rampage grew worse and worse, I could feel the fury inside me beginning to boil over.

What is *wrong* with this country? Who is going to do something, anything, to stop this gun slaughter?

I got to the office, and Jonathan could sense I was in a volatile mood.

"Try to keep it cool out there," he warned.

I began interviewing one of the victims, a young woman called Patricia Legarreta. She'd been at the theater with her boyfriend, Jamie, her four-year-old daughter from a previous relationship, and their four-month-old son. "At first we were thinking, oh, it's a prank, a joke," she said, her voice trembling. "But you see the flashes coming out of his gun and that's when I was like, this isn't a joke, this is real."

Suddenly, I had to divert to a live press conference with Aurora police chief Dan Oates, who revealed some astonishing new information.

Holmes had purchased six thousand rounds of ammunition on the Internet, and multiple magazines, including a one-hundred-round drum for his AR-15 assault rifle.

Chief Oates said: "I've been asked, was the weapon automatic or semi-automatic? I can't answer that question now. Even if it was semiautomatic, I'm told by experts that with that drum magazine, he could have gotten off fifty to sixty rounds within one minute. And as far as we know, it was a pretty rapid pace of fire in that theater."

Just unbelievable.

What on earth does any civilian need that kind of firepower for?

Chief Oates continued: "He was dressed entirely in black, wearing a gas mask, a ballistic helmet, a tactical ballistic vest. Tactical means places to put all kinds of gear and clips. In addition, it was bulletproof. He was wearing ballistic leggings in case he took a round in the legs. He was wearing throat protection and groin protection, and black tactical gloves. So that's what he looks like in the theater."

Dressed for war, and perfectly legal.

The press conference ended, and I went back to the survivors.

Patricia had been hit by a bullet, and Jamie had dived over their baby son's body.

"Every time a bullet flashed, you just hear the sound and your ears are ringing," he said. "You're like, 'This one's going to kill me.' People are falling all around, screaming right next to me."

I asked him what his view was of gun control, in light of the fact Holmes bought his guns and ammunition legally.

"It's not right. Like, I mean, yes, people are entitled to things—but how many weapons do you need? These are destructive, they're not just handguns. They're shotguns, assault rifles, they're just so fast at killing people. Like you just realize how many people it can kill so fast. Because, I mean, this only took three minutes and seventy shot, twelve dead.

"These are weapons of destruction. It's horrific."

My next guest was a Denver University professor called David Kopel, known for his progun views.

"People are saying it's time for gun control to be strengthened," I said. "What is your reaction to that?"

"Honestly, Piers, I think this is the wrong night to be doing this," he said. "And I really wish you'd waited to have this segment until after the funerals. This is a time in Colorado, and nationally, when it would have been better to have more of the segments like you did before with the family, and when people could be unified in helping the victims."

I couldn't believe what I was hearing.

"If I may, let me challenge you on what you just said," I replied, trying to control my rising temper. "A lot of people who don't want to strengthen gun control have said this is not the day to debate it. I'll tell you the day to debate it would have been yesterday, to prevent this happening."

My voice rose.

"When you have a young man like this able to legally get six thousand rounds of ammunition off the Internet, to buy four weapons including an assault rifle, and for all of this to be perfectly legal in modern America, allowing him to carry out the biggest shooting in the history of the United States, that, I'm afraid, means it's too late for this debate, for those people who lost their lives!

"So don't patronize me about when we should be talking about the gun control debate. You tell me a good reason why we should not strengthen the law now to stop another young man like him going into a store tomorrow, buying four more weapons, six thousand rounds of ammunition on the Internet, and killing and shooting another seventy people in America!"

"Because we don't even know the full facts of this situation yet," Kopel retorted. "I know you've said many times on the air, 'America's got too many guns.' You want to drastically reduce the number of guns. If your whole point is there's too many guns, we've got to get rid of lots of them, drastically constrict things, and you think somehow that's going to make it better, well, there's no real evidence that it will."

He stared at me defiantly. And I stared equally defiantly back.

"I respect the Second Amendment," I said. "I respect the average American's right to defend themselves in their own homes with a firearm, if they need to. That is a totally different issue from what we're talking about today. It's got nothing to do with that right whatsoever."

And it doesn't. The Founding Fathers didn't imagine deranged young students slaughtering fellow Americans in movie theaters when they drew up the Second Amendment. They imagined people having muskets to defend themselves against an invading army such as the British.

Well, let's get real here. The British aren't going to be invading America again anytime soon. Nor is anybody else, given that the United States has half the world's military firepower, including a reputed five thousand nuclear weapons.

And if, as some Americans believe, they need weapons to protect themselves against their own government turning tyrannical against them, let me point out the bleeding obvious: a few assault rifles aren't going to be much good against a nuke.

I came off air feeling utterly incensed.

"That was brilliantly handled," Jonathan said. "You were angry but not too angry, and you argued your point really well."

"I wanted to punch him," I replied.

"I know. I'm glad you didn't. You know something—I think you found your voice tonight."

A rare moment of levity for the Romneys during an intense,
bruising, and ultimately unsuccessful election campaign.

9

MONDAY, JULY 23, 2012

Perhaps the single bravest, most outspoken politician in America on guns is Michael Bloomberg, New York's mayor.

Tonight he came into my studio and laid into his more cowardly colleagues.

"I think there is a perception in the political world that the NRA has more power than the American people," he said. "I do not believe that."

I asked, "Why do so many Americans not feel angry enough to demand further gun control?"

"Well, I would take it one step further. I don't understand why the police officers across this country don't stand up collectively and say, 'We're going to go on strike. We're not going to protect you. Unless you, the public, through your legislature, do what's required to keep us safe.'

"After all, police officers want to go home to their families. And we're doing everything we can to make their job more difficult but, more importantly, more dangerous, by leaving guns in the hands of people who shouldn't have them, and letting people who have those guns buy things like armor-piercing bullets.

"The only reason to have an armor-piercing bullet is to go through a bullet-resistant vest. The only people who wear bullet-resistant vests are our police officers."

I asked him what the politicians should do to curb gun violence.

"Well, the Supreme Court has held that while it's a constitutional right to bear arms, the government also has the right to have reasonable restrictions. An assault weapon ban would be considered I think by the Supreme Court a reasonable restriction.

"Not selling guns to minors or to people with criminal records, or psychiatric problems, or drug addiction problems, would be reasonable restrictions. So you start out with that.

"Then we can have guns but not every kind of gun. I think everybody wants to preserve the right of people that want to use guns for sport, hunting, or target practice. But that doesn't mean that you have an assault weapon. That doesn't mean you have a rifle that's advertised as able to bring down a commercial airliner at a mile and a half, or bullets that are designed to go through bullet-resistant vests."

Then he said:

"I think the first question you might want to ask, if you could get the two presidential candidates sitting here across from you, would be: 'Why, Governor Romney, did you sign a bill outlawing the sale of assault weapons when you were governor of Massachusetts, but today don't believe it's the right thing? What changed your mind?'

" 'Why, President Obama, did you campaign three years ago on a promise to try to enact legislation that would ban assault rifles, assault weapons? What changed your mind? Why did you not during the last three years do anything?'

"And I think it's incumbent on them to explain what changed their minds."

One of the more stupid arguments gun rights people spout is that there's no point banning guns because bad guys will always find a way to get one.

The same argument could apply to terrorists, but nobody even suggests that.

"Can you imagine," said Bloomberg, "if there was a disease that we caught all of a sudden, some epidemiologist found a plague that was going to kill forty-eight thousand people in this country in the next four years? I suspect that there would be a lot of yelling and screaming and demanding, and everybody would want to vote money and personnel to try to stop it. This is exactly the same thing. Except we're not doing it."

I asked him to explain *his* interpretation of the Second Amendment text.

"I wasn't there, but we have a mechanism under our Constitution that the Founding Fathers put in to answer exactly that question. It's called the Supreme Court. The judicial system, up to the Supreme Court. And the Supreme Court has ruled that you have a right to bear arms, but reasonable restrictions can be applied in terms of the kind of arms, the number of arms, who can buy them.

"And that's what really matters. It doesn't matter what you think or I think. It matters what the Supreme Court thinks and what the legislature does.

"And you come back to the history of the country. We started out with our muskets. And today here we are where some people think everybody should be armed. There was a congressman that I heard quoted as saying, 'If we had armed everybody in that theater, then somebody would have pulled a gun and shot the young kid who killed twelve people and injured fifty-odd.' I don't know that you would want to have your kids in that theater when everybody starts shooting. It's a circular firing squad.

"We just cannot continue this kind of carnage. Now, someday there will be a shooting, which you would think would trigger in the American psyche this 'I'm not going to take it anymore' attitude—"

"I thought it would be this," I interjected.

"Wait a second. Maybe if you shot a president. But Ronald Reagan when he got shot didn't trigger it. Maybe if you shot a congresswoman. No. Maybe if you shot a bunch of students on campus. No. Maybe if you shot a bunch of people in a movie theater. I don't know what it is. We obviously haven't gotten there yet. But we just cannot continue."

He's right, what the hell *will* it take?

TUESDAY, JULY 24, 2012

Michael Moore vowed not to give TV interviews in the aftermath of any mass shooting, following the release of his stunning movie *Bowling for Columbine*.

But the Aurora shooting compelled him to break that vow on my show tonight.

And to my surprise, given he's an arch-Democrat, he blamed both sides of the political divide.

"I think that both conservatives and liberals are half right on this issue," he said. "The conservatives when they say guns don't kill people. I would alter that to 'Guns don't kill people, Americans kill people.' We do this more than anybody else. Of the twenty-three richest countries, over eighty percent of all gun murders happen in one country: ours.

"The left, liberals, believe that if we just have more gun control laws, all the problems are going to go away. Well, I don't think so. Yes, it will be reduced. There's no question about that. If that individual in Aurora had had not so many magazines, not so many bullets, not so many people would have been shot. There's no question that less guns will mean less murders.

"But it won't really get rid of the larger problem of our culture. What is it about us as Americans? You know, we're not any better or worse than you Brits, or the Japanese, or the Canadians.

"Yet in Japan, less than seven gun murders every year. In Canada, about two hundred. In the UK, around forty a year, in a nation of about seventy million people.

"So why here? Why us? You can't say it's because of the violent movies and the violent video games. Because I got to tell you, those Canadian kids right across the river from Detroit, they're watching the same violent movies and playing the same violent video games.

"And yet in that city across from Detroit, most years they have one, maybe zero, murders a year, in Windsor, Ontario."

"In Japan," I pointed out, "they made it law in 1958 that no person shall possess a firearm. The complete opposite, in other words, from America's right to bear arms. And Japan has barely any gun crime as a result."

"Yes, and we hear people say about Americans, we have this violent past. Well, Japan, violent past. Germany, violent past maybe? A history of maybe one thousand, two thousand years from the Huns to the Nazis. Very violent people. And yet they don't kill each other now. They don't shoot each other with guns.

"Why is that? What is it about us that wants to do this?"

It's a great question.

WEDNESDAY, JULY 25, 2012

I discovered today that Kinder Surprise eggs are banned from American stores, including Walmart, because of the risk to one's health from choking on the tiny toys inside them.

I'm also prohibited from purchasing more than six packets of Sudafed (in case I'm building a secret drug factory), and a variety of French cheeses (for bacteria-infective reasons).

Yet many of those same stores, again including Walmart, stock myriad guns including AR-15 assault rifles.

I'm sure there's a logical explanation for why a Kinder egg is deemed more dangerous than an AR-15. There has to be, right?

THURSDAY, JULY 26, 2012

Mitt Romney's in London for a brief Olympics stopover, and ran into immediate trouble by expressing concern over whether London was ready, questioning the public's enthusiasm for the big sporting event, and "security issues" in particular.

These have been the exact same criticisms hurled at Olympic organizers by many in Britain for the last month. But that's not the point—you don't visit someone's house for dinner and lambast the quality of their curtains, even if they don't like the curtains themselves.

I interviewed him at an outdoor venue next to the River Thames.

When we started, two hazards immediately reared their ugly heads: 1) it was very windy, sending Romney's hair into a permanent tailspin, not a cool look for a usually immaculately groomed would-be president, and 2) the skies were buzzing with helicopters flying on and off the nearby battleship HMS *Ocean*, causing filming to constantly stop and start, usually at a crucial moment.

To his credit, though, he saw the funny side.

"I'll have to deal with worse than wild hair and noisy choppers if I become president!"

Romney seemed more uptight than the last two times I'd interviewed him, which is hardly surprising given the stakes of this election campaign.

His attitude to guns was curious given he once signed an assault weapons ban.

"If you had a law saying guns were going to be regulated in some way that would end gun violence, there might be some merit to having that discussion. But the truth is there's no particular change to the law that's going to keep people who are intent on doing harm from doing harm."

"Shouldn't a political leader be the one that says actually we're going to do whatever it takes to make it as difficult as possible?" I replied, exasperated. "That's what we do with terrorism."

"I respect the right of the people to bear arms for any legal purpose. The real question is, what things can we do to prevent the kinds of tragedy from occurring that we saw? And the answer is to find people who are distressed and deranged and evil and do our very best to find them, to cure them, to help them, to keep them from being able to do harm."

"But this guy, James Holmes, the shooter in Aurora, wouldn't have been picked up by anything," I said. "He had no history of mental illness. He had no history of criminality. He was able to buy four weapons, including this assault rifle. Then on the Internet, thousands of rounds of ammunition. And a gun cartridge that could hold a hundred bullets, which enabled him to fire at seventy people in a matter of a minute or two. And I say to you, where is the movement now by political leaders in America to mean that there can't be another guy who can do that as easily?"

Romney looked just as exasperated as me.

"If he didn't have a gun, he'd have used a bomb! The idea that somehow the instrument of violence, if one can make it illegal, would keep a person from doing something illegal, is not a policy that actually will be successful."

Not with that attitude from a potential president, it won't!

I remembered Michael Bloomberg's question.

"When you were governor of Massachusetts, you extended a ban on these kinds of assault weapons because you felt there was a qualitative difference between shooting and hunting and the guns you need for that, and having guns where the only capability appears to be mass killing."

"Actually in Massachusetts," he replied, "we had the progun lobby and the antigun lobby come together and fashion a bill that both thought was an advance. So it was supported by both sides of the debate. That's one reason why I was able to support that."

"So if President Obama called you up and said, look, we need to get together in the wake of this worst ever shooting and do a compromise deal that makes it more difficult for people, would you at least in principle be happy to have that conversation?"

"Piers," he said firmly, "I don't support new gun laws in our country."

FRIDAY, JULY 27, 2012

Sad news. Jim Walton has resigned.

He's been a great president as far as I'm concerned—a smart, kind, and loyal man, who's been here for thirty years, since CNN started.

But the network's had a rough time in the ratings this year, mainly due to the markedly slower news cycle than last year's mayhem, and I guess he's falling on his sword for it.

SATURDAY, JULY 28, 2012

It emerged today that the AR-15 assault rifle, as used by Aurora shooter James Holmes, and his hundred-bullet magazine were both outlawed under a previous assault weapons ban signed by President Clinton in 1994. But in 2004, the ban expired and was not renewed.

The reason?

Numerous Democrats lost their seats after voting for the assault weapons ban in 1994, because the NRA aggressively targeted them with negative ads.

In fact, so many of them were forced out that the Democrats lost control of the House.

And that's why they're all so terrified of the NRA today.

SUNDAY, AUGUST 5, 2012

A white supremacist entered a Sikh temple in Wisconsin today, and shot dead six worshippers, wounding four others—including a policeman.

Once again, the gun rights lobby was quick to defend their "right to bear arms."

They always come out fighting in the immediate aftermath of these mass shootings, suppressing any cries for tighter gun control by just making more noise than their opponents.

The big question for America is whether, after the presidential election on November 6, Barack Obama or Mitt Romney will have the guts to stand up, say so, and do something about it.

I see absolutely zero will on either's part to do so.

MONDAY, AUGUST 20, 2012

A Republican congressman called Todd Akin has caused outrage by claiming women can't get pregnant from "legitimate rape" because their bodies instinctively rebel against the attacker.

We booked him to appear on my show tonight, but his representative pulled him out at the last minute, citing "scheduling issues."

So we replaced him with an empty chair, and I explained it to viewers by saying: "We booked Congressman Akin to tell his story himself. We kept *our* word. I'm here. But Rex Elsass, who's the political consultant to Congressman Akin, did not keep his. He pulled the interview at the last possible moment, having agreed to it on his behalf, leaving us and you looking at an empty chair. It's a very nice empty chair but it remains an empty chair. Why would he say yes, then no? We can only speculate.

"Congressman, you have an open invitation to join me in that chair whenever you feel up to it. Because if you don't keep your promise to appear on the show, then you are what we would call in Britain a gutless little twerp."

Within minutes, both "twerp" and "empty chair" were trending on Twitter.

TUESDAY, AUGUST 21, 2012

Prince Harry has been caught partying naked with a vast coterie of young ladies in his Las Vegas hotel suite, sparking an absurd new "privacy" debate.

Hard to feel that sorry for him.

If you're one of the senior heirs to the British throne, and you invite fifteen complete strangers to play nude billiards with you in your Vegas suite, then I think it's fair to say your expectation of privacy should be about the same as if you perform a moonie on the roof of Buckingham Palace—which Harry probably has at some point in his life.

WEDNESDAY, AUGUST 22, 2012

I've interviewed a lot of big, tough men, but few have looked more capable of handling themselves than the rapper LL Cool J.

He's a thoroughly nice chap, but built like the Hoover Dam and famously honed his fighting skills on the mean streets of Queens in New York.

In the early hours of this morning, he was the victim of a burglary at his L.A. home while his wife and children slept upstairs.

Well, when I say "victim," the police report made me laugh out loud:

"Mr. Smith [LL's legal name is James Smith]," it read, "confronted the intruder in his kitchen. The intruder, Jonathan Kirby, suffered a broken nose, jaw, and ribs. Mr. Smith was uninjured."

THURSDAY, AUGUST 30, 2012

I'm at the Republican National Convention in Tampa, Florida, and was doing a live hit with Wolf Blitzer inside the convention center this afternoon when the formal presentation of the colors began on stage behind us, followed by the Pledge of Allegiance and "Star-Spangled Banner."

Everyone began to stand up, but we were both strapped into our chairs with microphones.

I wasn't entirely sure what the protocol was in this situation, so I waited for Wolf to take the lead, as he was bound to know.

But confusion reigned.

"Do we stand?" Wolf asked the control room. "Because we need to disconnect all our mics if we stand."

As we sat there, slightly trapped, people looking down from the seats above us began heckling loudly.

"Stand up, Wolf and Piers! Show some respect! Shame on CNN!"

This was getting very awkward, especially when the band began playing the "Star-Spangled Banner."

The protests grew significantly louder, and nastier.

"Wolf, we've got to stand now . . ." I whispered.

"I know, let's just do it."

We ripped off our mics and stood up, by which time the anthem had already been playing for around twenty seconds.

A YouTube clip appeared later, showing the whole thing as it happened.

Not our finest moment. But not even the most awkward microphone-related moment of my day, as it transpired.

Each night at the convention, I've been anchoring a live show at midnight from the Grill, a rather fancy makeshift bar that CNN set up in a tent. Tonight, all my worst fears about broadcasting live from a bar came to fruition.

The plan was for me to interview a few guests at the top of the show from one area, then get up and walk to the bar itself, and interview a few more there.

Unfortunately, I'd forgotten that I was strapped into my chair with various microphone wires and cables. With the cameras still on me, I broke out of the chair, and disconnected the link between me and the control room in New York.

To compound the problem, we then suffered a second catastrophic technical breakdown, meaning we lost every camera apart from one, sitting on the shoulder of a guy walking with me.

This, in broadcasting terms, is like walking naked around Times Square. It feels good for about five seconds, then you realize you're on your own, and exposed as you've never been before . . .

I walked to the bar, sat at a table, and winged it reasonably successfully with my guest, Jon Voight, for the next ten minutes as our engineers raced to resolve the problem.

Finally, Jonathan burst back into my ear, shrieking like a banshee (his decibel levels in the control room during live shows have been known to rattle windows in New Jersey).

"PIERS! PIERS! Can you hear me?"

"Unfortunately, I can now, yes . . ." I replied calmly.

"Thank *fuck*!" he wailed.

"Actually, I found that all quite liberating," I said, and laughed. "Maybe we should cut out the middleman and do that every night . . ."

"Yeah, and maybe I should find an anchor who doesn't forget he's strapped into a chair!"

FRIDAY, AUGUST 31, 2012

Clint Eastwood was booked by Mitt Romney's team to make a brief five-minute warm-up last night to the party faithful before the nominee's big speech.

Instead, he rambled on for eleven minutes, most of the time interviewing an empty chair—pretending it was Barack Obama.

The whole thing was excruciating. Like watching a mad uncle make an impromptu train-wreck "tribute" to the bride at a wedding.

But it was still flattering to see Clint steal one of my ideas.

"What did we learn tonight?" someone tweeted tonight. "That Piers Morgan is much better at talking to an empty chair than Clint Eastwood."

WEDNESDAY, SEPTEMBER 5, 2012

One of the more self-defeatingly inexplicable laws in America is the Twenty-second Amendment, which states no American president can serve more than two terms in office.

This meant that Bill Clinton, for me the best U.S. president in my lifetime, had to give up the reins at the peak of his powers.

He remains an extraordinary political force though, as he showed tonight at the Democratic convention with a speech so rich in oratory, charm, and bite that it had the rare effect of reducing the media to the same fawning, simpering, cheering ranks as the audience.

Clinton brilliantly articulated the best argument for why Barack Obama should be reelected—despite America's continued economic woes and chronic unemployment—and did so way more effectively than Obama himself has done throughout the campaign so far.

"If you want every American to vote and you think it is wrong to change voting procedures just to reduce the turnout of younger, poorer, minority, and disabled voters—you should support Barack Obama."

As the audience roared, he continued:

"I love our country so much. People have predicted our demise ever since George Washington was criticized for being a mediocre surveyor with a bad set of wooden false teeth. And so far, every single person that's bet against America has lost money because we always come back. We decide to champion the cause for which our founders pledged their lives, their fortunes, their sacred honor—the cause of forming a more perfect union."

His voice rising to new heights of power and emotion, he then virtually yelled: "My fellow Americans, if that is what you want, if that is what you believe, you must vote and you must reelect President Barack Obama."

On cue, Obama walked on stage and the two men hugged.

They're never going to be best buddies, but they both need each other.

SUNDAY, SEPTEMBER 9, 2012

Tonight I was watching the Paralympics closing ceremony in London on TV, when Rihanna suddenly bounced up on stage sporting a weirdly unflattering new short-cropped elfin hairstyle.

Before I could stop myself, I tweeted: "Rihanna needs to grow her hair back. Fast."

As soon as she came off stage, she retweeted my comment with the simple yet devastating observation: "Grow a dick . . . *fast!*"

"Is this a good time to ask for an interview?" I replied.

"Haaaaa!" shot back Rihanna. "Only if it's not about cosmetics! But phuck yea let's do it!"

Booked, however incredibly.

WEDNESDAY, SEPTEMBER 19, 2012

I've now completed six hundred shows at CNN, which leaves me a mere sixty-four hundred behind Larry King (gulp . . .). In that time, I've had one person walk out on me, Christine O'Donnell, and one not turn up at all, Todd Akin—whom we replaced with an empty chair.

What I've never had, until tonight, is someone turn up and then walk out before the interview even starts.

The culprit was *Frasier* TV legend Kelsey Grammer.

What made it so bizarre was that I interviewed him last year and we got on so well, he greeted me backstage tonight with a cheery smile and the words: "I returned because I liked the last interview so much!"

We exchanged further pleasantries (he also became the father of a baby girl recently) before I walked into my studio and began the first half of the live show, which featured U.S. presidential election coverage.

Then, after twenty minutes or so, Jonathan uttered the immortal words: "Kelsey has left the building."

Given that Mr. Grammer was supposed to be the second half of the show, and we had no plan B, this was a rather unsettling turn of events.

"Is he coming back?" I whispered frantically.

"We don't think so."

It transpired that he'd been standing in the green room a few minutes before 9 P.M., and saw a rehearsal on the monitor of a pretaped opening to the show. It featured a tease for his interview, including a photo (one of five we used in the tease) of him with his ex-wife, Camille.

They've been through a bitter, very public divorce recently, but Kelsey had told our producers he was quite happy to answer questions about her.

Apparently this generosity didn't extend to a picture of her too.

"I want that picture removed," he demanded.

But it was literally too late to do it before we went on air.

The moment Kelsey saw Camille's photo flash up on screen at the top of the show, he began ranting and raving at my staff in an astonishingly rude manner. Then he left.

I decided the only thing to do was inform the viewers of what had happened.

"Kelsey Grammer was due to be on by now," I said, "but he appears to have left the building. We're not quite sure what's going on.

"He was here. I spoke to him. And he was happily looking forward to coming on. But he has exited stage left. So we have half an hour left. He may or may not come back. We shall see."

Fortunately, I had two smart, adaptable guests in Nick Kristof and Larry Kudlow with me. In the next commercial break, I asked them: "Could you possibly stick around, chaps?"

To my huge relief, they both said yes.

Kelsey never returned.

I came off set absolutely steaming. And grew even angrier when I learned just how rude he'd been to the team.

But that anger turned to incandescence when Stan Rosenfield, his publicist, and someone who's always been a good friend to the show, put out a statement saying: "Piers needs to take responsibility for what he did to Kelsey. It's called accountability."

SUNDAY, SEPTEMBER 23, 2012

The world's leaders are all gathering in New York this week for two of the biggest political events of the year—the United Nations General Assembly and the Clinton Global Initiative.

None will attract more interest than the president of Iran, Mahmoud Ahmadinejad—a man who inspires more fear and loathing in America than anyone alive since the deaths of Saddam, Gaddafi, and bin Laden.

This morning, thanks to the persistence of one of my bookers, Lisa Thompson, I landed his first major TV interview in America in a year.

Security around his hotel, the Warwick in midtown Manhattan, was insane.

Once inside, I sat waiting for half an hour as his staff finalized their boss's interview requirements.

His three main ones were: 1) the air-conditioning was to be turned off; 2) the lighting on his face was to be softened; and 3) most amusingly, the gold-shaded doorknobs on the cabinet in the backdrop of the set were to be removed as they were "too flashy."

Then, around 11 A.M., his vast entourage of at least forty people suddenly swept in and there, in the middle, was the president himself.

Ahmadinejad is a small, wiry, dark-eyed man.

He shook my hand with a beaming grin, and made a peace sign with his hands.

Certainly no fool—he's a scholar—he's a skilled political operator whose trick in interviews (from ones I had watched) is to avoid giving any direct answers to direct questions, and to keep talking for as long as you let him, eating up as much airtime as possible.

Like most despots, he's a weird mixture of charm, ruthlessness, outrageous opinions, and a very sinister stare.

It's not easy interviewing him because he claims not to speak English, so your questions are translated and his replies are then translated back into your earpiece.

This gives him plenty of time to plan answers, of course. And I suspect his English is perfectly adequate for Western interviews if he wanted it to be.

"Mr. President," I began, "welcome to New York. Many Americans see you as public enemy number one. How do you feel about that?"

He replied in Farsi, and I waited at least a minute for the translator to repeat it in English.

"The Creator, the Almighty, and most gracious and the most merciful, good morning to you. I wish to greet all of the wonderful people of the United States and all of the people who will see your program. At the end of the day, if you do have personal animosity toward me, don't transfer that on to the rest of the people of the United States. We love the people of the United States and they also wish in return peace and stability for all of the world."

Hilarious!

After discussing the Arab Spring uprisings, the revolt in Syria, and the wars in Iraq and Afghanistan, I turned to his infamous quote that he wants Israel "wiped off the face of the map."

"There have been many different interpretations of what you said. You have disputed the meaning that was then translated from the original Farsi. Let me give you this opportunity to say exactly what you did say, and to say exactly what you did mean."

He smiled and made a short speech that didn't even allude to the question I'd asked.

"The question wasn't any of that," I persisted. "The question was do you believe that Israel should—"

"I will get to that answer. Don't be in such a hurry."

"Should Israel be wiped off the face of the map? Is that your desire?"

"If a group comes and occupies the United States of America, destroys homes while women and children are in those homes, incarcerates the youth of America, imposes five different wars on many neighbors, and always threatens others, what would you do?" he replied. "What would you say? Would you help it? Would you help that entity? Or would you help the people of the United States? So when we say 'to be wiped,' we say for occupation to be wiped off from this world, for war-seeking to be wiped off and eradicated, the killing of women and children to be eradicated. And we propose the way. We propose the path. The path is to recognize the right of the Palestinians to self-governance. Allow the people of Palestine to make decisions regarding their own future. Imagine one day in Palestine there is no longer occupation, occupation no longer exists in Palestine."

No denial of that original quote, I mentally noted.

Next, I pressed him on his persistent intimations that the Holocaust never took place.

"Do you believe that the Holocaust happened?"

"The historic events that you speak of, I have two questions. I've had two questions for quite some time, never received an answer to either one. Everywhere they allow a certain amount of research, of looking into historical events. Whenever there are obstacles placed on this path, then a question mark or two will arise. Why such obstacles?"

"What are the questions that you have about the Holocaust?" I asked.

"Why in Europe has it been forbidden for anyone to conduct any research about this event? Why are researchers in prison?"

"There has been extensive research into the Holocaust. It is indisputable that over six million Jews were annihilated by Adolf Hitler and the Nazis. The question is, do you dispute that six million Jews were killed?"

"Do you believe in the freedom of thought and ideas, or no?"

"I believe in facts."

"And the freedom of research, do you believe in that and allow that, or no?"

"You're a very intelligent man. Do you believe that six million Jews were annihilated by Adolf Hitler and the Nazis? Do you believe that as a fact?"

"You pose a question and are willing to only hear what you want me to say."

"It's a simple answer, isn't it?"

"Do you want my answer or the answer that you want me to give?"

"You either believe it or you don't."

"Your answers and your thoughts seem to be quite clear on this. Why do you wish to impose your opinion on me?" he said.

"I believe it is an inarguable fact that six million Jews were killed in the war by Adolf Hitler and the Nazis. I'm merely asking you, as the president of Iran, do you believe that six million Jews were killed by the Nazis, or do you think that it's not true?"

"So in other words, I must accept the premise of your question in order to give you the answer? That's a dictatorship."

The sheer ludicrous irony of this statement was almost beyond parody.

"No, you either believe six million Jews were killed or you don't."

"You asked me a question."

"Yes or no. Yes, I believe it, or no, I don't."

"So, you see, what you're doing is you're seeking a response based on my thoughts. Why do you even care the origin, what the origin of my thoughts are?"

"The reason I care is because part of the damage to your reputation among Americans is because they believe that you question the validity of the Holocaust. So I'm simply asking you to state very clearly and simply whether you believe over six million Jews were killed by the Nazis in the war or not. And the answer is either yes or no. It's not a difficult question."

"I thank you for caring so much about me. And I do believe that it is commonplace for an interviewer to pose a question and wait for the proper response to be completed. If you keep wanting to interrupt me, it's not an issue, it's your show, here you are, and there's the camera."

He was smirking at me, challenging me to continue pressing him. It was both threatening and mocking, and undeniably intimidating. My heart began beating a little faster, and I could feel sweat building on my neck. It's not often you find yourself in an eyeball-to-eyeball confrontation with one of the world's most feared men.

But this was no time to blink first.

"Forgive me for my impertinence. I will allow you to answer in any way you see fit."

"I pass no judgment about historic events. I say researchers and scholars must be free to conduct research and analysis about any historical events, and have contrary opinion, pro and con. Why should a researcher be put in jail, one question? Question number two. Let's assume your parameter is right, your question is right. Your assumption is that this event took place. Where did it take place? Who were the individuals responsible for this event? What does this have to do with the occupation of Palestine? What role did the people of Palestine play in this event? These are very clear and transparent questions, sir. The third question I have, if a historical event has indeed taken place, why so much sensitivity surrounding it by politicians?"

At no stage in this lengthy exchange did Ahmadinejad ever say he thought the Holocaust happened.

His evasiveness gave me, and the viewer at home, the only answer we needed.

Things got even more heated over gay rights.

He ranted about how homosexuality was "very ugly behavior" that would "cease procreation" and insisted people became, and were not born, gay.

"Do you really believe someone is born homosexual?" he mocked.

"Yes, I absolutely believe that," I replied. And I found myself staring down the "most dangerous man in the world" for several long, slightly unsettling seconds.

I asked how he'd feel if one of his children was gay.

"Proper education must be given! The political system must be revamped. If a group recognizes an ugly behavior or ugly deed as legitimate, you must not expect other countries or other groups to give it the same recognition. This is an imposition of your will, sir!"

"How would you feel if one of your children dated a Jew?"

"I would have to see who that Jewish man or woman would be. I see love among people as completely acceptable. There are many Jews living in Iran with whom we are very close. There are some Muslims that marry into Jewish families or marry Christians. We have no such problems."

I was astonished by this answer, and told him so.

He feigned surprise at my surprise.

"We believe that color, religion, native tongue, ethnic background shouldn't create differences or distances between people," he continued. "Nor should it be the sole reason to bring people closer together."

"Mr. President," I concluded, "how many times have you been properly in love?"

He smirked. "I'm in love with all of humanity!"

Unless they're gay or a member of the Israeli government, presumably.

"God bless you," he said as we parted company. "I wish you success."

And with that, we were done.

MONDAY, SEPTEMBER 24, 2012

Woke to an email from Juliana, containing the following quote from William Gibson: "Before you diagnose yourself with depression or low self-esteem, first make sure that you are not, in fact, just surrounded by assholes."

TUESDAY, SEPTEMBER 25, 2012

I've met Bill Clinton once, for precisely eleven seconds, in a hotel foyer in Blackpool in 1998 as he headed out to speak at the Labour Party Conference.

I was so overexcited, I shouted: "Thank you, Mr. President!"

"For what?" he replied.

"EVERYTHING!"

It summed up how much Brits loved him at the time.

Today, I finally got to interview him, in return for me agreeing to moderate a panel at his Clinton Global Initiative conference.

He bounded into the room and up onto the small stage where I'd later be hosting the panel, looked out to a sea of 150 empty chairs, and burst out laughing. "Wow. I always feared the day would come when I'd end up speaking to an empty room!"

"We tried to sell the seats to people out on the street, Mr. President," I responded, "but you're just not the draw you used to be . . . sorry."

Clinton roared again.

"I know, right? This is the end of the road!"

The interview itself was compelling. He hammered Ahmadinejad and Iran: "So what they're really saying is in spite of the fact that we deny the Holocaust, that we threaten Israel and we demonize the United States, we want you to trust us."

"Do you trust him?" I asked.

"Not on this, I don't."

And then the chilling warning: "Their country, their civilization, their whole history would be destroyed if they ever dropped a bomb on someone, because the retaliation would be incomprehensible."

As I listened to Clinton easing his way through all manner of complex world issues, I bemoaned once again America's Twenty-second Amendment to the Constitution that prohibits any president serving more than two terms.

He remains, comfortably, the smartest, most eloquent and popular politician in the world today.

But perhaps all is not lost.

I suggested he become British prime minister instead, if I managed to force through a rule change, and his eyes lit up.

"There are only two countries I'm eligible to still run for the leadership position—Ireland, because of my Irish heritage. And because I was born in Arkansas, which is part of the Louisiana Purchase, any person anywhere in the world that was born in a place that ever was part of the French empire, if you live in France for six months and speak French, you can run for president."

He chuckled.

"I once polled very well in a French presidential race. And I said, you know, this is great, but that's the best I'd ever do because once they heard my broken French with a southern accent, I would drop into single digits within a week and I'd be toast!"

MONDAY, OCTOBER 1, 2012

Arnold Schwarzenegger has published his autobiography, addressing in painful detail his housekeeper baby scandal and subsequent breakdown of his marriage.

Today, we taped an interview for my show.

I went to see Arnold in the green room, and although friendly, he seemed oddly detached. The same demeanor continued when the interview started. Gone was all the old Schwarzenegger bravado, replaced by a somber, reflective, and astonishingly self-critical version.

"What has it been like to be you in the last year?"

"Everything was perfect," he said with a sigh, "and so all of a sudden, from one day to the next, the personal life totally crashed and I wiped out everything I had, and that thing I cherished most was my personal life, my marriage, my family."

He stared at me, deep sadness etched in his eyes.

"I love Maria, she's been truly the only love I've ever had. And that's what is so pitiful about it. She was the most perfect wife, extraordinary. And I ruined it by doing just about the stupidest thing any human being can do."

"If Maria's watching this," I said, "what would you say to her?"

"I would just say sorry for what I've done. I want to win her back, and I hope she can really forgive."

I looked at this still huge (he told me he still does five hundred sit-ups, an hour's bike ride, and two-hundred-pound weight training every day) yet undeniably diminished man and felt a pang of genuine sympathy.

WEDNESDAY, OCTOBER 3, 2012

The phrase "political earthquake" is often overused.

But tonight saw a real one.

Mitt Romney won the first of three presidential debates, and won it easily.

Where he was confident, Obama seemed oddly flat and unconvincing.

Romney's also been calming down his Tea Party–appeasing rhetoric on issues now that they're fading as a political force, and reverted to his old moderate positions once again. To widespread mockery, he said this week that he wouldn't seek any antiabortion legislation if he became president, a direct contradiction of what he said at the start of the year.

"There's old moderate Mitt!" chortled President Bill Clinton. "Where you been, boy? He shows up with a sunny face and says, 'I didn't say all those things I've been saying the last few years.'"

But how much does Romney's flip-flopping actually matter to the result of the election? Especially as all the polls say the main concern for Americans right now is the economy.

After all, when I asked Bill Clinton during our recent interview if he felt Romney was a "principled man," he smiled and said: "That's not the issue to me."

And I suspect it's not for most voters either. They just want to know which man, Romney or Obama, is going to revive the economy faster.

I don't sense that Americans hate Obama, which is why he may still scrape home despite this shocking night.

But there's definitely a distinct disillusionment about his general performance.

The great messianic tidal wave of optimism that Obama swept in on has been replaced by harsh reality. He promised Americans tremendous "hope" and "change" and, frankly, they don't feel he's given them much hope, nor changed very much.

Obama does deserve plaudits for improving the reputation of America abroad after the war-ridden years of George W. Bush, not least by ending the wars in Iraq and Afghanistan, for saving the U.S. car industry with a successful federal bailout, for bringing thirty million more poor Americans into health insurance, for killing Osama bin Laden, and for pushing down the barriers of homophobia by publicly supporting gay marriage.

But—and it's a big "but"—unemployment is still running at a frighteningly high 7.9 percent, meaning twenty-three million Americans are out of work. Meanwhile, the country's national debt has risen to a staggering

$16 *trillion,* up $5 trillion from when he took over. Add a still severely deflated housing market, and gas prices double where they were in 2008, and it all adds up to a pretty miserable economic picture.

That's where Romney can win. His track record as a businessman is better than almost any presidential candidate ever. He also almost single-handedly turned around the fortunes of the Salt Lake City Winter Olympics in 2002, after the International Olympic Committee chiefs turned to him desperately for help. He sees America as a struggling company, and himself as therefore the perfect person to rescue it.

New Jersey Governor Chris Christie told me during the party's recent convention: "Mitt's not the kind of guy you'd go for a beer with, mainly because he doesn't drink beer. But he's the kind of guy who gets stuff done."

There was great excitement around the world when America elected its first black president in 2008.

The possible election of America's first Mormon president will bring with it far lower expectations.

But that may not be such a bad thing for him, for America, or for the world. Especially if he actually gets things done.

TUESDAY, OCTOBER 9, 2012

One of the more amusing aspects of my CNN job is the sheer variety of guests I interview on a nightly basis.

Never was this better illustrated than this week, when I spent 95 percent of the time grilling politicians about the American election. And the other 5 percent of the time interrogating a collection of vicious, snarling wild animals.

Jack Hanna is one of the world's most famous zookeepers and animal experts. Nicknamed "Jungle Jack," he's an extraordinary character famed for his khaki safari outfits, deep perma-tan, and strong southern accent.

But it wasn't him that I was worried about.

Jack brought over thirty of his animals into my New York studio— ranging from cuddly little owls, beavers, and possums to not-so-cuddly snow leopards, alligators, boa constrictors, and vultures.

Nothing had ever quite prepared me for the tension of sitting in a chair three feet away from a giant cheetah, standing free outside of its cage, with raw hunger in its eyes.

It was massive, snarling, and straining on what looked to me like a rather skimpy leash being held by two smiling female animal trainers.

Jack gave me some cheery advice.

"Now, don't touch him. And remember, he's very quick on his feet—cheetahs can accelerate from zero to seventy mph in three seconds . . ."

"Yes, I'm aware of that . . ."

"Nothing should go wrong, but you never know with cheetahs, so be on your guard, and if he does attack you, just remember that cheetahs go straight for the neck. He'll bite you on the underside of your throat until he suffocates you, or punctures the vital artery in your neck. If he does kill you, then he'll try and devour your flesh as soon as possible before any of the other predators we brought here today can join in. They're quite selfish like that."

Suddenly, the cheetah roared and flew at one of my cameramen. And I mean *flew*.

The trainers both pulled hard on the leash, and somehow managed to stop this giant, seething cat from reaching its lunch—as the cameraman dived for cover.

Jack laughed.

"I think the lights are cranking him up a bit."

Jonathan, hiding in the safety of the control room, laughed: "If this goes wrong, can I have your office?"

FRIDAY, OCTOBER 12, 2012

Interviewed Oscar Pistorius tonight, the brilliant South African Paralympian sprinter with the nickname "Blade Runner."

He was soft-spoken, incredibly polite, and very charming.

But I remembered watching him lose the two-hundred-meter final in London this summer, and exploding with rage by the side of the track afterward because he thought the Brazilian winner had sought an unfair advantage with longer blades.

It was such a shocking outburst that I tweeted after watching it: "Wow, way to destroy your brand, Oscar Pistorius."

I asked him about it tonight, and he admitted: "I saw your tweet, that's OK. It was one of those days, hopefully I won't have another one of those. It's definitely a debate that needed to be brought up, it wasn't the right time to take it up. We all make mistakes. I'm still learning and I'm certainly going to learn a lot more lessons throughout my life."

I asked him how he was dealing with all the female fans he now attracts.

He smiled. "I haven't had much time to think about that. I'm seeing somebody in South Africa, she's a great girl."

After the interview, I asked if he could sign some photos for the boys.

"They're all huge fans," I said. "In fact, my middle son, Stanley, is writing a whole school thesis about how inspiring you are."

"He is? Wow, that's amazing. Please thank him for me."

I sent Stanley a text afterward passing on the message.

"That's so cool, Dad!" he replied. "I love Oscar!"

TUESDAY, OCTOBER 16, 2012

Woke to a touching email from Juliana: "Today is the national day to honor your boss. Thanks so much for being the worst boss ever!"

MONDAY, OCTOBER 29, 2012

Weather forecasts for a monster storm dubbed Hurricane Sandy have grown progressively worse for the New York area over the last few days, and some meteorologists were sounding positively apocalyptic this morning.

"How bad will this be?" I asked Jonathan, self-acclaimed New York weather obsessive.

"Bad," he replied. "They're saying this will be the worst storm ever to hit the city."

The rain started around midday, and the clouds darkened rapidly. I took a cab to CNN around 2 P.M.

An hour after I arrived, an enormous noise, which sounded like a thunderclap, boomed out.

I ran to the window of my office and saw that a giant crane on top of a skyscraper five hundred yards away (a building called One57, which will be New York's tallest residential tower at ninety stories) had buckled, and the top of it was now dangling precariously over the densely populated streets below.

In that moment, it was clear that Sandy was going to be on a different scale from any weather-related episode I'd ever been through before.

As the afternoon wore on, our newsroom lights began to flicker, and our building—the Time Warner Center is one of the biggest, newest, and supposedly strongest multiskyscraper edifices in America—shook and rattled like a cupboard full of steel skeletons.

Rain and wind lashed the windows with ominous velocity, and by 9 P.M., when I went live on air, the full force of Sandy had descended on the city.

What happened in the next hour was mind-boggling.

More than fourteen feet of water surged onto the mainland at the southern tip of Manhattan, swamping the subway system, and flooding the streets so badly that cars began floating away. House facades were ripped off, fires erupted as power lines collapsed (a hundred homes in Queens were destroyed by one blaze alone), thousands of trees smashed down (in a few tragic cases, onto people).

I interviewed numerous ashen-faced governors and mayors from all over the East Coast, all of whom said it was the worst storm they'd ever seen.

Sandy wasn't even that big by hurricane standards, registering only Category 1 for most of its terrifying journey. By comparison, Hurricane Katrina, which ravaged New Orleans in 2005, reached Category 5.

But what made Sandy so devastating was that it collided with an unusually early winter storm coming from the west, a fierce Arctic air coming from the north, and hit New York at the precise moment the city had a high tide and full moon.

It was a perfect storm of hell. Coincidentally, one of my expert guests tonight was Sebastian Junger, who wrote the book *The Perfect Storm,* and he explained why this was even worse than the 1991 monster he dramatized. "Sandy came ashore," he said. "My storm didn't. Big difference."

Later, Chad Myers, CNN's superb meteorologist, reported on my show that the New York Stock Exchange was submerged in three feet of water. This was a sensational development.

Unfortunately, it wasn't true.

Chad had read it on the National Weather Service bulletin board, usually a reliable source of information.

But CNN reporters down near the NYSE phoned in to say there was no sign of any flooding.

I had to correct it on air, and we rightly copped some flak for getting such a hugely important piece of information wrong.

I anchored a second live hour for CNN at midnight, by which time Sandy was on the rampage through Long Island, wreaking havoc everywhere it went.

The sheer scale of the damage was incredible.

I remember the 1987 "Great Storm" in Britain, the last version of a hurricane we suffered back home, and that seemed like a troublesome squall compared to this. (Eighteen people died in our Great Storm, over a hundred died during Sandy—and well over double that number on its lethal route through the Caribbean and Haiti.)

I left the office at 1 A.M. to walk one block up to the Mandarin, where I was staying for the night. The wind was still strong, and it was raining, but there was an eerie kind of calm to the sky now. Sandy was now barreling on to other areas.

From my fortieth-floor hotel room window, I looked down and saw a city of two halves—the lower half, downtown, was plunged into almost total darkness. The upper half, from around Fortieth Street onward, still had power.

I turned on CNN to see shocking scenes from the NYU hospital on the Lower East Side, where the backup generator had (shamefully—they'd had a week to prepare for this) failed, and mothers with newborn babies were being ferried on makeshift respirators down ten flights of stairs to other hospitals on higher ground.

Atlantic City looked almost completely submerged in parts (one of our guys was now reporting from a main boardwalk, up to his waist in seawater), and other parts of New Jersey were even worse.

I finally went to sleep at 3 A.M., exhausted and slightly shell-shocked.

TUESDAY, OCTOBER 30, 2012

Woke at 6 A.M., and caught up with all the aftermath of Sandy's appalling rampage. Millions of homes are without power on the East Coast, the subway may be out for a week, all airports and schools are closed for at least two days, the Stock Exchange shut for a second day, and the death toll is rising by the hour.

I walked home at 9 A.M. in surprisingly mild conditions. New Yorkers were back out walking their dogs, jogging, and doing everything they'd usually be doing on a Tuesday morning, except drinking Starbucks, which remained closed.

Outside my apartment, trees had fallen onto almost all the cars in the street (I don't have a car here—there's no point driving in New York). But the only damage we'd suffered was a broken flowerpot on the terrace.

We were the lucky ones.

Returned to the office late in the afternoon, and we had an inquest into the faulty NYSE flooding report last night.

It's always serious when CNN reports a significant piece of information like that, which transpires to be wrong. Our brand is "the most trusted name in news," and people turn to us in huge numbers on these stories because they expect us to report the facts.

It's one of the great advantages we have over rivals at Fox and MSNBC, who have reputations for partisan reporting.

Chad is an excellent, very experienced correspondent, and he had clearly reported the NYSE flooding story in good faith, but Jonathan and I agreed that I should have said something like, "Whoa, that's a huge development if it's true. CNN hasn't independently verified this story yet. We'll try to do that now," after he said it, to cover ourselves.

There are always going to be mistakes on big running breaking news stories; such is the fog of information.

But it's better to wait a few minutes and be right, than to rush to be first. Or cover any such claim with transparent qualification.

The NYSE story could have had major global financial repercussions had I not corrected it on air very quickly.

FRIDAY, NOVEMBER 2, 2012

Barack Obama has seen a spike in his poll numbers since the hurricane, which is hardly surprising given that he's dominated the airwaves, leading the country through a crisis—as poor Romney has been forced to sit in the shadows, cursing his luck.

Sandy may have changed everything.

There are two famous quotes from former British prime ministers that every politician needs to have tattooed on his or her forehead from birth.

Harold Macmillan, asked by a journalist in the late 1950s what he thought was most likely to knock his Conversative government off course, replied: "Events, my dear boy, events."

A few years later, Labour leader Harold Wilson came up with his own version: "A week is a long time in politics."

This is just about the worst thing that could have happened to Romney. Why?

Because it removed the election from the top of the news agenda in America for most of this crucial final ten days, meaning he's barely had any TV airtime for his campaign just when he needs it most.

Conversely, Obama's been seen giving orders, hugging victims, flying in Marine One over flooded areas, and giving press conferences in army jackets. In short, he behaved exactly like a president should behave.

Obama's been undeniably impressive. And there's nothing Romney can do about it.

Even worse for the candidate, the most popular Republican in the country, Chris Christie, has poured ecstatic praise on Obama—saying repeatedly what a brilliant job he's done throughout the disaster.

This is the same Chris Christie, of course, who's spent the past six months telling Americans what a terrible president he thinks Obama has been.

"This administration, at the moment, could give a damn about election day, it doesn't matter a lick to me, I've got much bigger fish to fry than that. I only care about what's happening to people in my state," Christie said, standing next to Obama at a disaster site.

It was a powerful display of nonpartisan politics. And absolutely the right thing to do with regard to the people of New Jersey, whom he was elected to represent. Yet at the same time, it's obviously been deeply unhelpful to Romney's electoral chances.

Despite all this, the polls are so tight it remains too close to call.

Mitt Romney may still pinch the election.

And if he does, it will be because Americans concluded they trust him more than Obama to revive the ailing economy.

But it wouldn't surprise me if come Wednesday morning, we now see Romney stranded at a drive-in, branded a fool, crying: "Sandy, Sandy, why, oh Sandy?"

MONDAY, NOVEMBER 5, 2012

The final Gallup and CNN swing state polls have the election race a dead heat.

But Nate Silver, a *New York Times* number-crunching blogger, has consistently forecast an easy Obama victory throughout the entire campaign, and says he's seen nothing in all his stats to change his mind.

His confidence is extraordinary.

WEDNESDAY, NOVEMBER 7, 2012

Barack Obama won the election last night.

In the end, it was nowhere near as close as the polls suggested. But almost exactly how Nate Silver had predicted.

There's no doubt that Sandy helped him tremendously, by knocking Romney out of the news agenda.

But I think Americans went for Obama again primarily because they bought into his repeated assertion that he inherited an unprecedented financial mess from George W. Bush and simply needs more time to repair all the damage.

They also just like him personally more than Romney, a man who never shrugged off his reputation as a rich, out-of-touch businessman who neither fully understands nor cares for the concerns of ordinary Americans.

Obama's not perfect, and has failed to fulfill much of his huge promise so far. But he's been given a second chance, and I hope he makes the most of it.

Ronald Reagan and Bill Clinton, two of the most popular presidents in history, both had rough first terms, then enjoyed a thriving economy in their second terms, which encouraged them to be bolder in their leadership—and they ended up heroes.

Crying children being led away from Sandy Hook Elementary School—twenty of their classmates were shot dead that day.

10

General David Petraeus sensationally resigned as director of the CIA today over a sex scandal involving an extramarital affair with his biographer, Paula Broadwell.

America can be a peculiarly puritanical place for a country so famed for defending freedom, and the revelation of Petraeus's infidelity has sparked the usual cacophony of moral indignation.

It's exactly the kind of outrage I'd have certainly embraced in my old tabloid editor days. But today, perhaps enlightened by my years in the real world, I'm not so sure.

Yes, Petraeus behaved badly, but really that's a matter for him and his wife to resolve unless it emerges there were genuinely serious security issues.

The bottom line is that America's lost one of its most brilliant military stars just when the country's security needs men like him most.

Three of the nation's greatest generals—Eisenhower, MacArthur, and Patton—all had affairs. As did great presidents like Roosevelt, Kennedy, and Clinton.

All were famed as bold, risk-taking high achievers.

MONDAY, NOVEMBER 12, 2012

Most depressing news since Obama's reelection is that gun sales have been soaring in America because of it.

In October alone, as polls began to suggest he might win again, background checks on people applying to buy guns rose by 18.4 percent.

The stock price of weapons manufacturers like Smith & Wesson surged too, especially since last Tuesday's result came in—due to massively increased demand.

The reason?

Simple.

Obama indicated during one of the presidential debates that he might bring in tougher gun control laws relating to high-powered assault weapons.

That was enough to trigger a mad sprint for guns.

Mel Bernstein, owner of the Dragonman gun store in Colorado Springs, said it all: "We're going from normally six to eight guns a day to twenty-five. I stocked up. I got a stockpile of these AK-47s, we're selling these like hotcakes."

It was in nearby Aurora, Colorado, of course, that James Holmes shot seventy people in a movie theater, killing twelve of them.

One of his four weapons was a Smith & Wesson semiautomatic rifle.

SUNDAY, NOVEMBER 18, 2012

CNN's medical expert Sanjay Gupta presented a show tonight on America's reliance on medication. It contained one astonishing statistic: 80 percent of the pain pills in the world are taken in the U.S.

That means a lot of pain, a lot of drug abuse, or a lot of hypochondria.

MONDAY, NOVEMBER 19, 2012

The Middle East has blown up in rockets and flames again, this time back in that most persistently inflammable of tinderboxes—Gaza.

The ongoing conflict between Israel and the Palestinians has always been the running sore of the region.

I've interviewed many senior figures on either side of this divide and both groups have compelling arguments: Israel abhors the relentless bombing of its people by what it views as Palestinian terror groups, led by Hamas. The Palestinians abhor what they see as Israel's equally relentless land grab of their territory, and oppression—through blockades—of so many of their people, particularly in the densely populated area of the Gaza strip.

But as was proved in Northern Ireland, seemingly implacable enemies can eventually be brought to peace—if there's genuinely courageous political leadership, and the will of the majority of the people behind it.

Tonight I interviewed Israel's president, Shimon Peres. He's an extraordinary man, who will be ninety next year, is the oldest legally appointed head of state in the world, and has served in twelve cabinets during a gargantuan military and political career spanning sixty-six years.

His face is creased with age, but his mind is as sharp as ever.

He was blunt about what needed to happen. "They [Hamas] must stop shooting, and start talking."

When I pointed out that the Israelis have fired numerous missiles into Gaza themselves this week, killing over a hundred people, he replied calmly: "We would appreciate if one of our critics will suggest an alternative. What can we do?"

It's a good question.

But he then asserted: "There is no siege in fact about or around Gaza, the roads are open, we don't think there is any shortage of food, or any other human needs. Their economic situation has improved."

All of which is palpable nonsense. Gaza's a desperately poor, hopeless place, crammed with 1.7 million suffering people.

In the end, I suspect lasting peace will only be achieved when—as the British government had to do with the IRA in Ireland—the Israelis bite the bullet, literally, and sit down and negotiate directly with the leaders of Hamas.

THURSDAY, NOVEMBER 29, 2012

Jeff Zucker has been announced as the new president of CNN.

You couldn't make it up!

MONDAY, DECEMBER 3, 2012

Bob Costas, the voice of American sports, has sparked controversy by using his halftime NBC segment in last night's NFL game to make a heartfelt statement about guns.

His decision followed the murder-suicide of a Kansas City Chiefs linebacker called Jovan Belcher, who shot dead Kasandra Perkins, the mother of his three-month-old daughter, then himself.

Costas quoted a Kansas writer called Jason Whitlock, who wrote: "Our current gun culture ensures that more and more domestic disputes will end in the ultimate tragedy. Handguns do not enhance our safety, they exacerbate our flaws, tempt us to escalate arguments, and bait us into embracing confrontation rather than avoiding it. If Jovan Belcher didn't possess a gun, he and Kasandra Perkins would both be alive today."

Costas has been attacked for "being political" during a football game.

But he just told the truth, however unpalatable it may be to many Americans.

Guns do not make the country safer, they make it more dangerous.

TUESDAY, DECEMBER 4, 2012

A staggering thirty-eight people were shot in fifty-eight hours over the weekend in Chicago.

The issue there is a very particular one involving mainly young black gang members killing each other with handguns.

Chicago has quite tough gun laws, but that's where the lack of any effective, consistent federal gun control is exposed for the farce that it is.

Because Chicago's criminals and gang members simply cross the state line into Indiana, where state gun laws are far less onerous, and buy them there.

Of all the guns seized by Chicago police between 2001 and 2012, and traced to their place of origin, more than half came from outside Illinois.

Gun laws in America should be federal, so you can't just skip from state to state exploiting weaker laws where you can find them.

SATURDAY, DECEMBER 8, 2012

Smith & Wesson posted record net sales of $136.6 million for its second financial quarter. This was up a staggering 48 percent from the same quarter last year.

"The increase was led by continued strong sales across all of the company's firearm product lines," a company spokesman said.

In other words, Americans are racing out and buying as many guns and as much ammo as they can get their hands on.

And that, analysts said today, is because Barack Obama was reelected, and they fear he's going to grab their guns—despite the president repeatedly making it clear he has absolutely no intention of removing a single gun from circulation.

The NRA has done what it always does. Used events like the tragedy in Aurora, and the election of a Democrat president, to drive fear into the hearts and minds of Americans.

It has nothing to do with safety, as they absurdly claim.

And everything to do with commercial greed.

The more noise the NRA makes, the more guns get sold, and the more money the grateful gun manufacturer community pours back into the NRA.

It's a vicious, horrible cycle.

MONDAY, DECEMBER 10, 2012

High drama at CNN today, as a man was gunned down in an apparent execution right outside our Time Warner Center offices in New York.

He was shot at point-blank range, in front of huge holiday crowds of tourists, and died immediately.

It follows an obscene few days in which a four-year-old boy accidentally shot and killed his younger brother with his father's handgun in Minneapolis, a seven-year-old boy shot his sister in Philadelphia, and another seven-year-old boy was shot and killed when his father's gun went off in the parking lot of a Pennsylvania gun store.

The sheer regularity and randomness of death by guns in America is what I find so startling. It's relentless, and filled with as much unspeakable tragic accident as cold, callous criminal murder, mass shootings, and gang violence.

Bob Costas was my special guest tonight, and I asked him to name the biggest problems with America's gun culture.

"Forty percent of all the firearms purchased in this country are purchased without a background check," he replied.

"There is no federal ban on assault weapons like AK-47s, or high-capacity ammunition magazines or a fifty-caliber sniper rifle, which can literally pierce an airplane fuselage, or the side of an armored limousine.

"There's no purpose for anyone outside the police force and the military to have weapons like that. And while there are tight gun controls in some areas, it's ridiculously easy for someone to purchase a gun online or multiple guns or at a gun show and then those guns wind up in the hands of people in Washington, D.C., or New York, which may have stricter gun controls, but it's so easy to get around the gun controls.

"You could literally be a felon, walk out of jail, and it would be very easy for you to purchase a weapon without any kind of a background check. You could be on a terrorist watch list, a no-fly list, but you could still acquire a gun in this country.

"George Zimmerman had an arrest record and he had a restraining order for domestic violence taken out against him in his past.

"I'm not commenting on the exact whys and wherefores that will play out in the court of law about what happened between him and Trayvon Martin, but what does common sense tell you about the likelihood of that confrontation ever taking place in the first place if George Zimmerman was not carrying a gun?"

"President Obama has flirted with banning assault weapons," I said. "Is it time for him to show some proper moral leadership here?"

"I would like him to, yes. I think people on both sides of the aisle cower before the gun lobby. The laws that govern us and the steps we take ought to be geared toward the larger public good. There are obviously some people out there who have some apocalyptic vision that the government is going to lean toward tyranny, and they're going to be holed up somewhere with their munitions plant and resist it. I don't think people with that mind-set ought to be having any undue influence on our national policy."

TUESDAY, DECEMBER 11, 2012

I sat down this afternoon with three of the most experienced senators in America—John McCain, Joe Lieberman, and Lindsey Graham.

And I quickly got into a heated exchange with Graham about guns.

"The Second Amendment came about because of your country," he said accusingly.

"You're going to blame the British?"

"Absolutely. When in doubt, always blame the British!"

"If you're worried about us invading again, I can probably relax you on that score."

"Why did we decide as a nation that individuals can have the right to bear arms? Because in England, the individual didn't have a whole lot of rights about religion or freedom of speech. I own more than eight guns. Why should my constitutional rights be limited because you don't understand why I want eight guns?"

"Why do you want eight guns?"

"Because I enjoy shooting. I hunt. It's something me and my dad did together. In the South, it's part of growing up. We are who we are as Americans, and we have our faults, but the Second Amendment is ingrained in our culture. Ninety percent of the football fans at South Carolina or Clemson home games probably own a weapon. And I really do believe it's how you act as a person that determines your fate, not the sensibilities of someone else. Because if my individual rights under the Constitution are limited by the sensibilities of others, I don't have a whole lot of rights."

This is, I'm sure, a mind-set shared by tens of millions of Americans.

Their "rights" supersede anyone else's "sensibilities."

The Obamas hosted a Christmas party tonight for media types.

I went with Jonathan, and when our time came, we lined up for a photo with the president and first lady.

"How many of these things do they do?" I asked one of the Secret Service agents as we edged toward them.

"There are twenty-four parties like this in December," he replied. "And they pose for over three thousand photographs."

"That's a lot of standing around!"

"Yes, Mr. Morgan, about thirty-two and a half hours standing around to be precise."

Incredible.

The American economy's in turmoil, war in Afghanistan still rages, and the Middle East is blowing up in flames. But amid all this, the president and first lady—as is the tradition for all their predecessors, apparently—spend more than an entire day standing to say hello to mostly complete strangers, and pose for photos.

You get about thirty seconds with them.

"Mr. President," I said. "We meet at last!"

He smiled in a slightly bemused way—suggesting he hadn't been waiting for this historic encounter in quite the same breathlessly excited manner that I had.

"Lovely party, thanks for inviting me!" I babbled on like a hyperactive One Direction fan finding himself in a lift with Harry Styles.

"My pleasure, great to have you here."

They both then automatically slid their arms around my back, pivoting us as a threesome to the cameraman waiting a few feet away.

"Do we say *cheese*?" I asked.

Neither of them replied, which meant that either they didn't hear me, or they were silently wondering why this crazy British guy was shouting about cheese.

Later tonight, I adjourned for dinner with a few of our team to a local D.C. restaurant.

Halfway through, news broke of another horrific shooting—this time at a shopping mall in Oregon.

"This is happening all the time," I said. "When will anyone do anything about it?"

None of my American colleagues seemed to share my exasperation.

They care, don't get me wrong. They just don't seem as enraged as I am, and I'm sure it's because they have grown up in a culture of guns, so have become almost immune to the shock of these events.

More than thirty-five Americans get shot dead every single day, another fifty kill themselves with guns. And this slaughter has been going on for decades.

I just can't stay as calm about it as they do, and I'm not even American! Or maybe it's because I'm not American.

WEDNESDAY, DECEMBER 12, 2012
Details of the Oregon mall shooting are horrible.

A twenty-two-year-old gunman called Jacob Tyler Roberts ran inside and fired off sixty shots with an AR-15 assault rifle at random strangers.

He killed two people, seriously wounded a third, and then shot himself dead.

Police said he didn't seem to have a real motive, he just wanted to kill as many people as possible.

I started tonight's show by telling viewers: "Here are statistics that you may find as shocking as I did. There are more than 129,000 federally licensed firearms dealers in this country. That's according to the Bureau of Alcohol, Tobacco, Firearms and Explosives. To put that number in perspective, there are a mere 36,000 grocery stores and 14,000 McDonald's restaurants. Far, far more places to buy guns in America than groceries or burgers."

Sandy Phillips, who lost her daughter Jessica in the Aurora massacre, appeared on the show tonight.

"It must take you right back to the nightmare that you went through," I said.

"Yes. Absolutely. Not only myself, but my husband and the other eleven families that lost a loved one in Aurora. We were all texting back and forth last night and all of us were shaking and some of us were crying and we understand the pain that those families that lost loved ones are going through.

"It's a horrible state of affairs that we're in in America right now and it really needs to be addressed. And when we have leaders like Lindsey Graham, who was on your show the other night, saying, 'We're not going to do anything about it because we believe in the Second Amendment,' it makes you even more curious as to where this country is heading.

"Because I too believe in the Second Amendment. I too am a gun owner. So is my husband. And to not address these issues is ludicrous.

"When forty percent of the guns that are bought and sold in America are bought and sold without any background checks, we've got a problem."

Another guest was Alan Gottlieb, founder of an organization called the Second Amendment Foundation, and I asked him about the AR-15 in the shooting.

"Why would anybody in America who is not in the military or the police force need to ever have one of these weapons?" I asked him.

After downplaying the power of the AR-15—"the weapon isn't that sophisticated"—he cited the L.A. riots of 1992, and how Korean shopkeepers used AR-15s to defend themselves, as an example.

"You're talking about a riot that was twenty years ago," I replied. "Unstable young people in America are able to walk in and buy AR-15 semiautomatic rifles and go into shopping malls and to movie theaters and to blow away as many Americans as they possibly can, using these magazines which can carry up to a hundred rounds a minute . . ."

"They don't do a hundred rounds a minute. It only shoots one round. I want you to be factually correct."

This was nonsense. I've seen people firing AR-15s on ranges, and they can easily fire a hundred rounds a minute in experienced hands.

I quickly got angry. I find it impossible not to, when confronted with people who seem to value their right to have guns over the right to life.

At one stage, Gottlieb even started laughing as he tried to insist I had called for all guns to be banned—which I never have. It's just not a practical solution to America's problem, as there are simply too many guns in circulation.

"It's not funny," I snapped. "Why are you laughing?"

"Because you're not telling the truth, that's why I'm laughing."

"Well, stop laughing, it looks creepy, right?"

Jonathan sighed in my ear. "Keep calm, debate him, don't lose your temper, don't be rude," he said.

But I carried on bickering with Gottlieb until we ran to a commercial.

"Sorry," I told Jonathan. "I can't keep calm with these people."

"Just remember that many of our viewers agree with these people."

Later in the show, I spoke to Mark Kelly, Gabby Giffords's husband.

"When I have this debate," I said, "a lot of Americans say to me, 'Listen, it's the Second Amendment. It's our Constitution. We have a right to bear arms.' Do you empathize with that?"

"Well, I personally believe that people have a right to have a gun to protect themselves in their home, and their family. But I also think that we have an issue with the access that people have to guns, that it's so easy to buy a gun, especially in certain states. And in certain circumstances, people that are mentally ill can acquire a gun or even, in some cases, a former felon can. So these are problems that I think need to be addressed. You know, we elect some smart people that should be able to work out these issues. They've just—they've just neglected to do it on this particular case. And there are reasons that politicians tend to ignore this issue."

They ignore it because the American public doesn't care enough to force them to do anything.

And I can't for the life of me understand why.

THURSDAY, DECEMBER 13, 2012

I interviewed Rudy Giuliani tonight and quizzed him about President Obama's lack of effective action on guns.

"Don't you have to try and make it harder for people like this Oregon shooter to get a gun when you're running a country with so many guns already?"

"There's no question about it. I think I probably—with Bill Bratton, Howard Safir, and Bernie Kerik—seized more guns in New York City than any mayor in history.

"Maybe Mike [Bloomberg] and Commissioner Kelly have met that record, I'm not sure. But I was the first one to really seize guns. I believe in it. I believe in getting them out of society, but I don't believe it really ends crime. Human behavior is much more important. If you want to do a factor, seventy-five percent is human behavior, twenty-five percent is the instrument. Weapons like this where people can kill multiple times very, very quickly, we should have some reasonable restrictions on the use of them."

This is the sensible voice of the Republican Party speaking, but I fear that voice is not getting heard.

FRIDAY, DECEMBER 14, 2012

I was sitting idly around my apartment this morning when Conor emailed: "Shooting at a school in Newtown, Connecticut."

Early reports on this kind of incident, as we both knew from our time working together at *The Daily Mirror,* are nearly always unreliable and completely contradictory.

It often takes at least an hour or two for any real hard facts to emerge.

At 12:30 P.M. though, the highly respected CBS crime correspondent John Miller tweeted: "Preliminary information indicates a couple of dozen shot in CT school."

Jesus.

A few minutes later, ABC reported: "Twelve people, including school-children, dead in CT school shooting."

I called Jonathan. "This is huge."

"Yes, do you want to go do the show from there?"

I stopped to think for a moment.

I've never done a breaking news show from the scene of a major incident since I joined CNN.

Not because I can't, or because I'm fearful of it, but because I know we have far more experienced field anchors like Anderson who do it so well—and because I feel more comfortable doing these big stories from my own studio.

The art of being a successful news anchor is sticking to what you know you do best. Viewers in these situations want anchors who sound and look calm, composed, and on top of things.

Jonathan agreed. "I think your strength is in the studio."

CNN showed a live scene outside the school, and my heart sank as I saw frantic parents running toward it.

My mind raced back to 1996, when the Dunblane massacre happened in Scotland. These were almost the exact same horrible images on TV that I had watched then.

Celia came back from a walk and I hugged Elise tightly to my chest.

In three years, she may well be off to an American elementary school like this herself. Newtown is only an hour up the road.

Twitter erupted with shock, anger, and outrageous comment—led by Ann Coulter, who declared: "More guns, less mass shootings."

So incredibly dumb.

Fortunately, there was reason amid the madness, from Lenny Kravitz: "I appreciate our American rights, but this is, again, why guns should go . . . doesn't one child's life outweigh that right? Wouldn't you give it up to bring them back?"

I'm not sure the majority of Americans would, actually; that's the problem.

But this horrific incident may be the catalyst for at least some much-needed self-examination among gun lovers.

Maria Spinella, my line producer, tweeted: "My family always owned guns, I've shot guns. I support gun rights. But America seems awash in guns and something's gone horribly wrong."

By the time I went on air at 9 P.M., the full scale of the tragedy was clear. A young man named Adam Lanza had shot his mother dead at the home they shared, stolen her gun collection, driven to nearby Sandy Hook School in Newtown, forced his way inside, shot and killed twenty-six people, including twenty children ages six and seven, with an AR-15 assault rifle, then killed himself with a handgun as first responders arrived.

It is the single worst school shooting in American history.

President Obama made an emotional address to the nation, making it clear he intends to do something "meaningful" about this.

I don't doubt his sincerity, but it's almost the exact same rhetoric every American president has come out with after every mass shooting in the last thirty years—something that was proved by a viral video on YouTube splicing almost identical clips from various postmassacre addresses by Obama, Clinton, and Bush.

As I spoke to CNN's reporters on the ground, Sandy Hook parents, and various politicians, I could feel the fury inside me start to spill over. Those poor kids, they'd gone to school, for God's sake—and had their brains blown out in their classrooms.

We'd booked a progun author called John R. Lott, whose book is *More Guns, Less Crime.*

"He fired over a hundred rounds and killed twenty children," I told him. "Twenty children! At what point do you gun lobby guys say, 'We get it. It's time for change'?"

"Right, it is time," he replied, to my astonishment.

"Time to do what?"

"To get rid of some of these gun laws that cause—"

"To get rid of gun laws?"

He nodded. "Look at what has happened, all these attacks this year have occurred where guns are banned. Look at the Aurora movie theater shooting . . ."

Unbelievable. This clown had actually come on my show on the night of this dreadful atrocity to advocate getting *rid* of existing gun control laws?

"What the hell has that got to do with it?" I exclaimed, raising my voice. "Seriously? What has that got to do with it?"

I stared at Lott, who has weird, pointy, bushy eyebrows, and a permanent sneery half smirk on his face. I wanted to reach across the desk and slap it off him.

"There are about thirty-five gun murders a year in Britain," I shouted. "There are nearly twelve thousand murders a year from guns in this country. When are you guys going to focus on that and stop telling me the answer is more guns? It is *not* the answer. Three hundred million guns in America isn't enough for you? How many more kids have to die before you guys say we want less guns and not more?"

Lott snorted with indignant defiance. "I'm upset because I worry that the gun control laws that you are pushing have killed people."

"Oh, what a load of nonsense!" I snapped back. "I've been debating this for months, if not years. I am so frustrated. I'm so furious for these kids who have been blown away again with legally acquired weapons. Some boy who has problems takes his mother's weapons, including this ridiculous assault rifle, and goes in the school and kills these kids. And you guys still want to tell me the answer is more guns? It is madness!"

Lott replied: "How else can you stop someone from shooting people?"

And there, right there, was the utter insanity of the progun lobby laid bare. They genuinely have no idea how you stop someone shooting people unless everyone else has a gun too.

It's like the Wild West has been beamed into modern-day America.

And it's as terrifying as it's stupid.

I ended the show by looking directly at the camera and saying: "It's time for action. It's time that America's politicians just did something. Stop worrying about the gun lobby, which makes billions of dollars out of this trade, in what often leads to appalling death. It is time for some moral conviction and some moral courage."

Then I stormed off home, feeling drained and furious. And so unbelievably sad for those poor children.

The final thing I read before going to sleep was an email from Barbra Streisand: "Keep up your fight for sanity! Go get 'em."

SATURDAY, DECEMBER 15, 2012
My exchange with Lott is attracting a lot of attention on social media.

But Jonathan is a bit concerned I went too far.

"All your passion will get lost and be seen as personal grandstanding if you aren't careful about how you frame all this," he emailed this morning. "As an American television viewer, I can tell you there's a fine line between seeking truth by fighting with people you invite on your show, and simply being rude."

I'm tired, still angry, and not in the mood to listen to reason.

"You're entitled to your opinion, I'm entitled to mine," I wrote back. "The segment in which you accused me of 'yelling' and now 'being rude' is one of our most talked about since we went on air—with the vast majority of people who've seen it totally agreeing with me. If you don't want me to continue berating these gun nut morons, then don't put me on the air. Because I'm going to."

"You did yell, it's not an accusation," he pointed out, entirely accurately.

"I didn't say you were rude, I said it's a fine line between seeking truth and being passionate and seeming rude. Again, that's a fact not an opinion. I want you to beat them at the debate, not berate them. Berating gets tired. Aren't you better than that?"

"I'm not going to curb my passion over this issue," I emailed back. "Sorry."

"Again, I didn't ask you to. I never would," Jonathan wrote. "But you can't just go off half-cocked at these guys and sound sane yourself. Just trying to help you. Not everyone is against you! I think it was riveting TV and that you showed true passion at the end of an emotional day. But everyone, even editors, needs editors from time to time."

He's right about the editing. But I don't agree about calming down.

"Now is not the time to rein things in," I replied. "But I'm not oblivious to the dangers of going too far. I actually feel completely distraught for these poor parents. I see my little girl in front of me now, and it enrages me that another wacko's ruined so many little kids' lives. I want to make this slaughter stop, and we are in a very good position to influence this debate. Doing it quietly isn't going to do anything."

"I think you were on the finest of lines," Jonathan responded, "and you ended up getting the benefit of the doubt because it was the day it happened and you captured a frustration many people share. If you keep having that same conversation in that way it will seem rude to many.

"I think you can own this issue, but it's a lot harder to do if you are seen as a Johnny-one-note than if you acknowledge the uphill battle and why it's different here than England, etc. That has nothing to do with how you carry yourself in an interview. If you invite someone on, let them speak. Disagree all you want but be civil. It doesn't make your case stronger to simply disagree. I would like to see you win at intellectual, not emotional combat, which will make for better TV because it will be sustainable. You'll save more lives in the long run (including that of your show) if you will at least have a discussion about having a discussion. You can be right and still not win. I want you to have both."

Everything he was saying was eminently sensible, and this is a guy who's worked with everyone from Matt Lauer and Katie Couric to Brian Williams. So he knows what he's talking about.

But I think it was perfectly justified to shout last night, given the hideous circumstances.

"So, to be clear, you don't ever want me raising my voice?" I persisted.

"I think the first person to raise his voice in an argument loses," he replied. "That's what I teach my children and try to live by, sometimes successfully. Average, everyday gestures and sayings get hugely exaggerated on TV. It's why Nixon lost to Kennedy on TV but won their debate on radio. You can raise your voice, but if you drown out the other guy you defeat the purpose of having him on."

"But by that yardstick, I'd have never done what I did last night. And it demonstrably worked. Just read all the reaction."

There was a pause of twenty minutes in our correspondence.

Then Jonathan emailed again: "Guy at the gym just said, unsolicited, 'Tell your boy he's going to have a coronary.' People want you to live!"

I laughed.

"I'll be fine, relax! Look, it's important that we debate these things, I get that. Just understand that I'm at my best when I don't feel restricted by 'what anchors usually do' convention, and go with my gut in the moment."

"Of course I get that," he responded immediately.

SUNDAY, DECEMBER 16, 2012

My music booker, Susan Durrwachter, revealed an extraordinary thing this morning on her social media.

"Covering these stories, we develop a hardened shell, but sometimes personal emotions seep in. Can't help but think of my vibrant brother who was taken because of a gun. Our family had twelve great years with Michael and for that I am grateful. RIP to all the kids gone too soon."

I knew absolutely nothing about this, and was completely stunned.

I emailed her immediately.

"Susan, I never knew this. I'm so sorry. What happened?"

"It was a hunting accident," she replied. "My dad took my brother hunting for the first time with another father-son duo. While hunting for turkeys, the other kid (fourteen years old) accidentally shot and killed my brother. My father told me my brother was shot in the chest and killed instantly. I've never, ever gotten over it and actually hate guns. My father grew up hunting and has since been a safety advocate at his hunting club. This shooting has hit me hard."

There must be so many American families whose lives have been affected like this by gun violence—quite literally, millions.

More and more details have emerged about Adam Lanza. A picture building of a misfit loner, living with his mother, suffering mental health issues, addicted to violent games, and obsessed with guns.

In other words, a human bomb waiting to explode.

The gun rights argument is always that you need guns at home to protect yourself. Yet Lanza's mother, Nancy, had six, precisely for that purpose. Her deranged son then stole them, shot her in the head as she lay in bed, and went on a rampage at Sandy Hook.

Nick Kristof has written another superb piece for the *New York Times*, pointing out a report by Harvard public health specialist David Hemenway that showed children from ages five to fourteen in America are thirteen times as likely to be murdered with guns as children of the same age in other industrialized countries.

As Kristof said, America's children are protected by myriad health and safety rules with regard to school stairways, windows, school buses, and cafeteria food.

"There are five pages of regulations about ladders," he wrote, "which kill around three hundred Americans a year. We even regulate toy guns by requiring orange tips. It is more difficult to adopt a pet than to buy a gun."

Kristof ended his op-ed by reminding us that the history of auto safety in America should be the inspiration for how to tackle gun safety.

"Some auto deaths are caused by people who break laws or behave irresponsibly. But we don't shrug and say, 'Cars don't kill people, drunks do.'

"Instead, we have required seat belts, air bags, child seats, and crash safety standards. We have introduced limited licenses for young drivers and tried to curb the use of mobile phones while driving. All this has reduced

America's traffic fatality rate per mile driven by nearly ninety percent since the 1950s."

The logic is inarguable.

But I don't think the gun rights activists want to hear logic. It interferes with gun sales.

What is an undeniable fact is that five of the eleven worst U.S. mass shootings in history have occurred since 2007.

People keep asking me what I would do to curb the slaughter. My immediate suggestions would include:

1. A national gun law policy. Same rules for everyone.
2. A new ban on all assault weapons and magazines over ten bullets.
3. A universal 100 percent background check on all gun sales.
4. Mandatory safety/training courses, minimum of three references, and detailed vetting over six to eight weeks for all gun applications.
5. A ban on all convicted felons and anyone with a documented history of mental illness from owning a gun. Period.
6. A ban on all guns for anyone under twenty-five, with the exception of those who secure special licenses to hunt, or shoot for sport.
7. A nationwide, incentivized gun amnesty to reduce the volume of guns in circulation—like the one that worked well in Australia.
8. Far higher sums invested in federal and state research into mental illness, and advice to teachers and parents on how, why, and when to raise a red flag over their concerns.
9. Make Hollywood and video game manufacturers come to the table and acknowledge that to a disturbed mind, their more violent material can act as a trigger.

None of these measures will stop gun violence. What they would do collectively is reduce it.

Tonight I read a fascinating piece in the *New Yorker* about the Second Amendment and the NRA by Jeffrey Toobin, CNN's top legal analyst.

For most of America's history, he revealed, the courts ruled that the amendment conferred on state militias the right to bear arms, but did *not* give individuals the right to own or carry a weapon.

Thus confirming what I've always assumed the Founding Fathers actually meant by their clumsily, ambiguously worded amendment.

Enter the NRA. Before the seventies, Toobin wrote, the NRA was predominantly a nonpolitical organization. But in 1977, there was a coup d'état at the group's annual convention that brought a group of committed political conservatives to power. And, Toobin claimed, they pushed for a new interpretation of the Second Amendment—one that gave individuals, not just the militias, the right to bear arms.

That view was widely scorned, Toobin said. Chief Justice Warren E. Burger, who was no liberal, even mocked it as "fraud."

But the NRA kept pushing, and they were helped by Ronald Reagan's ascendance to the presidency in 1980. He was a gun rights enthusiast and NRA member.

The NRA, said Toobin, commissioned endless academic studies to "prove" their new theory until it eventually evolved, by sheer force of pressure, into conservative conventional wisdom.

Finally, in 2008, the Supreme Court, led by Justice Scalia, ruled that an individual had the right, under the Second Amendment, to own a handgun because "handguns are the most popular weapon chosen by Americans for self-defense in their home."

But, and it's a big "but," it did allow the government to ban other weapons, acknowledging that there had to be limitations.

Toobin wrote: "In the eighteenth century, militias were proto-military operations and their members had to obtain the best military hardware of the day. But Scalia could not create, in the twenty-first century, an individual right to contemporary military weapons—like tanks and Stinger missiles."

So there we have it.

The NRA hijacked the meaning of the Second Amendment to suit its agenda—to arm every American and sell millions of guns.

MONDAY, DECEMBER 17, 2012
A new CBS poll shows that support for stricter gun control laws has surged eighteen points since spring of this year.

Fifty-seven percent of Americans now want tougher laws, the highest number in ten years.

But I won't hold my breath. After Gabby Giffords was shot, 47 percent backed stricter gun laws in a CBS poll, and that dropped to 39 percent by April this year.

I hosted a special town-hall-style debate tonight on guns.

One of my guests was Dianne Feinstein, one of the few American senators actually prepared to do anything about this madness.

"I'm going to do an assault weapons piece of legislation," she said. "It's going to ban by name at least a hundred military-style semiautomatic assault weapons. And it's going to ban big clips, drums, or strips of more than ten bullets. And in this particular category of weapon, the Bushmaster AR-15, which is a killer weapon. You can fire it very quickly. It has very little recoil, very little kick, and it's very high velocity. And it doesn't belong on the streets of our cities. And it doesn't belong in a place where a twenty-year-old like this particular twenty-year-old could get ahold of it and go in and do what he did. And this makes me very angry."

I wanted to stand and cheer.

I asked her, "What do you say to those who say, 'I have my Second Amendment rights, I'm entitled to bear arms, you are not entitled to take away that right by removing these kinds of weapons from the streets and from the stores'?"

"There is no Second Amendment right to bear every type of weapon that you know of. These are a certain class of weapons. They are designed to kill large numbers of people in close combat. I don't believe the Second Amendment covers them. The Second Amendment was written a long time before this class of weapons was founded, merchandised, and spread all over our country, where they fall into the hands of juveniles, grievance killers, people who go into our malls, our theaters, our stores, our businesses, and now our schools, and just kill people for no good reason. It's got to stop. These children, this is the straw that breaks the camel's back. People have to respond. They have to understand that the rights of the many to remain safe are more important than any right you may think you have to have a military-style assault weapon."

"Senator Feinstein," I said. "I applaud what you're doing and I wish you every success."

Another guest was Dan Gross, a very smart, eloquent guy who runs the Brady Campaign—a gun safety organization set up after White House staffer Jim Brady was shot and paralyzed in the Ronald Reagan assassination attempt in 1981.

"One in three Americans knows somebody who has been shot," he said. "And the only place where this is a partisan political debate is in the halls of Congress. What this tragedy is doing is exposing that disconnect between what the American people want and the conversation we want to have and what our elected officials are doing about it."

The problem is that the conversation is being dominated by loud, angry, and often offensively idiotic gun rights lobbyists.

Take, for example, Philip Van Cleave, of the Virginia Citizen Defense League. He was my final guest tonight, and reiterated remarks he made to the *Washington Post* yesterday, when he was asked why anyone would need an AR-15:

"I could ask you why anyone would want a Ferrari. Bushmasters are absolutely a blast to shoot with. They're fast, they're accurate. Guns are fun. Some of them are more cool than others. It's just like we have television sets that look cool and others are more boxy."

Just like television sets.

Unbelievable.

TUESDAY, DECEMBER 18, 2012

Watched a gun store owner on CNN this morning, smiling as he boasted how sales of AR-15s have been soaring since Sandy Hook.

I was left steaming with anger again.

What is *wrong* with these bloody people?

We booked Larry Pratt, executive director of a group called Gun Owners of America. He was sneeringly arrogant and defiant.

"America is not the Wild West you're depicting," he smirked. "We only have problems in our cities and in our schools where people like you have been able to get laws on the books that keep people from being able to defend themselves."

This moron was actually blaming *me* for the Sandy Hook massacre.

I stopped and stared at him for a second or two, trying to stay calm.

Then I lost it.

"YOU'RE AN UNBELIEVABLY STUPID MAN, AREN'T YOU?"

This ignited a heated exchange, which ended with me saying: "You are a dangerous man espousing dangerous nonsense. You shame your country."

He didn't bat an eyelid, and spat back: "Disarmament is dangerous."

Jonathan wasn't happy afterward.

"You shouldn't have called him stupid."

"Why not? He is."

"He's got an opinion you don't agree with, but one that many Americans *do* agree with. If you call him stupid, you're calling every American that agrees with him stupid. That's not smart."

But within minutes, the "stupid" clip was blowing up on Twitter.

And most of the reaction was strongly supportive.

The viewers are loving me tearing into these gun nuts. And that's because hardly any news anchor has ever done this on American television.

"I don't want to curb your passion, or anger," Jonathan added. "Just don't be rude to them, don't call them stupid."

"All right, all right . . . I'll call them idiots."

Jonathan sat back in his chair and sighed.

Earl Brien, an L.A. surgeon I met at a recent lunch party, emailed me after watching the show.

Piers, you are spot-on regarding military weapons. I have seen over ten thousand gunshot wounds in my orthopedic career and treated thousands of patients with both low- and high-energy gunshot wounds. The degree of destruction and devastation between handguns compared to assault weapons are so dramatic, there is no reason why any individual (other than law enforcement and militia) should have the right to own military weapons such as the AR-15. In South Central Los Angeles we would see multiple victims of military assault rifles in what the gang bangers termed "AK spraydowns." If such a bullet hit the bone, massive bone and soft tissue loss ensued. Entrance wounds were five millimeters to ten millimeters and exit wounds could be up to ten centimeters to fifteen centimeters.

Many of the gunshot deaths are crime on crime, but I have seen hundreds of innocent women, men, and children killed or maimed by stray bullets as well. It is unbelievable that it takes mass murders by deranged shooters to get our politicians off their asses to address such an obvious issue that has spiraled out of control. It is not enough that many of our citizens living in lower socioeconomic regions where gangs are prevalent are held hostage in their own houses and their children are at risk while sleeping in their own beds to make such important changes. We cannot turn back the clock and eliminate nearly three hundred million guns in our country because the bad guys would have no restraint, however a reasonable, thoughtful approach to our Second Amendment rights must follow. Unfortunately these tragedies often have multiple components to them, and isolating the argument to military arsenal shortchanges the complexity of the problem: mental illness, violent video game addiction, childhood isolation, parental denial. But it is a good starting point.

Earl's grandfather was Earl Warren, the fourteenth chief justice of the United States.

WEDNESDAY, DECEMBER 19, 2012

Another fiery live town hall show tonight about guns.

We invited John R. Lott back, and he and I soon got into another heated debate, this time over the specific power of an AR-15 rifle.

"How many bullets can it fire a second?" I asked him repeatedly.

And he repeatedly fudged his answer.

I knew why. Every expert I've now spoken to says that the AR-15, with some simple, inexpensive modifications, can fire up to six rounds a *second,* even in semiautomatic mode. And that's what the gun lobbyists are desperate to keep quiet, because it's their biggest selling rifle.

During our last commercial break, various relatives of mass shooting victims who were also in the audience turned on Lott, and the atmosphere became extremely tense and volatile.

He tried to argue with them, but his whole "the only answer is more guns" is so disgustingly offensive to people who've seen loved ones shot that he never stood a chance.

I liked watching him squirm. I just wish we'd been on air at the time.

After the show, a gun rights supporter started a Twitter hashtag called #piersmorganmovies—which was designed to be a tribute from firearm fans to both my general awfulness and my specific British awfulness.

Standout contributions included "No Country for Whiny British Men"; "Rebel without a Clue"; "The Good, the Bad, and the Real Frickin' Ugly"; "Careerfall"; "America's Just Not That into You"; and "I Am Bellend."

Finally got home at midnight and saw a tweet from Rosie O'Donnell: "U are doing a great job, Piers—carry on—we need your voice—stay strong loud and accurate—bravo. #guncontrol."

THURSDAY, DECEMBER 20, 2012

It's been a long, draining six days since the Sandy Hook massacre.

As we learn more about the short lives of these sweet little children, so the anger grows.

This afternoon, I interviewed a man called Neil Heslin, who lost his only son, Jesse.

"Jesse was my son," he said, "but he was also my best friend and my buddy too, and I'm just really lost for words."

He stopped talking for a few seconds, his face etched in torment.

"We did everything together. And he had so many favorite spots where we'd go: the diner in town, the grocery store, a bagel or muffin in the morning. The Misty Vale deli where he'd go to get his sandwich in the morning, also before school, and his snack . . ."

His eyes filled with tears and he stopped talking again.

"I'm lost for words."

Silence.

"My little boy said something to me the night before. He said, 'Dad, this is going to be the best Christmas ever.' And he was going on about it and I said, 'Jesse, we'll make it the best we can.'

"I don't have much family. So it's kind of a quiet time for me. And he makes—made—Christmas happy for me and joyful and he made it what it was. And the next day this tragedy happened, I thought to myself, 'Boy, was he wrong about that.' "

Silence.

Neil looked down, tears falling freely down his face.

"You know, he was right in a way. It is going to be a good Christmas, because it brings back the true meaning of Christmas. Him and I had this talk, what it was about. It's about giving and not receiving, and it's about helping, reaching out to others. That's what everybody in the world has done with this tragedy, and they've come together and they are looking to help and provide support and they've done that for me. And I just want to thank everybody. It just doesn't change my . . . loss or my . . . my . . ."

Silence.

"You know, my little boy is never going to come back."

I was glad to go to a commercial break, because I wanted to cry with him.

Tonight it was our own *Piers Morgan Tonight* staff Christmas party.

We thought about canceling it, but everyone's worked so hard this year, and in the last week in particular, that I wanted us all to have a night where we could come together, have a few drinks, and relax a bit.

But I was so tired, and drank way too much, way too fast.

The last thing I remember is sitting down in a chair inside the bar sometime around 10:30 P.M.

FRIDAY, DECEMBER 21, 2012

"What happened last night?" asked Celia when I woke.

Never a good question from one's wife after an office Christmas party. Particularly so when I have no memory at all of getting home.

"Er, why do you ask?"

"Because you were home by eleven fifteen P.M., about five hours before you normally return from these things."

"I was?"

"You were, and you fell over when you tried coming to bed."

I emailed Jonathan.

"I have no memory of leaving last night other than it must have been surprisingly early. Can you enlighten me?"

"Thought that might be the case," he replied. "You were quite wobbly so we got you in a car."

"Ah, I see. Did I actually fall over? I did when I got home apparently."

"It was more of a slump/lean. Cross-eyed."

"Well, it's been a long old year!" I wrote. "Did everyone enjoy themselves?"

"Yes, it was a blast. There was apparently a stretch limo to karaoke."

"Excellent. They're a good bunch."

"The best," he emailed back.

Later, NRA chief Wayne LaPierre gave a bizarre, ranting press conference, reiterating his belief that "the only way to stop a bad guy with a gun is a good guy with a gun."

Which, taken to its logical conclusion, means every single person in America needs to be armed. Because they are all either good guys or bad guys, and it's always *High Noon*.

Alex Jones politely explains to me that 1776 will commence
again if I try and take away his guns.

11

SATURDAY, DECEMBER 22, 2012

A petition has been launched on the official White House website to have me thrown out of America. It's been posted by an organization called InfoWars, led by an extreme right-wing radio host called Alex Jones.

Entitled "Deport British Citizen Piers Morgan for Attacking Second Amendment," it states: "British Citizen and CNN television host Piers Morgan is engaged in a hostile attack against the U.S. Constitution by targeting the Second Amendment. We demand that Mr. Morgan be deported immediately for his effort to undermine the Bill of Rights and for exploiting his position as a national network television host to stage attacks against the rights of American citizens."

I asked John if this could actually be successful.

"Well, they tried to deport John Lennon, but failed," he said, encouragingly. "Mind you, he did write 'Imagine.' "

MONDAY, DECEMBER 24, 2012

The petition has passed the twenty-five-thousand-signature mark required to compel the White House to make a formal response. In fact, by noon today it had reached thirty-one thousand. And by midnight, over fifty thousand.

The irony, of course, being that by demanding I be deported, these gun rights campaigners are attacking my own First Amendment right to free speech.

I am a U.S. resident, so covered by the same constitutional rights as any American.

To understand why they want me thrown out, look no further than the revelation today that Brownells, one of America's largest sellers of gun supplies, sold more than three years' worth of inventory in three days following the Sandy Hook massacre.

WEDNESDAY, DECEMBER 26, 2012

A second petition has now sprung up, again on the White House website, from a British man. It reads: "We want to keep Piers Morgan in the USA. There are two very good reasons for this. First, the First Amendment. Second, and the more important point, no one in the UK wants him back. Actually there is a third. It will be hilarious to see how loads of angry Americans react."

This instantly began attracting thousands of signatures too.

At this rate, I'll have to be dropped off somewhere in the mid-Atlantic.

THURSDAY, DECEMBER 27, 2012

The U.S. petition has soared to eighty thousand signatures, and is now sparking fear and panic in Britain.

"Americans," said TV host Jeremy Clarkson, "it took us forty years to get rid of Piers Morgan. Please don't send him back."

Michael Moore countered with: "So sad that the host on American TV to speak out the loudest against this madness is not one of us, but a Brit."

WEDNESDAY, JANUARY 2, 2013

We've been trying to book Michael Bloomberg again for my first show back on Monday.

Today, his office responded: "Mayor Bloomberg regretfully can't do the show Monday, but he will offer Piers asylum in NYC should the need arise."

THURSDAY, JANUARY 3, 2013

The cable news ratings have been published for 2012, and *Piers Morgan Tonight* was the highest-rated show on CNN for the year in total viewers.

I'm very proud of the team, and told them so today.

FRIDAY, JANUARY 4, 2013

The petition to have me deported has passed a hundred thousand signatures, and is now getting media attention all over the world.

The White House, having promised to respond to all petitions on its site that got over twenty-five thousand signatures, will have to say something.

Question is, what?

SUNDAY, JANUARY 6, 2013

I flew back into America tonight after a vacation, not entirely sure if I would actually be allowed back in.

But as I nervously approached the immigration counter at Newark Liberty International Airport, feeling like that drug runner in *Midnight Express*, a burly armed policeman spied me, smirked broadly, and said: "Relax, Mr. Morgan, we're not going to deport you."

Jonathan rang in a state of high excitement.

"We've booked Alex Jones for tomorrow."

"Who?"

"The guy who started the petition . . ."

I Googled Jones, and discovered a series of clips from his radio show that suggest he is a very noisy, and rather angry human being.

This could get lively.

MONDAY, JANUARY 7, 2013

Alex Jones arrived just before we went live on air, and was already working himself into a fearful frenzy—stomping around my studio, sweating profusely, and talking to himself like a UFC cage fighter seconds before a fight started.

I shook his hand, or rather the giant Texan paw he extended in my direction, and he laughed maniacally. "Ha-ha-ha, this is going to be gooooood."

"Well, I'm hoping we can have a proper debate," I replied.

"Yes, yes, we're going to have a *proper* debate, all right," he sneered in a ludicrously over-the-top English accent.

Well, I tried . . .

"Why do you want me deported?" I asked when the interview began. And off he went, ranting and raving like a gorilla at the zoo that's just seen the morning bucket of bananas arrive.

"Hitler took the guns, Stalin took the guns, Mao took the guns, Fidel Castro took the guns, Hugo Chavez took the guns. *And I'm here to tell you, 1776 will commence again if you try and take our firearms!*"

"How many gun murders were there in Britain last year?" I asked.

His eyes almost popped out of their sockets.

"How many great white sharks kill people every year, but they're scared to swim?" he yelled.

I persisted. "Let's try again, how many gun murders were there in Britain last year?"

"HOW MANY CHIMPANZEES CAN DANCE ON THE HEAD OF A PIN?"

We went to a commercial break, and Jonathan chuckled in my ear.

"You OK out there?"

I nodded, as Jones continued to shout and scream at me, even though we were off air.

"If this carries on," added Jonathan, "we'll have to cut him off—he's making no sense and refusing to answer your questions."

I shook my head vigorously, our prearranged sign for "don't end this under any circumstances."

I sensed that Jones's extraordinary behavior was turning into a more powerful advocate for gun control than anything I could possibly say.

I eventually wrapped it up after he informed me that President George W. Bush had deliberately caused 9/11—then suggested we settle things next time in a boxing ring: "I'll wear red, white, and blue, you wear your Jolly Rogers!"

Backstage, Jones continued to harangue my staff in an unhinged, explosive manner until he was led away into the streets of Manhattan by CNN security.

He owns fifty guns—a comforting thought.

Spencer, who'd stayed up to watch the show live in England, texted me: "Alex Jones. There are no words."

Jonathan was jubilant.

"That was great! And so much better because you didn't get angry, and you let the guy speak."

TUESDAY, JANUARY 8, 2013

The White House has confirmed it will be responding to my deportation petition. "In the meantime," noted Jay Carney, the president's press spokesman, "it is worth remembering that the freedom of expression is a bedrock principle in our democracy."

This sounds encouraging to me . . .

WEDNESDAY, JANUARY 9, 2013

The Jones interview has become a global Internet sensation, trending on Twitter for two days, gaining millions of views on YouTube, and sparking comment all over the world. Even better, Barack Obama has decided I can stay in America.

Tonight, as I was on air, a formal White House response to the deportation petition said:

> Let's not let arguments over the Constitution's Second Amendment violate the spirit of its First. President Obama believes that the Second Amendment guarantees an individual right to bear arms. However, the Constitution not only guarantees an individual right to bear arms, but also enshrines the freedom of speech and the freedom of the press—fundamental principles that are essential to our democracy.
>
> Americans may disagree on matters of public policy and express those disagreements vigorously, but no one should be punished by the government simply because he or she expressed a view on the Second Amendment—or any other matter of public concern.

Mark Kelly emailed:

Gabby and I are watching your show tonight. Congratulations on getting to stay in the U.S. We need you!

SATURDAY, JANUARY 12, 2013

The NRA has reported a hundred thousand new members have joined since Sandy Hook.

How depressing.

MONDAY, JANUARY 14, 2013

Tonight I appeared on Stephen Colbert's show, *The Colbert Report*. He asked, "Have you *any* idea how it feels to have someone with your accent tell us how to lead our lives?"

WEDNESDAY, JANUARY 16, 2013

President Obama today announced dramatic, wide-ranging gun control proposals, including a new ban on assault weapons, a ban on high-capacity bullet magazines, universal background checks for all gun buyers, and increased funding for mental health programs.

All the things, in fact, that I've been campaigning for on air.

For all the vitriol that's been poured on my "limey-ass" British head by the likes of Alex Jones, this may go at least some way to try to stem the country's gun carnage.

And contrary to what some think, that's been my only goal. Far from being "anti-American," I'm actually so fond of them I want more of them to stay alive.

But Obama now has to get these proposals passed by Congress, and that's going to be a very hard task. I wouldn't trust this particular Congress to pass gas when it comes to gun control.

SUNDAY, JANUARY 20, 2013

I've come to Washington for Obama's inauguration.

Tonight I was due to anchor a one-hour special live at 9 P.M.

I left my hotel at 7:45 P.M. for the short journey to the makeshift open-air studio CNN had erected at the National Building Museum on the National Mall.

But by 8:20 P.M., the car had barely traveled a mile due to the insane traffic caused by multiple police roadblocks for tomorrow's big day. I began to panic.

"How far is it?" I asked the driver.

"Another mile or so," he replied.

"OK, I'll walk."

I got out and began striding in the general direction of where I knew the studio was. But every time I tried to walk down a road, I'd find myself either in a dead end or at another roadblock.

By 8:40 P.M., I was sweating profusely, breathing heavily, and virtually running through the cold dark night.

Jonathan rang.

"Where are you?"

"I've no fucking idea!"

Fortunately, it turned out I wasn't actually that far away, and with some directions from a policeman, I eventually arrived at 8:55 P.M.

The makeup department dusted me with a quick powdering, and I used a hair dryer to blow off the sweat, while simultaneously gulping air to try to calm down.

I walked on set at 8:59 P.M., sat down next to Wolf Blitzer, and at 9 P.M. he handed over to me as if nothing had happened.

MONDAY, JANUARY 21, 2013

I got to meet Richard Schiff, who played one of the greatest dramatic political characters in TV history—Toby Ziegler, the tormented White House communications director in Aaron Sorkin's *The West Wing*.

In one episode, Toby delivered a devastatingly effective soliloquy about gun control:

"If you combine the populations of Great Britain, France, Germany, Japan, Switzerland, Sweden, Denmark, and Australia, you get a population roughly the size of the United States. We had thirty-two thousand gun deaths last year, they had one hundred and twelve. Do you think it's because Americans are more homicidal by nature, or do you think it's because those guys have gun control?"

As we finished our brief interview tonight, he said: "Thank you for not asking me about guns."

"Why do you say that?"

"Because I would have gotten very upset . . ."

"Really? Why?"

He then did indeed get very upset—launching a spectacular rant about gun violence in America. It was searingly articulate, stunningly evocative, and utterly uncompromising. Exactly, in fact, like Toby Ziegler.

I also interviewed Stevie Wonder.

"I heard you on TV talking about the whole gun thing," he said. "And I said to one of my friends, 'You should go with me to get a gun, to show how easy it is for me to get one.' Imagine me with a gun."

The crazy truth is that in many parts of America there's nothing legally to stop a blind man like Stevie from buying an armful of assault weapons.

TUESDAY, JANUARY 22, 2013

A Washington-based website called the *Daily Caller* has exposed me today as a shameless and relentless offender when it comes to talking about my brother Jeremy being an army officer.

They've gone back over all my debates on the show, and found endless examples of me dropping this fact into my argument.

It's something that Jonathan's warned me about before, but I don't intend stopping the habit.

It's very hard for the more rabid gun rights protagonists to harangue me for "knowing nothing about guns," when my own brother is an active soldier who's served tours of combat in Iraq and Afghanistan alongside U.S. troops.

My whole point is that assault weapons and high-capacity magazines belong in the military, not in civilian hands. What better way to reinforce this point than to constantly mention what my brother does for a living?

WEDNESDAY, JANUARY 23, 2013

In an interview set up by Buckingham Palace to improve his image, Prince Harry has hammered the press, bemoaned his lack of privacy when he plays naked billiards in Vegas with complete strangers, and boasted of killing Taliban with finger skills he honed playing Xbox.

Can I politely suggest that Harry heed the advice of the late, great queen mother about royal decorum: "Never complain, never explain, and never be heard speaking in public."

TUESDAY, JANUARY 29, 2013

Meghan and Steve Krakauer, my digital producer, fell in love last year while working together on promoting the show, and are getting married on Saturday in Houston.

"Why don't we do a show from there?" I suggested to Jonathan this morning. "It's time we went and heard the other side of the gun argument. And I'm going to be down in Texas anyway."

He agreed, adding: "You could go to a range and actually shoot an AR-15."

"Wouldn't that look a bit odd?"

"No. One of the arguments the gun rights people use against you is that you don't understand what these guns are like because you've never used one. This is a perfect chance to tackle that argument head on."

It's true that I have barely fired a gun before in my life. I shot a few clay pigeons once, and spent a few hours at an indoor gun range in Prague at a friend's bachelor party a decade ago.

But other than that, nothing.

By the end of the day, we had booked a huge gun store and range on the outskirts of Houston called Tactical Firearms for Monday night's show.

THURSDAY, JANUARY 31, 2013

Appeared on the *Tonight Show* and Jay Leno came for his usual chat backstage.

"Here's the problem," he chuckled. "For you to be telling Americans you want more gun control laws is like you going to Germany and telling them that they suddenly have to have speed limits on the autobahns."

Jay, a car fanatic who owns more than eighty new and classic vehicles, added: "They wouldn't want to hear it, and particularly not from someone with an English accent!"

I'm sure he's right, but that's not a reason to stop.

The latest CNN poll says that the majority of Americans are now in favor of a renewed ban on assault weapons (56 percent) and high-capacity magazines (58 percent).

President Obama faces an uphill battle in Congress to turn these numbers into new laws, but no tougher than Abraham Lincoln faced when trying to abolish slavery.

After the show, I asked Jay if he had any advice for me with regard to working with Jeff Zucker.

Jay, of course, was moved by Jeff at NBC to 10 P.M. to let Conan O'Brien take over the *Tonight Show,* then returned to his old slot within a year.

"Jeff's a great guy," he replied, "but if he offers you ten P.M. at CNN, *don't take it!*"

Then he fell about laughing.

I told Jeff. "That is *very* funny!" he replied.

FRIDAY, FEBRUARY 1, 2013

Flew to Houston and had dinner tonight with Shant and Juliana at a great restaurant near the hotel.

The maître d' was a well-spoken, smart guy in an expensive suit, and we got to chatting about guns. As I seem to with almost everyone at the moment.

"Do you own a gun?" I asked.

"Yes, sir," he replied. "I've got a lot of guns, including two AR-15s."

"Why do you need those?"

"I go hog hunting with them."

"Hog hunting?"

"Yes. We go out with night-vision goggles on, sometimes in helicopters, and shoot wild hogs with AR-15s. They're the best gun for it, because they're light, easy to use, and don't have much recoil."

"What kind of magazine drum do you use?"

"As big as I can get, but at least thirty rounds. You need them that big because the hogs come in large packs."

"And why do you need to kill the hogs?"

"They ruin crops. There are millions of them and they cause billions of dollars of damage to crops each year."

I've only been in Texas a few hours, and I've already heard a completely new argument for the "need" to have an AR-15.

There's clearly a massive difference culturally between big East Coast cities like New York and rural hunting areas.

I got back to the hotel and Googled hog hunting. The maître d' had been entirely accurate. The USDA estimates there are four million to five million wild hogs in America, and they cause between $1 billion and $2 billion worth of crop damage every year.

Food, quite literally, for thought.

MONDAY, FEBRUARY 4, 2013

Brad, who's been setting up tonight's show at Tactical Firearms, rang at lunchtime.

"Alex Jones just tweeted that you're going down there, and he's joining you, so there could be a reception committee."

Christ, that's all I need. That lunatic confronting me at a gun store. But it's too late to change plans now.

"The store has security, and we've informed the local law enforcement too," Brad added. "It should be fine."

The word "should" is always so discomforting in these situations.

By the time I arrived at 5 P.M., there was a small but noisy group of protesters wearing combat clothes, carrying rifles, and shouting from bullhorns.

No sign of Alex Jones, though.

My car sped past them, and I met the Tactical Firearms owner, Jeremy Alcede, a large, thick-set man who was in a very good mood.

"We've increased our sales four to five times [since Sandy Hook]," he boasted. "We were doing about $1 million a month and we started doing $1 million a week until we sold out. Right now, it's impossible to get guns in, and ammunition."

"Why?" I asked.

"My customers feel they're going to be banned and need to go get them now while they still can."

We went through to the range, and he gave me instruction on a variety of guns that I was going to fire, including a semiautomatic and automatic AR-15, both with thirty-round magazines.

I picked up the semiautomatic. It was amazingly light. Jeremy showed me how it worked, and it seemed extraordinarily easy to use.

We set the cameras, and I was about to start firing it, when there was a commotion at the door, and suddenly Alex Jones was standing in front of me, clutching a video camera.

"I've come to see you fire guns!" he cried jubilantly.

"Well, we're actually doing it for my show tonight, Alex, so I'll have to ask you to leave, I'm afraid."

He was hot and sweaty, and very overexcited. And I assumed he'd been tipped off by Jeremy, who knew Jones well.

But no matter. Jones tried throwing a few questions at me, but I batted them away as politely and calmly as I could.

"Will you shake my hand?" he yelled.

"Sure," I said, and I shook his hand.

This seemed to take the wind out of his puffed-up sails, and he eventually walked back out.

I picked up the AR-15 again and began firing at the target. My first few shots were slow, as I got the hang of it. Then I began to pump the trigger much faster, and pretty accurately.

I imagined one of these in the hands of James Holmes at Aurora, or Adam Lanza at Sandy Hook. It was the same weapon both used in their murderous rampages.

It made me feel uncomfortable and nervy. But I continued firing.

The bullets were exploding out, creating massive noise, and exuding an air, and smell, of raw, deadly power. That maître d' had been right. Very little recoil, and frighteningly easy to use.

It took me about a minute to unload the full magazine. And this was the first time I'd ever fired an assault rifle.

"How many rounds could someone who knows what they're doing, like you, fire in a minute with one of these?"

"If I had multiple magazines, maybe two hundred. But the true cyclical rate, if you had an unlimited magazine, is about four hundred rounds a minute."

Staggering.

"You can buy these at Walmart. Do you think that's a good idea?"

"For law-abiding citizens, I think it's an excellent idea. If you start banning one particular anything, I don't care if it's a particular type of ammunition, firearm, magazine, where is it going to stop? You give anybody an inch, they're going to take a mile. If you're a law-abiding citizen, there should be no more bans on anything."

I fired the fully automatic AR-15, which is illegal unless registered before 1986, and it was much faster, as I expected. But I was much less accurate.

"About twice as fast, and you missed the target so many times," Jeremy said. "That's why they are called 'spray and pray.' You spray bullets and pray it hits the target. Because they're not very accurate at all."

"How many bullets can it fire in a minute?"

"About six hundred and fifty rounds."

I fired several more guns, including a ludicrously large Browning M2 antiaircraft machine gun that looked like something even Rambo would blanch at. I had to sit down to use it, and it blazed away in a shocking orgy of noise and smoke.

"How many rounds can this fire?"

"About nine hundred a minute."

"These are illegal, right?" I asked.

"No," said Jeremy, "because it was made before the previous assault weapon ban. If you pay me twenty-five to forty-five thousand dollars, you can buy it today, and take it home once you've passed a few background checks."

"Other than home defense, why do you need assault weapons?" I asked.

"The way the world is going, the military and United Nations are going to come in and try to take our guns."

"Do you really believe that?" I said.

"Anything's possible."

"Could you honestly imagine U.S. Marines charging onto your property to try to steal your guns?"

"I would hope not," he said. "But if it's an executive order . . . who knows?"

"Do you think the American military would attack its own people?"

"If they're forced to, I don't know. I would think at least forty to fifty percent would."

"Do you think that's what many Texans feel about why they need a weapon like this?"

"They want it because they are law-abiding citizens and they know it's legal to purchase now, but won't be later. So they'd rather buy it now to be legal than do something illegal. Because these are law-abiding citizens we're talking about."

At the end of the show, Brad came up to me and said: "We have a slight problem. Alex Jones has got a load more of his supporters outside, and he's shouting stuff about you through a bullhorn."

I got into the car and we drove past the "protest." There must have been fifty large Texans, some armed with guns, baying abuse at me. I toyed with getting out and remonstrating with them on camera. But I actually think one of them might have had a pop at me. They looked mad enough.

We sped away, and I was relieved to get back to the hotel in one piece.

WEDNESDAY, FEBRUARY 6, 2013

Bobby Kennedy's daughter Kerry was just four years old in 1963 when her uncle John, then president of the United States, was assassinated, and eight when her dad too was gunned down.

I interviewed her tonight, and suggested it was time America's politicians showed some of the bravery of her father, a legendary campaigning senator and attorney general.

Particularly as a million more Americans have been shot dead since Bobby died, and, in the fifty-five days since the Sandy Hook School massacre alone, the gun-related death toll already stands at a staggering sixteen hundred.

"It's tough," she replied, "because the NRA is very strong and very threatening. But one of the women at this event I attended today, whose daughter was wounded at Virginia Tech, put it so eloquently when she said, 'You want to know what courage is? Courage is standing in a classroom and seeing a guy with a gun, and wondering what's going to happen to you, and if you're going to survive that moment, and being six or seven years old. Courage is not standing up to the NRA. So let's get this into perspective. If you lose your seat because you vote for this legislation and that saves a life, I think you've served well. You've served our country well.' "

THURSDAY, FEBRUARY 7, 2013

A deranged ex-policeman has gone on the rampage in Los Angeles, in apparent revenge for being fired from the LAPD five years ago.

Christopher Dorner shot dead the daughter of his old police captain, and her boyfriend, then murdered a policeman who tried to apprehend him, and wounded another. He posted a bizarre, rambling, twenty-page, eleven-hundred-word "manifesto" on Facebook, in which he listed the names of forty more people he wanted to kill—and expressed his admiration for a host of politicians, celebrities, and media figures, including Barack Obama ("Mr. President, I think you've done a heck of a job"), Charlie Sheen ("You're effin' awesome!"), and me.

"Give Piers Morgan an indefinite resident alien and visa card," Dorner wrote, before addressing me directly: "Mr. Morgan, the problem that many American gun owners have with you and your continuous discussion of gun control is that you are not an American citizen and have an accent that is distinct and clarifies that you are a foreigner. I want you to know that I agree with you one hundred percent on enacting stricter firearm laws, but you must understand that your critics will always have in the back of their mind that you are native to a country that we won our sovereignty from while using firearms as a last resort in defense and you come from a country that has no legal private ownership of firearms. That is disheartening to American gun owners and rightfully so."

He then went on to endorse the main gun control suggestions that I have campaigned for on my CNN show, and which President Obama is trying to push through Congress.

All of which now seems utterly, obscenely preposterous given his very next action after posting the manifesto was to go and shoot a load of innocent people.

MONDAY, FEBRUARY 11, 2013

I interviewed Lorraine Kelly, a British morning TV star, for my *Life Stories* show tonight, and among her guests were two parents who lost their five-year-old daughter in the Dunblane, Scotland, massacre.

Lorraine covered the story as a young reporter in Scotland, and became so close to Pam and Kenny Ross that she was asked to speak at the memorial for the devastating massacre.

She broke down and wept as she recounted to me how she'd gone to see the dead body of Joanna Ross in her bedroom. "I just lost it," she admitted, "seeing that wee beautiful girl lying there in her bed."

Afterward, I had a chat with Pam and Kenny, a delightful couple that has tried hard to recover their lives but told me: "You never get over it, obviously."

We talked about the parallels with Sandy Hook.

"It brought it all back to us," said Pam. "All those poor young children shot at school."

Then she said: "Did you realize it even happened at the same time— around nine thirty A.M.?"

I hadn't, and it was an eerie coincidence.

"Please keep going with your gun control campaign," she added softly. "We really do hope that your argument and passion will eventually pay at least some small dividends. Even if it saves one life, it will be worth it."

TUESDAY, FEBRUARY 12, 2013

Pope Benedict XVI sensationally resigned yesterday, and as a good (OK, goodish) Irish Catholic boy, I'm not entirely happy about this.

The papacy isn't just a job that you walk away from. It's a vocation, something you do until you die. Which is why no pope's resigned in six hundred years. He is, after all, supposed to be infallible—not prone to waking up one day and resigning because he's exhausted.

Benedict's predecessor, Pope John Paul II, survived two assassination attempts—including being seriously shot and stabbed—several alleged bouts of cancer, Parkinson's disease, and crippling arthritis. But it never crossed his mind to quit. And I found John Paul's utter determination to carry on despite all his physical frailties remarkably inspiring.

This might sound a bit harsh on Benedict (I'm not going to keep calling him pope, I'm afraid—that title goes with staying in the job, otherwise we'll end with a whole plethora of people out there called pope), but he has over a billion Catholics around the world relying on him for religious and spiritual guidance. And for fortitude.

I watched Benedict conducting mass at the Vatican after his announcement and he seemed fine to me. Old, yes, and a little slow on his feet. But otherwise, no less agile than any eighty-five-year-old.

To put his resignation into perspective, our own Queen Elizabeth II is a year older than him, but she'd rather streak naked down Pall Mall than retire.

It's called duty.

WEDNESDAY, FEBRUARY 13, 2013

Cop killer Christopher Dorner was tracked down and killed in the early hours of this morning after a dramatic shoot-out with police.

He shot one more officer dead before the siege was over, the fourth person he murdered—the official threshold the FBI cites as qualifying for the term "mass shooting." There have now been sixty-two of these in America in the last thirty years—but twenty-five of those have occurred since 2006, and eight in the last year.

A terrifying escalation.

FRIDAY, FEBRUARY 15, 2013

Back in London to tape my UK show.

Elise wasn't well all day, and by 5 P.M., she was running a raging fever.

We called the doctor, who said he'd come by in a couple of hours to check on her. But by 7 P.M., she seemed considerably better, so we canceled him. Then, as I sat downstairs watching TV, Celia suddenly called out for help. I ran upstairs, and Elise was lying on our bed, ashen-faced, rigid, and shaking violently. Her eyes were wild, and she was incredibly hot. It was a terrifying sight.

I called the emergency services immediately and explained what was happening. The operator said: "This sounds like a febrile convulsion. They can happen to small babies when they get high fevers, but shouldn't last long. I'm sending an ambulance. Keep her lying on her back, and don't try to do anything else until she stops convulsing."

Elise stopped convulsing after about two minutes. They felt like the longest 120 seconds of both our lives. The paramedics were at the house very quickly, and raced inside to treat her.

As they did so, someone rang the doorbell. I ran down to find an angry-looking man standing there.

"Is that your ambulance?" he snarled.

I looked to where he was pointing.

"Sorry?"

"I said is that your ambulance? It's blocking my route."

Unbelievable.

"My baby's sick, you moron," I spat back at him, slamming the door.

I ran back upstairs and Elise was much cooler and calmer.

"She's going to be fine," one of the paramedics said. "We'll take her in for a checkup, but you should be OK to bring her back home later tonight."

I relayed my exchange with the angry driver, and they shook their heads knowingly. "Happens all the time; people are just extraordinary."

TUESDAY, FEBRUARY 19, 2013

Woke up to shocking news.

Oscar Pistorius has shot dead his girlfriend, Reeva Steenkamp, at his home in Pretoria.

He denies murder, saying he mistakenly thought she was an intruder.

Either way, it's an appalling tragedy.

Stanley called. "Dad, I've literally just finished my two-thousand-word essay on why Oscar Pistorius is such an inspiration to me. I think that's what you call 'bad timing.' "

THURSDAY, FEBRUARY 21, 2013

Interviewed former U.S. President Jimmy Carter again in San Diego today, and asked him for his reaction to Sandy Hook.

"I've advocated a prohibition against assault weapons and against magazines that hold multiple bullets and also armor-piercing bullets and things of that kind."

"The main reason why the assault weapons ban may not pass," I responded, "is the power of the NRA in going after American politicians who then get cowed into silence. And I think it's just morally cowardly."

"I do too. I agree with you completely," he said. "And it happens not only at the federal level, but it also happens at every state level and every municipal level. The NRA is there pressuring weak-kneed public officials to yield to their pressures, when they know what they're doing is wrong.

"I'm a gun owner. I'm a farmer. I have two pistols, two rifles, five shotguns. And I've been a hunter all my life. I never have had a need for an assault weapon. I've never had a need for armor-piercing bullets. And I think it's ridiculous for our country to be in the forefront of killing people with guns."

SUNDAY, FEBRUARY 24, 2013

CNN asked me to anchor its Oscar Night red carpet coverage today, which was a lot of fun.

Especially when I spotted Rupert Murdoch and his wife, Wendi, walking past.

"Mr. Murdoch, a few words for CNN?" I shouted, mindful of the fact that he'd told me two years ago my chances of securing an interview with him for CNN were "zero in a hundred."

Wendi heard me and persuaded Rupert to come over.

"We have breaking news," I announced to viewers. "I'm about to interview the boss of our rival network, Fox News."

After some chitchat about the movies, I couldn't stop myself asking: "How do you feel about CNN doing so well against Fox at the moment?"

He laughed.

"I think we're doing OK . . . I suspect we'll survive!"

MONDAY, FEBRUARY 25, 2013

Everywhere I've gone in L.A. over this Oscars weekend, I've had stars come up to me wanting to talk about my gun campaign on CNN.

Jamie Foxx collared me in an elevator at Soho House about it, and was so animated we had to step outside and wait for another one. "We have to deal with this problem now," he said. "It won't be easy, but I grew up a young black man in Texas. I learned how to compromise with people on emotive issues."

Tonight I was dining with friends when Kiefer Sutherland walked over, shook my hand, and said: "I just want to say something to you. I've been watching all the gun stuff you've been doing on CNN, and it's one of the bravest things I've seen anyone do on American television for a very long time."

I was genuinely astonished.

"Thanks, Kiefer," I replied. "Coming from you, that means a lot."

"Just don't stop," he added firmly. "It's too important. We're all behind you."

And then he was gone. Jack Bauer had given me my orders.

WEDNESDAY, FEBRUARY 27, 2013

A pizza restaurant owner from Virginia Beach is offering customers a 15 percent discount if they arrive carrying a gun.

He claimed he's doing this to protect his Second Amendment rights. But after further questioning from me tonight, he revealed the real reason he thinks his fellow civilians should be armed to the teeth (and rewarded with cheap pepperoni specials), and I quote directly: "The United Nations may attack us."

WEDNESDAY, MARCH 6, 2013

There's absolutely no reason now not to change the show's name to *Piers Morgan Live*, given that I'm no longer doing *America's Got Talent* and can now do the show 100 percent live.

I emailed Jeff Zucker, who replied two minutes later: "Yes, let's do it."

FRIDAY, MARCH 8, 2013

Justin Bieber's chaotic trip to Britain took an ugly turn tonight when he got into a highly abusive argument, and nearly a physical fight, with a paparazzo in London. Watching the video closely, I was appalled to see the photographer, a large, bald, middle-aged Neanderthal, repeatedly screaming, *"Fuck off back to America, you fucking little moron,"* at the top of his voice.

All because Bieber had the audacity to brush past him because he stood in his way to a waiting car.

I met young Justin last year at an Oscars party, and he's absolutely tiny—like the human equivalent of a Chihuahua. He couldn't hurt a stick insect with his minuscule frame, let alone a gigantic, blubbery, battle-scarred snapper.

The vast majority of paparazzi that I encounter are perfectly polite, and do a job that sustains many a flagging celebrity career. Morons like the revolting Bieber-baiting bully sadly give them all a bad name.

MONDAY, MARCH 11, 2013

I finally got my man.

Tom Hanks agreed to an interview today, and didn't cancel at the last minute because he was tired.

He's performing on Broadway for the first time in a play written by Nora Ephron just before she died last year. It's called *Lucky Guy*, and Hanks plays scandalous crime-reporting legend Mike McAlary.

"So you play a hard-drinking, controversial, Irish tabloid hack plying his trade and seeking journalistic redemption in New York?" I said, as we sat down to start the interview.

"Yes, Piers," replied Hanks. "You should be able to relate to him pretty well!"

TUESDAY, MARCH 19, 2013

The U.S. Senate looks likely to throw out proposals for new gun control measures, including a renewed assault weapons ban and an expansion of background checks, in one of the more appalling acts of political cowardice I've seen in a long time.

Tonight I debated this debacle live with Michael Moore. And in the middle of the show, Yoko Ono sent us both a tweet containing a photo of her late husband's blood-spattered glasses, with the words: "Over 1,057,000 people have been killed by guns in the USA since John Lennon was shot and killed on 8 Dec., 1980."

MONDAY, MARCH 25, 2013

Robbie Parker, who lost his daughter Emilie at Sandy Hook, wrote to thank me for an incredibly moving interview we conducted on Friday.

I feel like our society is so quick to point fingers and find blame that they fail to realize the power within us all if we have the determination to just do what is right. Unfortunately, that demeanor starts with our "leaders" in Washington, and they've had a deteriorating effect on so many people with their lack of real leadership. If our leaders had half the courage as all the families affected by this we could start to visualize a culture change in the way things get accomplished.

To be honest, my feelings on this subject are very powerful. I have to practice extreme restraint to not just "go off" about how ridiculous it is that people continue to be influenced and intimidated into doing nothing. I sincerely appreciate what you have done and will continue to do to fight gun violence.

FRIDAY, APRIL 5, 2013

Roger Ebert, America's greatest movie critic, died yesterday.

He once said: "Never marry someone who doesn't love the movies you love. Sooner or later, that person will not love you."

When Celia declared that she couldn't watch horror, science-fiction, "goofy," or fantasy films, I knew we'd have to get married.

MONDAY, APRIL 8, 2013

Margaret Thatcher has died.

I first met her at a cocktail party in London thrown by Rupert Murdoch in 1994 soon after I'd become editor of the *News of the World*. She was clutching, and drinking liberally from, a vast tumbler of whiskey, and was in splendidly bombastic mood—haranguing me loudly for daring to suggest that interest rate rises were hurting ordinary people.

"What a load of nonsense! It's much better for them because they'll have a lasting, smooth recovery without inflation coming back again, which it was tending to do."

I replied that this wasn't going to help families with mortgages—the same families she'd encouraged to buy homes in the first place, especially if house prices collapsed.

She stared at me for several seconds, then began physically jabbing me hard in the chest with her firm, bony fingers.

"You don't know what on earth you're talking about, young man! And I suggest you think very carefully before putting any of that rubbish in your newspaper!"

Murdoch, who'd heard all this, laughed: "I wouldn't tangle with Margaret if I were you, Piers—there'll only be one winner."

Love her or loathe her, Margaret Thatcher was the most transformative, domineering, dominant, bold, and unique prime minister of my lifetime.

MONDAY, APRIL 15, 2013

News broke this afternoon of a huge explosion at the finish line of the Boston Marathon.

Within minutes, that was upgraded to two explosions, and reporters at the scene were saying there were bodies everywhere and at least dozens of seriously injured people.

By the time we went on air, three people were confirmed dead, including an eight-year-old boy. Several hundred more have been wounded.

A shocking video emerged showing the exact moment of the first bomb. An elderly male runner could be seen jogging to the finish line, then being physically blown off his feet and onto the ground. Nobody seemed sure what had happened to him, with many fearing the worst. But one of our bright, young interns tracked him down so I could interview him exclusively tonight.

His name was Bill Iffrig, he was seventy-eight, and he'd competed in forty-five marathons.

"I was approaching the finish," he said, "and had a good day, and was feeling really good, when there was this tremendous explosion and the shock waves hit my whole body and my legs started jittering.

"I knew I was going down, so I ended up on the blacktop. And I didn't feel any severe pain; a little scratch on my leg but nothing too bad. One of the finisher assistants came over and asked if there was anything he could do for me and offered to give me a hand, help me get up, and get over the finish line so I could complete my race."

TUESDAY, APRIL 16, 2013

There's been considerable debate over how to try to stop bombing attacks like this happening again.

What I haven't heard yet is a single NRA member argue that the only way to defend oneself from bombs is for everyone else to carry bombs too.

WEDNESDAY, APRIL 17, 2013

The U.S. Senate today made its decision on gun control—and rejected every single proposal. No curb on assault weapons, no banning of high-capacity magazines. Not even universal background checks got passed, despite all recent polls saying 90 percent of the American people want it.

I watched as tearful Newtown families broke down inside the Senate, and shared their sense of utter disbelief and fury. They have been betrayed in the most cowardly way imaginable.

Politicians, in many cases, voting against their conscience to save their seats.

Power before principle.

President Obama spoke angrily about his disappointment, but the truth is that he's failed those families too. He promised he'd get something done, and he got nothing done.

Sarah Palin raced to Twitter to declare a jubilant "victory."

What a revolting piece of work she is.

THURSDAY, APRIL 18, 2013

The FBI has released photos of its prime suspects in the Boston bombings, and they were quickly identified as two Russian brothers, Tamerlan and Dzhokhar Tsarnaev. Both have been living in America for years, and are now the most wanted men in the country.

I anchored both a 9 P.M. and midnight show, and, as I was finally coming off air, reports started coming in of an incident on the outskirts of Boston. Local news outlets on Twitter seemed to think it was gang related, and some kind of local shoot-out with police.

"What if it's the brothers?" I said to Jonathan. "Shall we stay on air?"

"Nothing's pointing to it being them."

My sound technician, Jenna, was following a Twitter feed called "Newsbreaker" that specializes in breaking news.

"They're saying that bombs and grenades are going off. This has to be more than just gangs, doesn't it?" she said.

It was now 12:55 A.M., and we were due to hand over to CNN International, which would pick up live coverage.

I spoke to Jonathan again. "What do you think?"

"There's still nothing suggesting it's them. Let's wrap."

I ended our show and walked back to the control room, where the general view from our reporters on the ground was that it had nothing to do with the missing brothers.

But it was still nagging in my head that it might be.

As we watched the monitors, one screen suddenly showed footage of a young man lying flat on the ground, and another clip of a naked man being led into a van. Neither looked anything like the brothers.

"Good call," I said to Jonathan.

Then, a few minutes later, at a different location, an FBI vehicle raced into the camera picture at the scene. And another one.

"Shit," I said. "They wouldn't be there if it was a gang thing."

"Nope," said Jonathan, equally exasperated.

Sure enough, within an hour, it was obvious that it *was* the brothers, and they were engaged in an unbelievably violent ongoing shoot-out with police. If we'd stayed on air a few minutes more, we'd have been covering it all night.

FRIDAY, APRIL 19, 2013

Woke to discover that one of the two brothers, Tamerlan, had died in the shoot-out, but the younger one had gotten away and was still on the loose.

Boston was effectively locked down all day as thousands of police and FBI hunted him down. Finally, in incredible scenes tonight just before we went on air, he was found hiding in a boat in someone's backyard, and captured after more rapid-fire gun exchanges.

It was an extraordinarily dramatic end to an extraordinarily dramatic week.

SATURDAY, APRIL 20, 2013

Jonathan sent the ratings for last night. They were by far the biggest in our show's history—more than five million in total viewers, and 2.3 million in the demo.

The network as a whole had its best ratings day outside of general elections for a decade.

Further proof, not that any is needed, that when big news breaks, everyone watches CNN.

MONDAY, APRIL 22, 2013

Until tonight, I thought that Alex Jones was the most obnoxious human being I'd ever interviewed.

But that was before I interviewed New York state senator Greg Ball.

After the police captured one of the Boston Marathon bombers alive, he tweeted: "So, scumbag number two in custody—who wouldn't use torture on this punk to save more lives?"

The slight problem being that Dzhokhar Tsarnaev is an American citizen who committed a crime on American soil—so torturing him would be a breach of the U.S. Constitution. The same Constitution that Mr. Ball demands is never infringed when it comes to guns.

I asked him if he stood by his tweet, and off he went, like a ranting madman.

"A lot of politicians are full of crap! I think I share the feelings of a lot of red-blooded Americans! Dude, you're talking to a guy that supports the death penalty for cop killers and terrorists!"

He was almost foaming at the mouth.

"Let me ask *you* a question," he said. "What would you do if you were given the opportunity before Osama bin Laden was shot? If you had thirty minutes in a room with him, what would you do—*play cards with bin Laden?*"

Bin Laden, of course, was not an American citizen, but this minor detail was lost on the good senator.

"Maybe I should have said it in a British accent!" he sneered. "This man *killed innocent men, women, and children.*"

He was now smirking like Jack Nicholson in *The Shining*.

"Can you stop being such a jerk?" I suggested wearily.

"You get paid for it!" he shot back. "I figured I'd give you a taste of your own medicine! You don't like it when you don't have another *bobblehead* you can beat up and treat like a coward! If given the opportunity to be in a room with Osama bin Laden, it would be me, Osama, and a baseball bat. And yes, I would use torture!"

"Very macho," I observed.

"It's not about being macho! If I wanted to be macho, I would challenge you to an arm wrestling contest!"

Mr. Jones, move aside.

TUESDAY, APRIL 30, 2013

The monthly ratings have come out, and my show registered its second-highest numbers ever, up a whopping 119 percent from last April.

I'm pleased, obviously. But what I've learned the hard way at CNN is not to enjoy these moments too enthusiastically. Because the only certainty is that the ratings will fall again when interest in this Boston story drops, which it will do very soon.

The challenge remains to try to make our "normal" show outside of breaking news as compelling as possible, and as distinct from the rest of CNN as possible.

Jeff Zucker's made it very clear to everyone that he wants us all to expand our ideas of what "news" is, away from focusing on boring politics (when it's boring) and into stuff that people actually care and talk about.

He's absolutely right.

WEDNESDAY, MAY 1, 2013

A two-year-old girl in Kentucky has been shot dead by her five-year-old brother—with a rifle he was given by his parents as a gift.

It was purchased from a company called Crickett, whose website is full of photos of little kids gleefully brandishing deadly rifles.

What hope is there for any change in America when this kind of nonsense is legally permissible?

Lennox Lewis shared my dismay.

"You need a license to drive a car," he tweeted. "To do hair, to fish. I even needed one to box, but you don't need one for a gun. Why?"

There's just no sensible, logical answer.

FRIDAY, MAY 3, 2013

The NRA is holding a conference in Houston, and Wayne LaPierre attacked me in his speech.

"We know how they play the game," he sneered. "President Obama or Michael Bloomberg or some other official trots out on national television to scold and shame us, suggesting that there's something wrong with law-abiding people who want to own firearms.

"And then what happens—all the Piers Morgans, Lawrence O'Donnells, and Rachel Maddows, they pound the message over and over again."

Then he addressed the Boston bombings.

"How many Bostonians wished they had a gun two weeks ago? When brave law enforcement officers did their jobs in that city so courageously, good guys with guns stopped terrorists with guns."

Ka-ching! More gun sales guaranteed.

LaPierre ended by saying: "They're coming after us with a vengeance to destroy us and every ounce of our freedom. We don't care if it's round one, round two, or round fifteen, the NRA can go the distance. To the political and media elites who scorn us, we say, let them be damned! We will always stand and fight for our American freedoms!"

Cue thunderous applause.

I addressed his comments on my show tonight:

"That's right, Mr. LaPierre. I will continue to pound that message until people like you realize the damage that guns are doing to Americans every day."

LaPierre won't be happy until America is a complete military state, with every citizen armed. He's one of the most dangerous people in the country.

TUESDAY, MAY 7, 2013

The Brady Campaign honored me tonight for my gun control campaigning.

I was presented with the Sarah Brady Award, named for the wife of Jim Brady.

The event was held over dinner at the Beverly Hills Hotel, in front of 350 people, including Stevie Wonder—who was there to support my co-honoree, top Hollywood lawyer Laura Wasser.

My award was presented by Sandy Phillips, whose young daughter Jessica was murdered in the Aurora movie theater massacre.

I used the occasion to say what I really thought about the gun control fiasco.

"America's politicians, with a few notable exceptions, have betrayed the people of this great country. They did nothing when one of their own congresswomen was nearly murdered with a gun. They did nothing when seventy people were shot in a movie theater. They did nothing when twenty young children were annihilated in their elementary school.

"Well, you know what? Doing nothing when it comes to America's relentless tide of appalling gun violence is just not good enough anymore. Especially when so many of these cowardly politicians are doing nothing because they're scared the NRA will bully, threaten, and drive them out of their seats of power.

"America has been very good to me in the seven years I've worked here. I love the country, and I love its people. Well, apart from those who signed that petition to deport me, obviously.

"I also fully respect the Constitution, which is a magnificent document. But the true meaning of the Second Amendment of that Constitution has been dangerously and deliberately misinterpreted to protect and promote the commercial interests of the NRA and the gun manufacturers that pour money into its pockets.

"The Founding Fathers never intended the 'right to bear arms' to mean the right of a deranged young student to legally buy six thousand rounds of ammunition on the Internet, four assault weapons, and a clutch of hundred-bullet magazines; dress up like the Joker; and open fire on Americans, including Sandy's daughter Jessica, as they watched a movie.

"Nor, surely, did they intend the reaction to an atrocity like Sandy Hook to be that Americans raced out to buy the very same type of AR-15 assault rifle that Adam Lanza used in record numbers.

"That is not the way a great nation behaves.

"American civilians don't need military-style assault weapons. They don't need high-capacity magazines. Nor do they need absurd loopholes in the current background check system, meaning forty percent of all gun sales are conducted without the seller being required to even ask the purchaser's name, let alone their criminal status, or mental illness record.

"If the NRA wins this war, as they put it, America will lose.

"I urge each and every one of you to stand up and say, loud and clear: enough is enough."

The audience stood up and roared their approval.

Sandy Phillips walked over and hugged me.

"Please, please don't stop your campaigning. You are our voice."

"Don't worry," I replied. "This fight has only just begun."

Me firing an AR-15, the gun used at Aurora and Sandy Hook.
This killing machine has no place in civilian hands.

EPILOGUE

Since I finished the manuscript of this book, three stories happened that collectively sum up the insanity of America's gun laws.

WEDNESDAY, JUNE 5, 2013

A man called Ezekiel Gilbert was acquitted of killing a female escort by a jury in Bexar County, Texas. He shot her after she refused to have sex with him, nor return the $150 in cash he had given her, supposedly for that purpose. The woman was paralyzed in the shooting, then died several months later.

Under Texas law, people are allowed "to use deadly force to recover property during a nighttime theft."

Gilbert's lawyers successfully argued that his actions were justified because he believed sex was included as part of his fee to the escort. If this had happened in Iran or Saudi Arabia, we'd all brand it a revolting medieval monstrosity.

Here in America, it barely made national news.

THURSDAY, JUNE 27, 2013

Bill and Tricia Lammers, a couple from Missouri, committed their troubled son Blaec SEVEN times to mental institutions.

Last November, they found a receipt in his pocket for an AR-15 assault rifle. He'd bought it from his local Walmart store.

His horrified parents reluctantly reported his purchase to police, who arrested Blaec—and he then confessed he bought the rifle to carry out a mass shooting at possibly a shopping mall or movie theater.

It transpired that he had passed Walmart's background check, which supposedly prohibits anyone with a criminal record, or recorded mental illness, from buying a gun, because all his seven stays in mental institutions had been voluntary, not ordered by a court.

They didn't know what else they could have done, when I interviewed them tonight.

I had no answer.

SATURDAY, JULY 13, 2013

George Zimmerman was today acquitted of any wrongdoing over the death of Trayvon Martin.

A jury in Sanford, Florida, decided he was not guilty of either murder or manslaughter when he shot the teenager dead, despite the fact that Trayvon was unarmed and walking home at the time.

I don't blame the jury. They applied the law of Florida, which allows self-defense with a gun if you can justifiably claim you were in fear of your life.

But one thing is certain: If Zimmerman had not been armed with a gun that night, he would probably have never left his car to follow Trayvon, the altercation would never have happened, and that poor young man would have never been shot dead.

I blame the gun.

ACKNOWLEDGMENTS

A book like this is a team effort, and I am lucky to have a great team behind me.

I'd like to thank the following people:

Eugenie Furniss, my peerless literary agent.

John Ferriter, my irrepressible manager.

Jeremie Ruby-Strauss, my splendidly judicious and stylish editor.

Jennifer Bergstrom, my terrific publisher, and her excellent staff at Gallery Books.

Meghan McPartland, my publicist extraordinaire.

Rob McGibbon, my oldest friend in journalism, and my brother Jeremy, who both gave typically forthright—yet much valued—opinions on the manuscript.

Rick Davis at CNN, for his helpful and meticulous advice.

Alan Goldman, Lisa Robinson, Jim Jackoway, and Eric Weissler for keeping me out of debt, court, and trouble.

And four women without whom I would probably curl into a ball and cry, "No more of this madness!" My fabulous personal assistants, Juliana Severo (U.S.) and Tracey Chapman (UK), whose hard work, loyalty, professionalism, and sense of humor make my life a million times easier. My wife, Celia, who makes me laugh when I want to punch walls. And my mother, who's always there to make everything sound just a little better than it seems.

Finally, I'd like to thank all the people who work in any capacity on my CNN show. It's been one hell of a ride. This book is a tribute to each and every one of them.

Note: I deployed a team of fact checkers, skillfully masterminded by Juliana Severo, but if any eagle-eyed reader should still spy a factual error, please contact the publishers and I will fix it for later editions.